12 95

Yours to Finish the Task:
The Memoirs of W. Cameron Townsend

Part four: 1947-1982

Yours to Finish the Task

The Memoirs of

W. Cameron Townsend

Part four: 1947-1982

Hugh Steven

Wycliffe®

Partners in Bible Translation

ISBN 0-938978-37-3

Library of Congress Cataloging-in-Publication Data

Steven, Hugh.
    Yours to Finish the Task: the memoirs of W. Cameron Townsend, 1947–1982 / by Hugh Steven.
       p.   cm.
    ISBN 0-938978-37-3
    1. Townsend, William Cameron, 1896–1982. 2. Wycliffe Bible Translators—Biography.
  3. Summer Institute of Linguistics. I. Title.

CIP

10 9 8 7 6 5 4 3 2

Dedicated to the foundation-laying generation of WBT, SIL and JAARS personnel together with their praying and financial partners who faithfully stayed the course to bring about the Kingdom of God in the lives of countless thousands of ethnic minority people throughout the world.

"After this I looked and there before me was a great multitude that no one could count, from every nation, tribe, people and language, standing before the throne and in front of the Lamb." Revelation 7:9b.

William Cameron Townsend speaking by radio to a translation team in their village allocation. John Shanks, radio operator at his side. Radio communication on the field was an early development in Peru. Cameron Townsend spent 60 years of his life in Latin America, on the front lines, actively engaged in the work of Bible translation.

Contents

Elaine Townsend and Peruvian educator help Peruvian teachers learn a new method for teaching reading in the Spanish language to Quechua and Mestizo students. Elaine was commissioned to prepare materials for this reading campaign by the Peruvian Minister of Education in August 1946, just four months after her arrival in Peru.

Acknowledgments

Whender I answered the phone, the words I heard were like an echo coming from the halls of my memory, such as "You can do it," "It should be done," "You are the right person for the job," and "We need you." I had often heard such comments from Cameron Townsend whose ability to encourage and affirm one's gifts was legendary. However, on this day it wasn't Townsend's voice but that of Stephen Board, friend and editor, who was asking me if I had begun writing the last book in the Townsend series. When I said "No," Stephen said simply, "It should be completed."

For that spark of affirmation and encouragement I here thank him. I thank him also for volunteering without remuneration to typeset and design this book. Said Stephen, "I am committed to publishing books that will endure and that will inspire us all to greater heights of faith and commitment."

I thank Cal Hibbard, archivist of the Townsend papers, who has been a constant supporter, critic, editor and friend for this project from the very beginning. It was he who arranged for more than 25,000 items including letters, memos and other primary source material to be photocopied and collated by month and by year. The four-year writing project would have been impossible without this technological help. And, of course, without the very practical hands-on job of collating this material, this book would also not have happened if it hadn't been for the dedicated and time-consuming work of Beth Brennan, Dave and Vivian Robbins, Irene Smith, Alice Peterson, Hattie and Carolyn Dyk, as well as Cal Hibbard. I also thank my two grandsons, Jonathan and Andrew Steven for their help in collating the many hundreds of documents.

I also want to give a special word of appreciation to Roy Peterson, former president and CEO of Wycliffe USA, (now president of the SEED Company) who after my retirement from Wycliffe wrote:

> My desire for you to complete this project is now stronger than it's ever been. What you and Norma are doing is an enormous service to the work of Wycliffe Bible Translators and to the great history God has given us in this book. So clearly we very much want you to press on in your retirement years to serve as a volunteer and to complete the work you have started.

I am deeply grateful to my colleagues Ben and Adelle Elson, George Cowan, Bob Schneider, Bill and Marjorie Nyman, Elaine Townsend, Marianna Slocum, Florence Gerdel and Evelyn Pike, all still living as of 2004, also to Ken Pike and Dick Pittman, both now with the Lord, for clarifying historical facts and giving their interpretation and reflections of Uncle Cam and the early history of Wycliffe and SIL.

I add my thanks and appreciation to Don Burns, Gene Burnham, Vernell Cobbey and Corrine Hatch and Grady Parrot of MAF for their help and reflections. Also to Valarie Stevenson, long-time personal friend and friend of Wycliffe, who has been an energetic copy editor for all of the books in the Townsend series. Special thanks also to Jim Wylie for his careful copy editing.

At this point in my previous acknowledgments it was my custom to pay special tribute to my wife Norma who has been my editor, critic and full partner in our writing ministry. Just shortly after I began this project in 1999, Norma suffered a small stroke that left her unable to continue in this role. However, I here thank her for all the years as my dearest friend, editor and, before the days of the computer, my typist for almost thirty books on the worldwide ministry of Wycliffe Bible Translators. I could never have done it without her help and encouragement. I also want to thank God for His enduring faithfulness and for restoring Norma's health.

I also want to thank God for our prayer and financial supporters who, for over 45 years have joined Norma and me as full partners in our Wycliffe ministry.

And since God is always faithful and often supplies our needs before we ask, I here thank Him for putting on the heart of Allan Farson, with his wife Elaine, to take Norma's place as editor and critic. The Farsons are longtime friends and colleagues. Allan was an early Wycliffe member (1942-1943) who later felt called to be a printer of Christian literature in Mexico and as such, printed a number of ethnic New Testaments. Also much appreciation to Jewel Fink for her creative cover design. Lastly, I offer my thanks and appreciation to Bob Cruzen and Susan Van Wynen of Wycliffe USA, Orlando, Florida for their willingness to act as publisher for this, the last book in the series of the Life and Times of William Cameron Townsend.

Foreword
Uncle Cam and His Vision

As a biographer I am often asked how I decide "what will make a good story." In the case of Cameron Townsend, I was interested in his basic worldview. What were the tensions and misunderstandings that might have caused him to stumble or lose his God-given vision? What were the many social, religious, or political agitations he had to deal with in his ministry? How did he resolve conflicts with colleagues as well as those outside the organization who tried to subvert or undermine his person and ministry?

I began to look for answers to these questions by examining his diaries and personal letters. What I discovered was that even in the most heated exchanges, he dealt with everyone with grace and courtesy. I then asked myself, "What was the inherent wisdom that guided the corporate actions of Wycliffe Bible Translators?" The answers to these questions, and an in-depth look into the foundations of Wycliffe and the Summer Institute of Linguistics (SIL) are to be found in four books, *A Thousand Trails*, *Wycliffe in the Making*, *Doorway to the World*, and *Yours to Finish the Task*.

You won't find a list, however, or a how-to manual. What you will find is a story, the story of a young man's journey of faith as he grappled with his own idealism and lived in countries torn apart by revolution and reforms, by plagues of flu and malaria, and a world in the cold grip of depression.

As I moved into the history of Townsend's early life, I began to see that many of Wycliffe's operating principles were forged out of Townsend's life experiences, which came into focus during the early days of his ministry in Guatemala. As I probed deeper into his life, and remembered my own personal impressions and observations of Uncle Cam, I began to realize that these were more than just sterile principles. In a profound way they defined him as a person. These principles were criteria for evaluating his convictions about the nature of mission and about how SIL understood itself as servants to its host countries. Thus, through the sifting of facts and theories, in the light of additional knowledge, a new historical truth about Wycliffe and the men and women who were first drawn to Cam's vision began to emerge with greater clarity.

Throughout Townsend's life, his peers often misunderstood him. Some had little appreciation for his creativity and vision. Dick Pittman told me that Cam was always "floating trial balloons," hoping that some of his ideas would take. "And in my opinion," said Dick, "his batting average was over 400!" Some of those who seemed to understand Cam remind us that he was usually twenty years ahead of everyone else.

In the early stages of Cam's ministry in Guatemala, a number of his mission board members viewed translating the New Testament into the Cakchiquel language as an aside to real mission work.

Cam never seemed to live in a world of timidity or anxiety. Nor did he ever respond in kind to his unfair critics. He had the utmost confidence in God and in the Scriptures. It was said of Winston Churchill "conformity was his enemy," and "that he liked to break the rules." Those who knew Townsend were aware that he, like Churchill, had the courage and conviction to go against popular opinion, to take a position in faith, to push forward against all kinds of odds. Cam was always open to the serendipitous experience, which, in fact, he felt might be the nudging of the Holy Spirit. And he wanted always to be sensitive to that still, small voice of the Holy Spirit.

One important thing about Cameron Townsend is, to quote a phrase Bonhoeffer used to describe Jesus, that he was "a man for others."

Many have said that Townsend was a "one-dimensional man," that his vision for Bible translation was never turned off. This is both true and false. It is true that his vision for Bible translation was never turned off, but it is equally true that he had more than a single string on his violin. Cam had a spiritual force burning within that drew people to him. One had a sense of joy just being with him. He wasn't an ascetic; he had a sense of humor and liked to laugh. He loved parties, picnics and social gatherings, and would often say, "Let's put as much pie in pioneering as we can."

Cameron Townsend was an educator, linguist, and Bible translator. He completed a New Testament in ten years, yet during that period he had time to establish a public school that continues to this day, a clinic, and a Bible institute. He wrote an anthropological novel about the inequity and servitude of ethnic peoples in Guatemala (*Tolo the Volcano's Son*). He wrote an important biography and dozens and dozens of lengthy papers on everything from mission strategy to crop rotation. He hand-wrote hundreds of letters to friends, family and colleagues. He had an interest in architecture, agriculture, botany and much more.

When people met Cam, they knew intuitively he was sincerely interested in them as persons. When he spoke to a person, he engaged them fully, with warm eye contact and always let them finish speaking before answering a question or taking part in a discussion. At public meetings, informal services, or meetings when members gave reports from their allocations, Cam sat in a front row seat. He wanted always to pay close attention to what the speaker had to say.

Cam was also a superb mission statesman and visionary. Yet there was always the juxtaposition of the dream and the reality, the visionary and the practical, imagination and faith. It was this unique combination that captured the hearts and minds of hundreds of people, young and old, inspiring them to become part of that vision. Cameron Townsend also had a thirst for God. His mind was open to the Word of God and to the absolute standards of the Word. When he used the famous aphorism, i.e., "God said it, I believe it, that settles it," as an argument, many smiled politely and chalked it up to an overly simplistic and naive view of God.

In reality, Cameron Townsend had a highly developed understanding of God as the final authority and reference point for his own worldview. That worldview was based on God's self-disclosure in the person of Jesus Christ, and of course, in the Bible. Out of this came his view of humanity, namely, that since man is the highest form of God's creation, persons are significant and have a unique purpose in the creation order. Persons, he believed, need to be protected and encouraged to reach their highest potential. He actively tried to help people achieve their potential. He believed that to give a person a boost up, support, or open an avenue of opportunity was to serve God's highest purpose, particularly when he was able to connect persons to some aspect of Bible translation.

One of the important lessons I learned from Uncle Cam was the lesson of servant leadership. (See "Uncle Cam's Leadership Style," Appendix B.) The uniqueness of Cam's servant leadership style was found in his willingness to deflect credit from himself. Ben Elson's remarks about Cam's leadership style, which I have used in another book, are worth repeating here:

> Uncle Cam had the ability, as do all great leaders, to bring out the best in the men and women he led, to lead them forward toward the goals they believed were important, yet without violating their own individuality. His leadership was marked by a deep, personal concern for others. He always had a smile, an attentive ear, a word of encouragement and support. I remember him as having a forgiving, compassionate attitude toward those under his leadership.

Cam was also a peacemaker. His principles of peacemaking grew out of his deep understanding of the Scriptures, particularly from the instructions of the Sermon on the Mount. Thus emerged the principle of never striking back in anger or revenge at someone who had deeply offended him. Here, once again, are his words from the preface in *Wycliffe in the Making:*

> I told our workers that we must at all times remember that we are called to serve all people. We are called to serve with humility and compassion, and most of all, with a spirit of true human love and friendship. This must always be our attitude, even when we might have to face an unfriendly or hostile crowd, as I did in my early days in Guatemala. When that happened, I greeted everyone with a smile. I refused to regard anyone—even when there was a danger

of being chopped up by their long knives—as my enemy. My motto then, as now, is, 'By love serve one another,' even when you think they might kill you.

In one of my last conversations with Uncle Cam just before he died, he said he felt that few, if any, had understood his soul. I took that as a challenge to try to indeed interpret and understand this man of many paradoxes. The soul of Cameron Townsend was a soul that throbbed with great moral conviction, with an idealism that was sustained by faith and imagination. It was also a soul that believed anyone who trusted God could, with faith the size of a mustard seed move a mountain. William Cameron Townsend had that kind of faith, and the ongoing ministry he began, with two students and a dream, is a living testimony to that faith and trust in Almighty God.

Hugh Steven,
Santa Ana, California, 2004

Cameron Townsend believed passionately that the Bible is God's unique revelation to all humankind. As such, he believed it has divine authority in all matters of faith and practice. Thus, when he faced dark times, roadblocks and evidence that seemed contrary to his vision for Bible translation, he gained strength and confidence through prayer and daily reading of the Word of God. Photo by Cornell Capa.

Introduction

The vision of our future runs through our past." This is a phrase I hear frequently from a new generation of Christian young people in the United States. Their firm conviction is that God shapes us through our experiences, and through these experiences, he prepares us for future service.

I think Uncle Cam would have related well to the youth of today. I also believe that all those who have gone before us contributed to who we are today as an organization. It's important for us to remember the lessons of the past.

We owe a debt to Cameron Townsend. God gave him a vision to reach the Bibleless peoples of the earth. His experiences and the experiences of so many others have shaped both Wycliffe and SIL. That's why I'm pleased to write a few words in this final volume of Hugh Steven's comprehensive work on the early history of Wycliffe. I want to take this opportunity to acknowledge Hugh for his many years of service to Wycliffe that have continued long into his "retirement."

Over the years, Hugh demonstrated tremendous patience, stamina and skill to collect, sort, and research the thousands of historical documents and facts he's used in telling the story of Cameron Townsend and

Wycliffe. Yet no amount of data tells the whole story—it's a snapshot. Hugh faced this dilemma of data collection, and what to include of the past in his work *Yours to Finish the Task*. And, one of the challenges of compiling, editing and publishing historical data is that it may provide only a one-dimensional picture of people, events, relationships, organizations and the world. Some may find this to be the case in these pages.

But still, the past can inform our future. And the vision God gave Cameron Townsend lives on in the thousands of people who now work, pray and give on behalf of completing the task of reaching the Bibleless peoples. I'm sure I speak for many colleagues and friends when I express my appreciation for Hugh's labor of love in documenting the history that brought us to where we are today.

Bob Creson
President
Wycliffe USA

First group of SIL members that arrived in Lima, Peru, April 20-25, 1946. *L to R* front row: SIL friend, Elaine Townsend, Cameron Townsend, Gloria Gray, Olive Shell. Back row: Ray Liedtke, Pete Fast, Irene McGinnis, Esther Matteson, Ellen Ross, Lulu Reber, Florence Nickel, Titus Nickel, Mary Beth Hinson.

Chapter One

An Impossible Challenge

The year 1947 had been an incredible first year in Peru for William Cameron Townsend. In April 1946 Cam, with his new wife Elaine Mielke, and nineteen inexperienced but eager men and women in their twenties[1] began a new chapter in the history of the Summer Institute of Linguistics (SIL) and its sister organization, Wycliffe Bible Translators (WBT).

The focus of SIL's immediate attention was the Quechua and Aymara people, descendants of the Incas, in the Peruvian Andes, for whom Spanish had never become their heart language. But the greatest challenge facing the fledgling SIL group were 300,000 jungle dwelling ethnic minority people groups speaking nearly forty different languages. Most of these indigenous people groups were secluded in 278,000 square miles of the forbidding jungle and rainforests of Peru's Amazon basin. The jungle is the most culturally and linguistically diverse region in Peru.

Within the first few months of their arrival SIL linguists had been assigned, as per the SIL contract with Peru's Ministry of Education, to work in seven different language areas. And Cam, doing what he did best, was making friends and establishing cordial relations with Peruvian educators and government officials.

Bob Schneider, an affable and skilled public relations man in his own right, was often invited by Cam to accompany him on visits with government officials (as were several others of the newly-arrived SIL workers.) "At first I was sometimes bewildered by Cam's leadership style."[2] Said Bob:

> I was anxious to get out to an isolated tribal village to begin translation. But "Uncle Cam," as we called him, immediately had us inviting embassy officials to dinner at our "group house." Later, these dinners included top Peruvian educators, anthropologists, physicians, scholars and intellectuals. What I didn't realize was that Cam, in his own inimitable style, was leading us into a life of initiating friendships, of entertaining our Peruvian hosts, and thereby educating and introducing us to a broad spectrum of Latin American life. I often marveled at the intelligent and winsome way he explained SIL's purpose, successes and problems. Frequently he would ask an official's help in solving a particular problem and he would act on the advice he received.
>
> I remember visits with the Minister of Agriculture where Cam discussed the problems of rain forest farming, and the need for government experimental agricultural stations. He regularly carried vegetable and fruit seeds from Mexico to Peru and later to Ecuador.
>
> I also remember well our visit at the Ministry of Public Health where the Minister introduced us to the head of tropical diseases, including leprosy, which was endemic in Peru's jungle. This particular physician was an outspoken critic of Christian ideology. When Cam realized this he invited him to visit the jungle tribes. This resulted in the physician becoming a lifelong friend and supporter of SIL. Years later, when certain political factions, ultra-nationalists and anti-religious groups attacked SIL, it was our early friends in our host country who defended us in the press and in other ways.

In August, the head of the Linguistic Department of Peru's University of San Marcos invited Cam, Elaine and Bob Schneider to give a series of lectures on linguistics and life in the United States.

High on Cam's agenda that first year was an immediate and concrete demonstration of SIL's commitment to its contractual agreement with

Peru's Ministry of Education. The contract called for SIL to do serious linguistic analyses of Peru's indigenous, mostly monolingual language groups. Along with the scientific linguistic investigation, SIL personnel were to begin applied cultural research and literacy development. This included creating and publishing primers and other reading materials. Coupled with this work SIL was to produce nonsectarian translations of the Scriptures. Ingrained in Cam's mind was SIL's three-fold purpose, namely, to serve others *scientifically*, *materially* and *spiritually*.

From the beginning Cam was committed to each of these three areas of involvement. He argued that relevant and effective service must be motivated by more than high ideals. "Rather," he said, "service must be based upon a foundation of scientific investigation and thorough understanding of the people being served." But Cam wanted more for the ethnic peoples than simply amassing scientific data about their language and culture. He believed ethnic peoples should have choices and a way to better their daily lives. Cam thought it was important for indigenous peoples to learn something of the acquired wisdom of mankind. Without such choices these people could sink into apathy or despair.[3] The antidote to despair and meaninglessness in one's life, Cam believed, was to experience God's love in a personal way. This, he said, was to be found in the person of Jesus Christ as revealed in the Scriptures. For this reason Cam was committed to making the Scriptures available to people in their own language who could not otherwise hear the good news of the Gospel.

Cam also wanted government officials, as well as SIL workers, to learn that the SIL model was one of cooperation with the national government's aims, programs and goals for its people. SIL would not compete with the government. Dr. Benjamin Elson, Wycliffe's Executive Vice President wrote:

> One of the things Uncle Cam did when he first went to Mexico was to ... identify with [the goals and aspirations of the Mexican government] ...to provide a better way of life for the Mexican people. [He showed this solidarity by writing] a biography of then-president of Mexico, Lázaro Cárdenas. Some critics thought this was a waste of Cam's time, since it required a great deal of work on his part as well as that of several SIL members. The aim of the Cárdenas biography was not only to explain the Mexican Revolu-

tion to English speakers, but also to show the solidarity and identification that Uncle Cam felt for Mexico and for the aims and
aspirations of the Mexican people.

In Peru, when SIL began a bilingual school system at Yarinacocha, SIL's
jungle center, it was a cooperative effort. The school was an official part
of Peru's educational system, with a government-appointed director
and with government paying the salaries for the Indian schoolteachers.
SIL provided the location for training and technical expertise and for
the preparation of study materials in the indigenous languages. In other
words, Uncle Cam felt that service programs should be essentially government programs in which SIL merely helped.

A beginning step toward implementing these goals in Peru came
when Dr. Luis Valcárcel, the Minister of Education, gave Cam and
Elaine the responsibility of conducting a reading campaign to address
the problem of illiteracy among the highland Quechua and Aymara
peoples of the Lake Titicaca area. At 12,500 feet, this massive body of
dark blue water laps at the borders of Peru to the west and Bolivia to
the east. It is noted for being the world's highest navigable lake. The
area is also known for the buoyant *totora* reeds that people pull from the
shallows on the Peruvian side of the lake to build their homes and reed
boats called *balsas.*

The Quechua languages, with twenty major dialects, and Aymara,
also with several dialects, are Peru's largest indigenous ethnic language
groups. In the 1940s these descendants of the great Inca empire were on
the government's list to receive improved health care, agricultural and
literacy education. In October of 1946, Professor Jorge Alberto Paniagua
from the Ministry of Education and SIL workers Olive Shell, Ellen Ross
and Elaine Townsend, who was seven months pregnant with her first
child, prepared a set of primers for Quechua teachers and began literacy
classes in the Andean highlands. In her journal, Elaine wrote:

> The [Peruvian] government has asked me to work on a large read-
> ing campaign in the Quechua and Aymara languages. The govern-
> ment will print 50,000 primers. I'll be going to an area called Puno,
> about 12,500 feet elevation, in the Andes. There are fifty-six teach-
> ers being trained for this reading campaign. Sixteen of them are
> from Bolivia and the rest are from Peru. When the teachers return

to their own areas they will in turn conduct literacy classes. This means they will reach well over a thousand teachers. What a wonderful opportunity to help these teachers! This means thousands of children and adults will be learning to read in Quechua and Aymara. I will introduce the primer (that I have prepared ahead of time) as well as literacy helps like games and flash cards. I am hopeful the government will adopt the alphabet Ken Pike worked out when he was here. The Minister of Education has had forty different alphabets submitted to him for Quechua alone.

In her report Ellen Ross wrote:

After searching for a suitable site we began our classes on October 16, at Puno, an important Indian center and provincial capital. Our assignment was to find a monolingual school-age class of Aymara Indians and demonstrate that children could learn to read and write in their own language. This necessitated, of course, that we prepare primers, flash cards and flannelgraphs as teaching aids. While Elaine Townsend found it difficult to work in the high altitude, her considerable experience in reading campaigns was invaluable to us. News of the "school" spread quickly and in a short time we had twenty-one day students and a night session as well.

Classes were held on a cobblestone patio, where the rays of the sun warmed the highland air. Stone benches skirting the sides of the houses served as desks. The Aymara girls sat with chapped bare feet pulled in under their long woolen skirts. The boys, however, had no such refuge. Their bare feet and fingertips were often swollen with chilblains, and their ears turned red from the cold. With every syllable the boys and girls could see their breath. In spite of the cold and uncomfortable seats, the children made surprisingly rapid progress. During recesses it wasn't unusual to see one or more of the children clinging to their primers, preferring to study rather than play with the beanbags we teachers had brought for them. The campaign lasted seventeen and a half days. Dr. Julián Palacios, Director of Rural Education for Peru, visited us at the conclusion of our program and was impressed with the children's reading ability. He termed the campaign a good beginning. As a follow-up among the Aymara there are plans for three more primers. The first will be in four sections. All except the last reader will be bilingual (Aymara-Spanish), the last will be entirely in Spanish. A similar series of readers is to be published in Quechua.

Ellen Ross ended her report by saying, "All of Indo-America will follow with deep interest Peru's aggressive effort to solve its long-standing problem of illiteracy among the many ethnic minority peoples."

Cam was gratified with this modest beginning. In future years there would be several New Testament translations and remarkable literacy progress among the Quechua and Aymara. Cam's mind and heart however, were focused mainly on the languages of the Amazonian jungle. His chief concern in 1946 and 1947 was how to secure enough airplanes to support the isolated translation teams who, without air support, would have to rely on dangerous, unpredictable and tedious river travel. On July 12, 1946 Cam signed a contract to buy a J2F5 amphibian biplane (Grumman Duck) formerly used by the U.S. Naval Mission in Lima to rescue downed pilots in the Pacific Ocean. In a report entitled *How God Has Provided an Answer to Prayer,* Cam revealed how God used "means" to answer his prayer for an airplane:

> In 1946 I providentially learned the American Naval Mission to Peru was taking a surplus Grumman Duck to Panama for disposal. We were in desperate need of air support. One couple on the Marañón River had been out of touch with us for five months. Two other young women translators on the Urubamba River had been gone for the same length of time. When I learned about the Grumman Duck, the price was set at $45,000. We were without funds, but our need was great and I felt God would somehow provide the funds.
>
> I went to the American ambassador, whom I had met in a very providential way, to ask if he would delay disposing of the plane for ten days to give me an opportunity to bid on it. I also asked if he would give us special consideration. Jim Truxton, president of Christian Airmen's Fellowship [later to be called Missionary Aviation Fellowship, MAF], called on the State Department in Washington to also ask for special consideration. When the American ambassador, the Honorable Prentice Cooper, agreed, I immediately sent cables to three businessmen, one in Philadelphia, one in Chi-

cago and an old friend in Santa Ana, California. I told each of them about our critical need for air support, of the plane's availability and of its low price. Two weeks later I heard from the first two who promised to "pray about our need." But from the old friend in Santa Ana, I received an immediate reply by cable telling me he was sending $3,000 toward the purchase of the plane. In an amazing way, this was almost half of what I thought we needed. I knew the price was lowered, but I didn't know the exact amount until the moment I signed the contract. The price was $3,500. I was able to persuade the Ministry of Education and the Ministry of Health to pay half the cost of the plane ($1,750 each) and become co-owners with SIL. They agreed.

On July 20, 1946 at 10:30 in the morning, in a ceremony attended by five Peruvian cabinet members and numerous other invited guests, Mrs. Cooper, the mother of the American ambassador, christened the Grumman Duck. Mrs. Cooper poured out a cornucopia filled with red, white and blue flower petals over the nose of the plane saying, "Amauta shall be thy name, for thou shalt bring science to serve the peoples of the jungle." *Amauta* is a Quechua word reserved by the ancient Incas for the wise men and engineers of the Inca Empire. Since the purchase of the plane was a partnership with the government, the Peruvian Ministry of Aeronautics also signed an agreement to provide free aviation gasoline and regular airplane maintenance.

On July 24, 1946 Prentice Cooper, United States ambassador to Peru, wrote to Dr. George G.L. Cross, the president of the University of Oklahoma, to express his appreciation for the work of SIL in Peru:

Dear President Cross:

This is to tell you how favorably impressed I am with Dr. William Townsend and the Institute of Linguistics, Inc., with which the University of Oklahoma is associated. Dr. Townsend is a great leader and has the confidence of the Peruvian government as well as the American Embassy here. It is a great pleasure for me to assist him in securing an $80,000 Grumman Amphibian for use by the expedition for a total of $3,500. More than $3,500 in spare parts was furnished without charge.

Very sincerely yours,

Prentice Cooper
United States Ambassador to Peru

From the beginning, Cam insisted that SIL be a nonsectarian servant within a Christian framework, a Good Samaritan organization at the disposal of any and all who needed assistance. This meant that if a government official, an atheistic anthropologist, a materialistic businessman or a Catholic priest needed to be flown out of the jungle, Cam was more than willing to help them. This distinctive SIL concept of service-to-all-people without regard to ideology did not sit well with many conservative religious groups in the U.S. When Cam and SIL came under fire for exercising these services, Cam would tell them this story:

> A priest was about to leave for a long riverboat trip when the river was running dangerously high.
>
> He decided to ask if he could pay for a flight on one of our airplanes to get him to the village near his destination. The question now becomes, should an SIL pilot refuse the priest on the basis of what some evangelicals called "giving aid and comfort to the enemy"? If the pilot refused, the priest would have to get his food, rain clothing, mosquito netting and other supplies and begin a month-long river trip. Such a trip would include the discomforts of sitting unprotected in an open canoe under either an intense equatorial sun or in a drenching tropical rainstorm.
>
> Some time later, whether hours or days, the priest, now sick of his river travel, would look up and see the JAARS plane on its two-hour flight to his destination. At that point the priest might well curse JAARS, the pilot and the God whom SIL purported to serve. And he would be right to do so. Our experience is that great friendships have been established through loving service to all without respect to creed or ideology.

This was no apocryphal story.

Cam knew what it was to endure leaden skies with pouring rain that would turn lowland jungle trails into slippery, greasy mud that stuck to your feet like great globs of bubble gum. He knew firsthand what it was like to hike through a rain forest, through the dense underbrush of ferns, stinging nettles and slippery moss-covered vegetation that lined the small streams along the trails. He could not ask young women translators to take month-long canoe trips in order to reach a tribal location.

However, in January of 1947, Cam did travel down the Aguaytía River in an open canoe to allocate Canadian SIL member Olive Shell and Gloria Gray from Little Rock, Arkansas. Later that month, Betty Greene, on loan from Mission Aviation Fellowship (MAF) flew the *Amauta*, carrying Cam as he helped allocate Ellen Ross and Lulu Reber, two SIL translators. However, Betty could only fly them from San Ramón to Atalaya. From there Ellen and Lulu continued up the Urubamba River by canoe for twenty-seven days to reach the village of Timpía, where they began their study of the Machiguenga language.

Like SIL, MAF, begun in 1945, was a pioneer service organization. Its first leaders, Jim Truxton, Grady Parrot and Betty Greene had come out of the United States military. Each felt a call of God to serve Christian missions through aviation. When Betty Greene first joined MAF she was assigned to fly a 220-horsepower Waco biplane to support SIL in Mexico. Bob Schneider, who grew up with Betty in Seattle, said:

> Betty earned her pilot's license in a pontoon plane on Lake Washington. Later she joined the WASP (Women Air Force Service Pilots) and served during World War II ferrying aircraft and transporting high-ranking Air Force officers. In many ways Betty was the complete antithesis of the stereotypical woman jungle pilot. She was tall, attractive, refined, and when she spoke she enunciated her well-formed ideas with a cultured accent.

When Betty was reassigned from Mexico to fly the *Amauta* in Peru, Cam spoke highly of her as a person and as a pilot. In a letter dated January 25, 1947 Cam wrote:

> *How beautiful above the jungle are the wings of them that bring good tidings.* I am writing this paraphrase as we are flying up the Tambo River from Atalaya to San Ramón. To my right is a range of mountains and a plateau about a mile high where very few white men have ever gone. It is considered a "no man's land" of the Campa Indians. To the left the jungle stretches out in a vast level plain till it disappears in the horizon not far from the border of Brazil. Soon the

Tambo River will make a bend around the mountain range and turn west toward San Ramón, the end of the central auto road from Lima. We flew there last Wednesday to get Lulu Reber and Ellen Ross on their way to the Machiguenga Indians.

Betty Greene, who sits at the controls in the front cockpit, has proven to be God's own choice for this flying assignment. She is expert, cautious, calm and full of trust in the Lord. Her tact, courtesy and humility have completely won the members of the Peruvian Air Force with whom we cooperate. In turn they do all they can for us. (We are dependent upon them for mechanics, repair shops, gasoline deposits, hangars and radio stations. With just a smile from Betty, we secure one hundred percent cooperation. Betty had won many friends for the work during these months of almost daily trips to the repair shops. She has been a great testimony for us and for her Lord.

It is my privilege to go along on these allocating trips. We as yet do not have a mechanic and someone has to get out on the wing when we land on the river to throw a rope to a man on the bank to tie the plane to the shore. I also need to make arrangements for living quarters for our workers. Last month Sylvester Dirks made a trip by canoe with Henry Osborne to reach the Amahuaca Indian people. It took them nine days up one stream and three down another. It takes an hour by air. Another couple is to join us (Larry and Beulah Montgomery). We'll then be a group of twenty-five here in Peru. Larry is an expert pilot, aviation engineer and mechanic. He will be a great help to Betty. Immediately after Larry arrives, Elaine and I, with our precious three-month old daughter Grace, will leave for the Jungle Training Camp in southern Mexico.

Cam did not know then that this seemingly routine trip would involve a near-fatal accident for him, Elaine and baby Grace.

Notes

1   The SIL members who arrived in Peru in April and May, 1946, with Cam and Elaine were: Sylvester & Mattie Dirks, Titus & Florence Nickel, Pete & Mary Fast, Bob & Lois Schneider, Mary Hinson, Gloria Gray, Ray Liedtke, Irene McGinness, Lulu Reber, Esther Matteson, Ellen Ross, Ralph Sandell, Olive Shell and Henry Osborn. In November 1946, Dr. Ken & Lucille Altig arrived with their two children Charlene and Howie. In early 1947 Ken and Vivian Watters arrived with their son John. In May Dale Kietzman, Larry and Beulah Montgomery, later Dave Beasley and in November Harold & Juanita Goodall arrived followed in December by Harriett Steinhilber (Dale's fiancée).

2   Cam's leadership style was unique in that he would often provide a framework or opportunity for a younger worker to assume responsibility for a project that he himself had initiated. He allowed the younger and less experienced worker to exercise his or her own initiative. The further genius of Townsend's leadership style was his own attitude. He did not micro-manage. When he gave control and authority to younger workers he seemed not the least troubled by his own ego. He was confident enough of his own ability and moral authority to see that "if the young members ran too wild and got out of control" he could rein them in. See Appendix B, "Uncle Cam's Leadership Style."

3   There were a number of isolated indigenous peoples who, before coming in contact with SIL translators and learning something of God's love for them related that as a group they were often depressed and longed for death. Harriet Fields and Hattie Kneeland discovered this when they first made contact with the elusive Mayoruna people.

William Nyman (left) with Cameron Townsend, was Wycliffe's secretary-treasurer. Beginning in 1942, he served for 22 years in that position.

Chapter Two

The Crash

"The only one to escape injury was three-month-old daughter, Grace. She was being held safe in the arms of a Tzeltal Indian man who was on the scene moments after it happened."

This was part of Cam Townsend's letter dated February 25, 1947, written from Jungle Camp at Yaxoquintelá, Chiapas, Mexico and addressed to Dick Pittman, then-director of the Mexico branch of SIL. Cam continued:

> We have just had a commercial airplane accident in Joe Urquidi's Super Cruiser. Elaine seems to have a broken ankle and I definitely have a broken leg, but little Gracie came out without a scratch. The pilot is seriously injured. We had just taken off when, for some unexplained reason, the pilot suddenly banked, possibly to go back to the airstrip. The maneuver caused the plane to lose altitude and the tail to hit a tree in a small ravine. Fortunately, the plane itself did not crash until we were over the ravine. Before the Jungle Camp staff and students got to us, Elaine and I were able to extract Grace and ourselves from the plane. The pilot, however, had to be pulled

out. As I write this, three and a half hours after the accident, he is still unconscious.

We are grateful to the Lord that the plane did not catch fire, although the gasoline poured out in a stream—some of it on the baby and on us. We are thankful it happened to us and not to any of the Jungle Campers. We also praise the Lord that Dr. Culley is here. You can imagine how busy he has been after the accident and still is, giving injections and preparing to set bones.

We hope and pray the pilot's life may be spared, but it looks doubtful. [The pilot did survive.] Except for this we are thankful for the accident because it shows conclusively that for such an important project as the one in which we are engaged, it is absolutely necessary to have the best aircraft and pilots possible. The accident also shows us the importance of establishing our centers close to medical help. It seems we will be here for at least two weeks.

P.S. Please advise all that any mention of this accident must stress that it was a commercial aircraft and not our own.[1]

This was the first of many letters, telegrams, news bulletins and press releases that Cam and the group sent out. On April 12, 1947, Cam wrote his dear friend Albert (A.M.) Johnson[2] (whom everyone called Uncle Al) and painted a complete picture of how and why the accident occurred:

The pilot arrived a little after noon on Tuesday, February 25, in the same Piper Super Cruiser that had brought us to Jungle Camp a week before. When we got to the landing strip with little Gracie in her basket and a small amount of baggage, the pilot was in a hurry to take off. He expressed concern about his landing gear, because earlier that day he had hit a dog. As you know, the landing gear on the Piper is very light.

The pilot had us get into the plane as quickly as possible; he was first, then Elaine, and then me. A week before when we had flown out from Tuxtla we had strapped ourselves in, but because we got in so hurriedly, and because there was only one seat belt for the two of us and, for some reason it was out of sight, we forgot to strap ourselves in. I don't think the pilot strapped himself in either. We were terribly crowded; Grace's basket filled all the space between the pilot and us. I had to put my left leg a ways under the pilot's seat. The small amount of baggage we had was just behind my head.

Without giving us time to do much more than close the door, the pilot started off at the beginning of the runway. I watched the speedometer closely, a habit I had gotten into when flying in Peru with Betty Greene. By the time we got to the middle of the field, we had attained a speed of only about thirty-eight or thirty-nine miles an hour (when it should have been between fifty and sixty) and with that we took off and made altitude quite abruptly. As we passed the group on the field, waving goodbye, the plane was four times as high as the Waco would have been when Betty would take off clear at the end of the field. By the time we reached the end of the field, however, the plane seemed inclined to settle. (Betty thinks we hit an air pocket.) At that moment the pilot began to look around from one side to the other as though wondering what to do. He should have nosed down slightly and gone straight ahead and picked up speed and could have landed in the grass without much damage.

Instead, he turned sharply to the left, losing altitude and causing the tail of the plane to hit a tall tree. With that we came down sharply hitting one side of a small ravine and bouncing to the other side where we came to an abrupt standstill. Everyone on the ground said we would have been killed if we had landed in the middle of the ravine.

Immediately after the crash I looked down at little Gracie in her basket. I had my arms over her to prevent her from bouncing out. She had awakened and was looking at me with an astonished expression. By this time gasoline was pouring out between Elaine and me. (The pilot was unconscious and was unable to turn off the ignition.) I realized there was danger of fire. I tried to get out as fast as I could but my left leg was entangled around the supports of the pilot's seat. I had to disentangle it and then tumble out of the plane with Grace in my arms as best I could using only one leg. Elaine followed me as rapidly as she could; her left foot was pointed off at an odd angle. Later Dr. Cully said it had been dislocated from her leg. I began to drag myself further from the plane, but the ground was quite broken. I had a deep gash in my thigh that was bleeding and I was making very little progress. Just then an Indian man came up and I handed him the baby, telling him to take her away from the plane. The students also began to arrive and a little later Dr. Culley with his medical kit. He immediately administered the most necessary first-aid. The students then started taking Elaine to camp on an improvised stretcher and attending to the pilot. By the time they got around to taking me in it was getting late and threatening rain. Fortunately, it only drizzled. As I sat on the ground waiting for my turn to be carried back to camp, the only thing I could think of was that God was going to use the accident in a wonderful way for the furtherance of our aeronautical program in reaching pioneer fields that are almost inaccessible by any other means of travel. In a strange way it was a wonderful experience because the Lord gave us the assurance that something good was going to come of this. Later we rejoiced that the accident had come to us and not to any of our workers.

Eight months before the accident, on the morning of July 9, 1946 (Cam's fiftieth birthday), he wrote to a group of friends telling them that a Quechua washer-woman in the SIL group home had given him a birthday verse—Isaiah 40:31: *They that wait upon the Lord shall renew their strength.* Cam said this was a most appropriate verse to remind him that with the immense amount of work he and others had been doing, there had indeed been a renewal of strength. In fact, Cam said:

It seemed more like relaxing while watching a stronger one than Samson do the work. The responsibilities are increasing, and the jungle type of work we are forging requires more strength than in the past. But God will give us strength, as we need it. Praise His name.

Besides telling people how great it felt to be fifty, Cam said how wonderful it was to have Elaine by his side "Working with her is fun. God has fitted us for one another in an exceptional way. She is my joy!" In her letters to Cam, Elaine often signed her name as "Joy." [Later, when a second daughter was born to them, she was named Joy.] At the conclusion of that letter, Cam returned to a theme he had been talking about for months, even years—the need for airplanes to support the isolated translators in Peru. Cam was also aware that the newly acquired Grumman Duck airplane posed a new set of challenges:

Even though we have the amphibian here in Peru, and the Waco in Mexico we should not be over-confident. We must be undergirded *daily* with unseen wings of prayer. There must not be a single accident of any importance. The experience and skill of the MAF pilots will enable them to do their part. Prayer will do the rest. In this regard please pray also for adequate radio equipment for the base and for each lonely river operation. The safety of the workers as well as the airplanes may often depend upon this feature [radio contact].

While Cam expressed parental concern for the safety and well-being of translators in the field, his letters reveal almost no concern for his own safety. His faith and trust in the sovereignty of God in matters of life and death during his younger days in Guatemala and Mexico had always been rock-hard. Challenges in Peru, however, were proving to be more daunting than those Cam had experienced previously. For one, there was the vastness of the jungle itself. In a letter to American Ambassador Prentice Cooper, Cam wrote:

The trackless, ocean-like expanse of jungle east of the Andes [makes] the contacting of the many tribes, mastering their languages and extending them a helping hand, a most difficult task.

Other atypical incidents included the near drowning of Florence and Titus Nickel. In an understated description of that experience Florence Nickel (who was four months pregnant) wrote:

We had quite a strenuous trip. When we left on December 6 to come to Lima we were completely out of food and trade goods. The river was high which made traveling in the canoe extremely difficult and rather dangerous. When we reached the end of our canoe travels we had a four-day walk through the jungle. That was the hardest part of the trip. We then rode mule back for a day and a half, then were in a truck for thirty hours and finally rode down to Lima in a bus. Although we rested in between times for a day or so, we had nineteen days of actual travel. We will certainly be thankful to the Lord for the change the plane will make in our journey to and from our tribal allocation.

Yet another translator had to be evacuated to Lima for an emergency operation and some were becoming ill with hepatitis and malaria. These and other life-threatening experiences put Cam in touch with his own mortality in a new way. In a December 10, 1946 letter to Ken Pike, Cam seems to step out of character when he admits to being concerned for his personal safety and the danger involved in an upcoming trip:

> If anything happens to me on this trip resulting in a belated return or none at all, I would like you to become general director. Our family relationship has nothing to do with this wish [Ken was married to Cam's niece Evelyn] but rather it is your experience, unusual close adherence to our Wycliffe policies, gifts, vision, spirituality and love for your fellow workers. I write this because so many mention the dangers of this week's jungle flying.

As founder and general director of SIL and Wycliffe, Cam took a keen interest in all matters dealing with staff, individual workers and future developments of the group. Nothing, it seemed, was too insignificant for his attention. He was even known to play the role of matchmaker. But change was in the air; the group was growing larger year by year. The U.S. home office, charged with receipting monies and forwarding them to the individual translators in Peru and Mexico, needed more office space and personnel. William Godfrey Nyman Sr., a retired lumber company businessman, long-time friend, and avid Townsend supporter, was the group's secretary-treasurer. He had provided office space in an apartment over the three-car garage at his family home on the corner of Louise and Randolph streets in Glendale, California. But now the demands for more office space and personnel required him to move from the apartment to a larger storefront office, also in Glendale. The Wycliffe board was now assuming more responsibility for the direction of the group. However, Cam's casual and informal administrative style was sometimes at variance with the board. Cam often made major decisions not in a corporate boardroom, but at a dinner party or on a casual walk. The creation of bylaws for the group, however, had put in place legal administrative procedures that Cam often bristled at. In a November 12, 1946 letter to the Wycliffe board, Cam entered into a fray over what he considered to be the board's arbitrary "remote control" appointment of two members to the Peru executive committee:

I don't understand your logic. First you instructed me not to place the person I wanted on the committee. Then you arbitrarily picked two others and instructed me to use them. By doing this you manifestly felt that you at a distance knew more about the qualifications of the workers here than I, who am on the "front line," and have worked with these people for months. Also, two of you suggested I submit my nomination to you for approval by the executive committee, a thing I was never required to do in Mexico. There the Branch always trusted me to make my own appointments of someone to act in my stead. I honestly feel you would be a better board if you wouldn't do such things.

Several paragraphs later, Cam, following the example of the Apostle Paul in his second Corinthian letter, wrote:

While I am dead against "remote control" I need to beg your pardon if I have hurt anyone's feelings. I apologize if I have acted contrary to my customary procedure and have exceeded what is generally expected of me in the way of direction or interference. However, I am fully convinced that my opinions made good sense and were in line with what have been and should be our policies.

There were, however, some hurt feelings. The board did not receive Cam's letter well. This was a board that took seriously their responsibility to act in the best interests, goals and aspirations of the organization. On November 25, 1946, at board member Dr. John Hubbard's urging, William Nyman responded to Cam's letter. In the first paragraph he commended Cam's unique leadership and expressed how privileged all of the board members were to be part of what God was doing through "the Lord's great program in Peru." Then came the second paragraph:

We were all deeply grieved by your November 12th letter. We thought we detected an attitude on your part that was unwholesome for the organization of which we are all members. Although we have always attempted to be quick to respond to your reasoned statements, and often to your impressions of the Lord's leading, even when they have caused us to reverse our own earlier judgment, we cannot believe that by following the implications of the general tone of your letter we would become a better board, or one more serviceable to our Lord and our fellow workers. On the contrary, it might ultimately result in the board's weakness, indecision, and inability to give thoughtful consideration to any issue unless you were present.

This was not the first, nor would it be the last time Cam and the board clashed over some administrative policy procedure. There would come a time in the seventies when a new board would force the issue of Cam's retirement. His response to that notion was:

Retire, how can I retire when God's Word is still not available in over 2000 ethnic languages. Retire, never.

In the face of these scattered conflicts, two key elements of Cam's leadership style remained constant: The first, notwithstanding his letter to the board, was that he never wanted to make unilateral decisions.

A second key element of Cam's leadership style was that he never held a grudge or was vindictive, even with people who strongly disagreed with him. Anyone who clashed with Cam at noon could expect to sit down with him at dinnertime without the slightest hint of animosity, anger or judgmental comments. Cam's mind had moved on to other things.

Thus, Cam's letter appointing Ken Pike to be his successor in the event of his death—without first getting board approval—was normal for Cam, but a little unsettling for Ken. Ken Pike had a high regard for *Robert's Rules of Order,* and respect for corporate procedures and feelings of the board. Ken responded to Cam's letter by citing Wycliffe articles under which officers of the Wycliffe Corporation "shall be appointed," which by inference did not include Cam's impromptu approach to appointments. Ken's response to Cam's letter explored the legal avenues whereby, under the organization's bylaws and constitution, the office of deputy general director could be created with board and membership approval. The last part of Ken's letter, however, was much softer and reflected Ken's love and high personal regard for Cam in spite of the importance Ken placed on the preservation of democratic rule:

In the event of a disaster that would remove you from us we would be most dreadfully handicapped. Since, though, you wish to face the issue now, let me say that I personally hope that in such an event the entire senior membership at the annual meeting would have an opportunity to express itself in regard to the next leader. I think anyone without such backing would encounter a trying situation. Undoubtedly, though, the membership would give earnest attention to any suggestion you left with them, or with the board.

Let me say, Uncle Cam, that it has been wonderful to work with you. I do not know of anyone with whom I could possibly have labored so happily and harmoniously. Certainly no one has influenced me more in forming my specific missionary goals and attitudes. I am more deeply indebted to you than I can ever state, for opening up under God the way to do this task of getting out the Word of God.

For several months prior to the February 1947 crash at Jungle Camp, Cam had been sending and receiving a considerable amount of correspondence to and from Charlie Mellis, MAF's Secretary-Treasurer in Los Angeles. Much of the correspondence related to the activities of the Grumman Duck. Cam lobbied for yet another plane with supporting personnel and against any kind of "remote control" by the MAF home office. Clearly MAF and SIL were united ideologically and motivated by the same spiritual and altruistic values. They had every reason to find common ground and mutual cooperation. When Cam saw the need for an aircraft engine mechanic for Peru, MAF circulated an urgent appeal for such a person:

> An aircraft mechanic with the heart of a missionary is urgently needed to work in the jungles of South America. The candidate should be willing to leave very soon. To delay will jeopardize the advance of over twenty young pioneer Bible translators in their effort to give God's Word to seven needy tribal peoples.

However, there continued to be a major philosophical difference between Mellis' and Cam's understanding of how a flying program should be conducted. The stylistic difference related to Cam's fiercely held view that policy decisions should be made on the field. MAF, on the other hand, believed just as strongly that policy decisions, regarding who might pilot and ride in their planes, when flights should be made and under what conditions a plane should fly, must be cleared with the MAF home office in Los Angeles. Additionally, MAF had strong convictions as to the kind of aircraft they wanted to deploy in the field. This too, was at variance with Cam's view. Cam said that since most of the tribal people lived along rivers or beside lakes, the aircraft of choice was the pontoon plane. MAF favored planes with wheels. But the central feature of Cam's argument was control. Mellis wrote that the MAF position was, that "no major decisions in missionary aviation should ever be made by any one person." He continued:

> Since MAF is in a pioneering stage of development, and while our programs are small, and based upon previous experience, we believe there is need for a certain amount of "remote control." We fully realize the disadvantage of such "remote control" and are trying to keep it to a minimum. A single individual in the field naturally handles any problem that directly affects only the field in question. However, the executive committee must handle any problem that affects the work as a whole, such as movement of personnel, selection of aircraft, etc., after collecting *full* information from all fields and all sources.

The Wycliffe board favored the MAF administrative model, seeing it as parallel to their own. When Cam noticed this, he wrote a letter dated January 16, 1947, to Ken and Evelyn Pike [Ken was a Wycliffe board member] to lobby his own position:

> Now that Larry Montgomery is due to arrive shortly [he would replace Betty Greene] I feel that MAF in Peru should have the right to decide aviation matters *on the field*. For the sake of clarity let me draw a parallel between General Wedermeyer in China. He was not an aviation man, but in planning his campaign he knew what he wanted to do with his Air Force. He then told a competent aviation staff what his desires were. They in turn told him what they needed to carry out his wishes and he saw to it they got the necessary equipment. Here in Peru I feel I should have the authority to tell the aviation staff what I feel is needed and to do my best to secure

what they need to comply with my program. I feel we need to have our own permanent staff that understands our specific needs. I have a strong personal interest in seeing that the Word is being taken to the jungle tribes of Peru.

As was typical of Cameron Townsend, his vision was often larger than his grasp, or so it seemed to many of his contemporaries. Cam's letters to MAF in 1946 and 1947 outlined what he sometimes called the "Herculean task" of securing pilots and mechanics that were trained for the special challenges of jungle flying and living. Cam considered two pilots to be an absolute minimum. MAF thought one pilot was enough for the program in Peru. Cam disagreed. He wanted to have back-up pilots and planes to be ready for an emergency or to cover for a pilot who might become ill. Furthermore, in one of Cam's letters to Charlie Mellis it became clear that Cam wasn't just thinking of Peru:

> Captain Briggs who has flown the jungle and the Andes for almost four years and has flown all the way from the Philippines to Europe in all kinds of conditions for twenty-five years, says the day-in and day-out flying we will do is as tough as any he has ever seen. Besides the general flying a pilot must do, there will be a hangar to build, a shop to install, odds and ends of many descriptions to take care of, not to mention that he will have to learn Spanish, and attend to family responsibilities. The work that must be done will therefore require the efforts of more than just one or two pilots. Aviation simply has to succeed in this project if we are going to take the Gospel to over three hundred tribes scattered through the greatest jungle in the world that includes portions of Peru, Ecuador, Colombia, Venezuela, the Guyanas, Brazil, Paraguay and Bolivia. There is no reason in the world why the Lord cannot give us two pilots and a mechanic from the very start.

And so the debate continued. In the meantime, Cam's other concerns included the need for more members. To Max Lathrop, one of the early members who went with Cam to Mexico in 1934, he wrote:

> With doors of ministry opening and the Macedonian call coming from many parts of the world, we should have at least five times as

many volunteers next year [1947] as we did this year. The small
number this year has been a disappointment to me. I fear we didn't
have enough united prayer this year for recruits. I hope too, that a
number of our members will write articles about our work for
Christian magazines. Several recruits have joined us in the past
through reading such articles. The task ahead of us will require a
new kind of missionary.

To his long-time friend Charles Fuller, of *The Old Fashioned Revival Hour*,
Cam wrote to ask if he would "roll up his sleeves and give out a challenge" for Bible translation on his radio program. In his diary Cam
wrote: "If he does, it will help a lot. We should get a hundred and fifty
new workers in 1947."

There was also a growing need for workers other than Bible translators, to perform the many supporting roles such as finance personnel,
secretaries, teachers, government relations personnel, radio operators
and people to buy medical and food supplies for translators in the remote villages. Without support personnel, translators were being asked
to leave their prime linguistic and Bible translation responsibilities to do
what was called "group service." Cam also wanted to establish a clinic
and therefore needed a competent doctor and a nursing staff. The first
doctor to respond to this need was Dr. Kenneth Altig with his wife Lucille and their two children, Charlene and Howard. Altig was not only a
competent physician, he was also a passionate amateur "ham" radio operator and was responsible for bringing the first ham radio receiver and
transmitter to SIL in Peru.[3]

The SIL members who spent time with Cameron Townsend soon became aware that there was about him an overwhelming sense of expectation that God was working in some new and exciting way. The
membership also knew that Cam used strong, intentional language,
like, "we must," "we urge," "we should." He expected the members not
only to be in prayer partnership with him about his projects and vision,
but also to put hands and feet to those prayers. In two general letters to
the membership in October and December of 1946, Cam wrote:

> God has blessed us here in Peru beyond our fondest hopes. The op-
> portunities for service are great. I feel we should issue a special call
> to our membership for praise and prayer that the Lord will thrust

many more workers into His harvest. In this connection, there is a need to further develop our work in Canada. We have a wonderful Institute there, but very few recruits came from Canada this year. Something must be wrong and I am tempted to believe it is partially due to not having a permanent home office there. We should have one as soon as possible.

In 1942 we prayed for fifty new workers and God sent fifty-one. Last summer we felt led to pray for twenty-five new recruits. At the time such a prayer seemed impossible. There are now twenty-three accepted candidates in training in Jungle Camp in southern Mexico and several more applicants have come in. We plan to pray and work toward ten major prayer requests for Peru and Mexico in the coming year. We do this in the strength of Him who, time and time again, has done for us "exceeding abundantly above" during the twelve years since our humble beginning in 1934. As we plan for the future we commit our organization anew to the policy of serving all mission agencies that are giving out the Word in pioneer fields. May God renew the vision and give each of us faith to claim all of this and more. God can quicken our stride even as the world quickens its pace. May He find us ready!

Notes

1   For further details on this accident see Hugh Steven, *Doorway To The World, The Mexico Years* (Wheaton: Harold Shaw, 1999), 225.
2   It was in A.M. Johnson's home that Cam's first wife Elvira died on Christmas Eve, 1944. See *Doorway*, 191 ff.
3   Dr. Altig also pioneered in treating leprosy that he discovered existed among a number of extremely isolated ethnic peoples in the Amazon jungle areas.

Cameron Townsend with early aviation personnel in Peru
in front of the Canadian-made Grumman "Duck", first SIL
aircraft which he purchased for $3,500, were instrumental
in making safe transportation available to Bible translators
working in areas where no other means of transport were
available or feasible. Townsend once wrote: "How beautiful above the jungle are the wings of them that bring
good tidings" referring to his aviation pilots and mechanics. Left to right: Larry Montgomery, Don Smith,
Cameron Townsend, Les Bancroft, Bill Eddy, Roy Gleason,
Leo Lance, Bernie May.

Chapter Three

Nineteen Forty-Eight

It was the year Israel became a nation, Mahatma Gandhi was assassinated and Congressman Richard Nixon gained notoriety by prosecuting Alger Hiss. When the Soviet occupation army blocked all roads, rail and water communication with Berlin in 1948 the U.S. responded by flying over the blockade in what became known as the Berlin Air Lift.

In 1948 SIL had personnel working in forty-nine language groups in the U.S., Mexico and Peru. And also in 1948 on January 31, the Wycliffe board, meeting in the southern California home of William Nyman, voted to block Cameron Townsend's proposal to form SIL's own aviation and radio organization.

Ever since the summer of 1926 when U.S. Army planes under the command of Major Herbert Dargue landed in Guatemala City on a goodwill trip to South America, Cam's compelling dream was to use airplanes to reach the isolated tribal peoples of South America with the gospel. Five years later, in August of 1931, Cam, full of expectation about the practical use of airplanes to contact ethnic peoples attempted an aerial survey of the rugged Petén area of Guatemala. Unfortunately, forty minutes into that flight, bad weather and engine trouble forced the pilot to abort the trip. In a report to the Pioneer Mission Agency, under whose sponsorship Cam then worked, he wrote: "Bad weather and engine trouble convinced me that God's time has not yet come for us to use air travel."[1]

But that was then, and now in nineteen forty-eight, Cam felt the time for airplanes to implement the task of Bible translation in the Amazon jungle had arrived. The need was immediate and absolutely critical for the success of what he termed the "Peruvian advance." This "advance" had the support of the Grumman Duck and a superb pilot in Larry Montgomery, a former captain and instructor in the U.S. Army Air Force. But Cam strongly felt the need for more planes, plus pilots, airplane mechanics and radio operators, and all under the direction and control of the Peru branch director of SIL.

This was where the board, on that January afternoon in 1948, differed with Cam. The board argued that Missionary Aviation Fellowship (MAF) was the best, if not the only, viable resource for the aviation programs in Peru and Mexico. The Wycliffe and SIL leadership, including Dick Pittman and Ken Pike agreed with the board's unanimous decision not to form a new, separate aviation organization. "Planes," they said, "are expensive to buy and maintain. There is never enough money to meet the growing demands of other group programs." And besides, argued the board, "SIL is a linguistic organization, and should not be involved with airplanes. That's the prerogative of the experts in MAF." Ken Pike supported the board's decision and backed up his views by sending Cam a telegram that said "I strongly support MAF's recommendation [for Peru]. I absolutely oppose rupture with [Mission] Aviation Fellowship."

The board did, however, make two concessions at that critical 1948 meeting: one was to reaffirm his authority as general director, particularly as it related to the safety of workers assigned to remote jungle areas. The board also recognized Cam's unique gift for maintaining SIL's government relations in Peru.

While Cam was pleased that the board recognized his authority as general director, he felt that the reaffirmation was a kind of smoke screen. The members' safety and health were always uppermost in his mind. This was precisely why he wanted the authority to develop SIL's own aviation program. As far as government relations were concerned, Cam was the consummate diplomat. The board's concession was merely a vote of confidence in what he had done so successfully all of his career.

Another concession granted by the board was more to Cam's liking. In a letter to Dr. Torrey Johnson, head of Youth For Christ International, and Wycliffe board member Dawson Trotman, head of the Navigators, Cam explained what Wycliffe had decided:

> The Wycliffe board has just appointed a committee to be known as the Jungle Aviation and Radio Service (JAARS). This is a very important unit for the purpose of furthering the entire [translation] program for the hundreds of tribes in all of South America.

Cam was unhappy with the board's decision not to form a new separate aviation organization. Immediately after that January 31 meeting, before making plans to leave Southern California for Mexico, Cam began to dig in his heels and lobby more vigorously for JAARS to become an official aviation arm of SIL. In his letter to Dick Pittman, director of the Mexico Branch of SIL, written just days after the board meeting, Cam is unambiguous about his feelings toward the board and MAF, and gives his reasons for rejecting the board's decision:

> The Board's action on the aviation matter will probably be satisfactory to you. Since you were not present at that meeting I want to give you a full account of what happened. First, let me say there is no ill will toward MAF. All of us appreciate MAF and the fine spirit of its leaders. However, the fact remains they do not see what I see as an immediate need. MAF feels there is little need for another pilot-mechanic, and they feel Larry Montgomery went to Peru too soon.
>
> As leader of the Peruvian expedition I am responsible for the safety of our workers and the efficiency of their endeavors. I believe the aviation program is to be the lifeline of our entire work in the Amazon. I will not send young women translators to out-of-the-way places without air support.
>
> You spoke of the need for a translation center and a children's home in Mexico. These are worthy projects, but I am convinced the work in Mexico could continue without these valuable adjuncts. The work in Peru, however, cannot exist without aviation and radio communication for all of the translators in jungle allocations. Other methods have failed to accomplish their objective on anything but a

minimum scale. Since MAF does not comprehend the need, even after our having outlined it to them for over a year, we cannot continue to open up new allocations in Peru, much less plan for an entrance into Venezuela. The board saw no need to form another organization that would be independent of Wycliffe control the way MAF is. I disagree. I want JAARS to be a new organization that will be under my control. The problem in Peru is there are two heads for the same program. Such an arrangement does not work. But for some reason you and others of our board have felt such an arrangement will work with our aviation program.

As the responsible leader of the Peruvian advance this [two-headed] situation has caused me no end of grief, headaches and heartaches for over a year. I see the need for more aviation personnel—MAF does not. I see the need of a landing strip at the base, a hangar, a shop and homes for the pilots and other staff members. MAF feels these matters can be left to the future. Also, MAF and I differ on the types of planes we should use. They feel the Grumman Duck is too expensive and difficult to operate and repair. In the flood season I am inclined to believe that anything less sturdy than the Grumman Duck will not be safe. MAF wants to use lighter planes. I too, think we should have some lighter planes and I advocate for a four-seater instead of a two seater Piper Super Cruiser. I am pleased MAF has agreed with me on this point. We have prayed for such a plane for over a year. I still hope and pray we can secure an amphibian rather than a seaplane. MAF favors the seaplane because of its economy. But had we not had an amphibian last year when Ellen Ross took seriously ill and had to be flown out, she might not be alive today. Scores of tribes in Amazonia will never be reached with the Word of God unless our translators are taken to their otherwise inaccessible areas by airplanes and are kept in touch with help and supplies by the same means. In this region where commercial aviation is almost nonexistent, there is no alternative, we must have our own planes and they must be under our own supervision.

Always in the forefront of Cameron Townsend's thinking was the vision of what SIL and Wycliffe might become under God. While the board and a host of friends and colleagues supported Cam's general vision for

SIL and Wycliffe, many had great misgivings about moving the group into the field of aviation. On this point, he was virtually alone. But Cam's conviction through the faculty of faith was so real, and seemed to him so logical, that it baffled him why no one else could see what he saw so clearly. To him, Peru was the gateway to Venezuela, Ecuador, Bolivia, Colombia and Brazil. The lessons learned in Peru he believed would enable future translators to move with greater efficiency and understanding into each of these countries' ethnic minority peoples with the Word of God. But before this could happen, it was absolutely critical, from Cam's point of view, that JAARS replace MAF in Peru.[2]

So consumed was Cam by this vision that he was frequently unable to understand MAF's position, which often was not only reasonable but correct. While Cam was enamored with the Grumman Duck, and was negotiating to purchase another from Ecuador, MAF contended that such a plane was far too cumbersome and expensive to operate and maintain. Cam did acknowledge that the Duck was frequently in for one repair or another including an engine overhaul within months after it was purchased. In fact, one reason for buying another Grumman Duck would be to cannibalize the older one for spare parts.

One of Cam's distinguishing tendencies was to create alliances by asking others to speak for his particular point of view. Most often, the person speaking for Cam was in basic agreement with Cam's position. But after the board's decision, Cam asked Ken Pike to be his ambassador—to try to persuade the MAF leadership to agree with his point of view. In the past, when Ken was given an assignment outside his scholastic and linguistic expertise, he would often feel ill-equipped to meet Cam's expectations. In spite of feelings of inadequacy, Ken at first would accept the assignment, trusting God to work out the details. Sometimes, however, Ken would begin an assignment and then ask to be relieved, as when Cam asked him to spearhead the development of a mission children's home in Oklahoma City.

Cam now wanted Ken to venture into an area outside his expertise, and to represent Cam's views with vigor and conviction. Ken believed Cam was asking him to advocate a policy that had radical implications for the future of both SIL and MAF. Fundamentally Ken did not want a professional rupture between the two organizations. Ken also felt a greater sense of responsibility to represent the feelings of the board, of

which he was a part. In his report to Cam, Ken wrote not as Cam's ambassador, but as his critic:

> Your reasoning startled the MAF leadership, but they were sympa-
> thetic to your position. In my conversations with them I deliber-
> ately refrained from forcing the issue. It seemed to me we would
> ultimately gain more by voluntary (even if slower) cooperation
> than by immediate coercion. Furthermore, your present attitude, as
> expressed in your February 8 letter to Dick Pittman, if pushed vig-
> orously, would seem to be in danger of giving the impression that
> you are more interested in imposing your will on MAF than in
> coming to some workable jurisdictional arrangement with them.
>
> With regard to your request that "You will not need to try and
> represent the board in this case, or even mention your own opin-
> ions—simply be my ambassador," I decline this new commission
> for three reasons. One, I have already accepted certain commit-
> ments, as when the group put me on the board, and therefore I can-
> not ignore these responsibilities, even for you, when in my
> judgment, as one of their representatives it would not be in their
> best interests. Were you here, I think you would agree. Two, your
> stated concept of an ambassador seems to me surprisingly limited.
> Three, freedom of thought, judgment and speech are some of my
> priceless possessions.

It's not exactly clear how Cam reacted to Ken's letter.

In keeping with Cam's desire to preserve unity within the group, and
his basic premise never to allow an opposing view to paralyze his personal feelings toward a colleague, Cam, without giving ground, simply
turned his attention to other things.

One of the "other things" high on his agenda in January of 1948 was
the need for a new jungle center or base from which the Peru branch
could expand. Since their arrival in 1946, the group had occupied eight
rooms in half of an old hotel. The hotel was located in the foothills of
the Andes in the town of Aguaytia on the bank of a river by the same
name. For two years the group had been praying and doing aerial sur-
veys for a new center. The Aguaytia River with its seasonal rise and fall
and rocky river bed was completely unsuitable as a base for the
floatplanes. A handwritten prayer list found among Cam's personal papers

offers a glimpse into how seriously he prayed for people and projects in Mexico and Peru. At the top of the page of prayer requests Cam wrote, "Thy mercies are NEW every morning." Then he wrote out the prayer requests:

A *new* person who will come to faith among the Piro people in Peru and among the Amuzgo people in Mexico, both of them being "first fruits." James 5:7

A *new* Aeronca Sedan airplane with new Edo floats to make it into a seaplane for work on the smaller rivers of the Peruvian jungle where our heavier planes cannot go.

A *new* pilot; a new aviation mechanic; new translators. Primer in another language.

A *new* hangar for our planes, and a shop to repair both planes and radios.

Little homes for our aviation and radio personnel (a thousand dollars) is not too much to spend on a home for a fine aviator or radio technician.

Little huts for the Indian families who will come in from different tribes to help translators.

A *dormitory* for our translators when they are in from their allocations to work on translation.

A *headquarters* building with offices, mess hall, storeroom, etc., etc.

And every day a *new* reminder that God is faithful.

Through faith we can see a new base for our Peruvian work even though it's still largely in the prayer and planning stage. Termites are eating up the old base house and earthquakes have cracked the roof. A cracked roof in a climate where it may rain five inches (by actual measure) in one night is bad. Furthermore, the base is only loaned to us by the Peruvian government and too, it is not located properly for airplane operation.

A new base is basic (maybe the pun will be a reminder to pray) for our whole Peruvian program. Our new base should be on a lake where our seaplanes can be kept safe from floods that are frequent on rivers. The base should be near the center of the jungle, measuring north from the Bolivian border and south from the borders of Ecuador and Colombia.

When one views the life of Cameron Townsend during the early days of 1948, it would seem his world consisted only of problems to be solved. Bob Schneider wrote to ask for a date when the Peru branch could hold their first general meeting. The membership was anxious to discuss issues of growing importance, including the drawing up of bylaws and a branch constitution. There were hints that several members were unhappy about some of SIL's basic operating principles and this needed to be discussed openly. There were also overtures from Australia to begin an SIL school affiliated with the University of Sydney. And just a day before Cam was rushed to the hospital for an emergency appendectomy, Ken Pike received the following letter from E.H. Mickelson, of Biak, Indonesia:

> The interior of Dutch New Guinea is mostly unexplored country. Expeditions into the interior have been made at various places from the coast. These expeditions could be likened to the pressing of a finger into an inflated balloon, and the withdrawal of the same from it. There remains no evidence of anyone ever having visited the area.
>
> The only way one can reach the interior is by plane. Government officials in New Guinea estimate the population of the interior to be approximately 750,000. The population is divided into less than ten tribes.[3] I am most anxious that these languages of the interior be reached with the Word of God translated into them. Would your organization consider accepting such a responsibility? I am most anxious that you cable me your disposition relative to this point.

The popular definition of a visionary is one who believes that all things are possible. Cameron Townsend embodied that definition perfectly. He was also generally practical, as evidenced by his prayer list which included requests for a new Base home and new pontoons for a seaplane. Yet many members of the Peru branch in 1948 saw chiefly what they considered to be Cam's impractical, idealistic ideas about running an organization that was having trouble paying its way. On January 14th and 25th Cam received two letters from the chairman of the Peru branch executive committee, Canadian member Sylvester ("Syl") Dirks. Sylvester wrote about the deplorable condition of the group house, and the lack of personal support for half the Peruvian membership, and he called into question the need for a Jungle Camp, radios and even the need for the *Amauta*.

Sylvester began his first letter by expressing concern for Cam's health. (After an emergency appendectomy on December 13, 1947, in California, an abscess had developed in Cam's incision and he had to return to the hospital to have the abscess drained.) As the letter continued, Sylvester laid out his concerns and those of several others in the branch:

> As you know, the Peruvian Branch has been low financially for several months. The airplane fund was nil and even in the red until a week ago when funds did come in for *Amauta*. Even with the generous contributions received during the last few days the account is still not solvent. There is a general feeling that something needs to change in our program. Members' monthly support quotas have not been met. People have been living on emergency funds and our folks in Lima are especially hard hit, having received only half or even less of their monthly quotas. It is evident that this cannot continue without seriously affecting the work and the morale of the group. The enemy of our souls is busy taking advantage of this situation and real efficient work cannot be expected. We fear that the unity and spirituality of the group are in danger.
>
> I am also uneasy over the poor state of the hotel. During a rain we have to rush to place tubs and pails in a half-dozen different places to catch the dripping water. Absolutely nothing is being done to maintain this building. Major repairs on the roof and verandas are long overdue. But there are no funds to make the necessary repairs. After occupying this building for two and half years I feel the Peruvian authorities (who are not charging us rent) should expect us to be responsible for the upkeep. Uncle Cam, I feel if something is not done about this situation immediately we will lose our testimony and be considered by our host country to be undesirable tenants.
>
> I am convinced, at least to a certain degree, that we as an organization are laying too much emphasis on non-essential projects. They absorb too much of our funds. I am personally in favor of diverting the funds spent on jungle training toward the purchase of this hotel to be used as a permanent base of operations. I don't

think the training at Jungle Camp is all that essential. Personally I feel it is an unnecessary expenditure of precious funds and the time of the young people who are anxious to get out to the field. I also think we should sell the *Amauta* and buy a smaller plane that wouldn't cost as much to operate. I believe a couple of outboard motors could fill the place of the plane, one on the Marañón River and the other on the Ucayali. This would meet our need and would be something we could afford. I also question whether the radio system we're planning is really essential. I admit it is a good idea, but with funds so low, I am inclined to drop it for the present. At least we, the Dirks, do not consider buying a short-wave radio set during this first term on the field.

When Bob Schneider received a copy of Sylvester's letter to Cam, he reported that several in the group did not fully understand the relationship of Wycliffe to SIL and that Cam should by all means come to the Peru conference to clarify this dual approach to mission. But Cam said no—the director of the Mexico branch, Dick Pittman, would represent him at the conference.

Cam said he wanted to give his attention and energy to writing publicity materials for the new JAARS committee. He also said he could not return to Peru until there was an "adequate" budget raised for JAARS. To his friends the Nymans, Cam wrote that he believed God would provide according to Ephesians 3:20. In a March 3 letter to the Peru branch executive committee, Cam wrote:

> I think it will be fairer for those who are troubled over my policies for me not to be present. If I am not there, people will be able to present their problems with greater liberty. I also feel that the members of the board of directors who will be present will be less biased than I am. You see I am convinced there is no other way to give the Word of God to all the tribes of Amazonia than in the way we have been following.
>
> I have given a great deal of thought and prayer to our jungle aviation problem. I am firmly convinced it will be impossible to reach the Indian tribes without aviation and radio support. I know planes are expensive and need constant maintenance. But let's not put economy ahead of getting our people in and out of their tribal

allocations safely and efficiently. Using planes for this purpose will cut weeks of travel through damp, unhealthful forests, infested with countless insects, reptiles, wild beasts and sometimes-hostile [local people]. In the long run using planes will cost less than to dilly-dally around with outboard motors. If my program is rejected, perhaps you all can discover some other way. My only request is that those long-neglected tribes be given the Word of God soon.

Notes

1   Hugh Steven, *Wycliffe in the Making, The Memoirs of William Cameron Townsend, 1920-1933* (Wheaton, Illinois, Harold Shaw Publishers, 1995), 22.

2   Cam did not feel this way about MAF's role in Mexico. In fact, MAF served SIL translators with distinction for over five decades, with a great spirit of unanimity, personal fellowship, and friendship between the two groups.

3   In 1949, Australia's Territory of Papua and the Australian trusteeship, Territory of New Guinea, were administratively united to become the Territory of Papua and New Guinea. In 1972, the territory's name was changed to Papua New Guinea. The figures recording one indigenous group numbering 150,000 and there being only ten tribal groups are incorrect. There are estimated to be over seven hundred ethnic people groups in Papua New Guinea, with only a few hundred indigenous people in each group, and each speaking their own distinct language.

SIL's Norseman aircraft unloading supplies on the Tambo River at an Ashaninca Campa village. Planes were the only practical means of transportation to the language allocations from the home base of Yarinacocha.

Chapter Four
The Revolt

Cameron Townsend's instructions in April 1948 to Bob Schneider, who was now his deputy director in Peru, could not have been clearer:

> I had hoped the JAARS committee would be busy by now getting people interested and generating support for the aviation program. But Jim Truxton of MAF has written to the JARRS chairman objecting to any publicity about JAARS, and requesting the committee to wait. As a result, the committee has done nothing and I have no idea when they will start, if at all.
>
> This means no new allocations should be opened. And those already established that are extremely isolated should be suspended until radio and aviation communication have been established on a regular schedule. We should also be slow in encouraging officials in Venezuela and Bolivia about the possibility of our beginning work in those countries.
>
> The reasons for this are, in addition to the hopelessly weak status of our aviation and radio communication program, a far more critical deterrent; the almost disastrous revolt in our ranks in Peru. It breaks my heart but I have to recognize our work in Peru is stalled and we are in no position to advance.

The dynamics of group coherence and unity are often mysterious and difficult to quantify. In the same way, Cameron Townsend believed unity and *esprit de corps* between the SIL membership came from belonging to the whole family, to a team, to a company of colleagues—men and women of kindred spirits who felt a singular call of God to do a singular task. And implicit in that call was an unwritten agreement for the membership to work out their ministry using the God-given principles and core values that were forged and refined during Cameron Townsend's years in Guatemala and Mexico. Unity, operating as a team, is one of the stated SIL and Wycliffe core values. While Cam understood that each member was unique and that at times the group would have diverse opinions, he also knew that for the group to develop as a unified team, there must be mutual trust and respect and a willingness to sometimes suspend one's personal agenda for the well-being of the team, as one might do in a nuclear family.

It was this concept of Wycliffe as a family that in Cam's mind defined the ethos of Wycliffe Bible Translators and the Summer Institute of Linguistics. An early Wycliffe brochure began with the tag line, "You really ought to know about Wycliffe, it's all in the family." Because Cam thought of Wycliffe as family, with him as the titular head, it was difficult for him to accept a challenge to his well-thought-out "rules of engagement."

This challenge to Cam's operating principles came in the form of a fourteen-point opinion paper from the 1948 Peru branch conference. Each point was tallied with the number of members who voted for or against the proposal. The paper began with a deferential preamble in which all affirmed their confidence in the board of directors and for their "heartfelt affection and confidence in Cam as their general director." The group did admit they were submitting their proposals with some hesitation. However, the preamble went on to say:

> Nevertheless, there are problems, which have deeply troubled some of us. We appreciate most cordially that we have been given the opportunity to state our concerns and opinions. These opinions are in no way to be considered an ultimatum to the directors. We still [as a group] recognize the principle of obedience to properly constituted human authority. It is our intention to continue to coop-

erate to the best of our ability with the authorities in the group as long as the Lord leads us to continue as members of the group.

Some of the opinions had to do with public activities like Cam's recommendation that group members not attend evangelical church services *en masse*. Cam was keenly aware of the religious sensibilities of Peru, and did not want to draw undue attention to the group as a whole. Another opinion raised by some members was that Cam should not attend government receptions and official functions where liquor was served. Still others objected to SIL's cooperative government arrangement with the Grumman Duck airplane. (This was MAF's concern as well.) Others were upset when Cam, because of his certainty as to what could be accomplished, appeared to exaggerate SIL's track record when speaking to Peruvian officials. But by far the most talked about and debated opinion was over the double name of Wycliffe/SIL. Some voiced concern over what they felt was the duplicitous nature of SIL. Some felt the group was saying one thing and doing another. Interestingly, the very way they framed the question and their use of WBT/SIL showed some misunderstanding of the original relationship between the two organizations. It was never Cam's intention for the membership to think of the two organizations as a single entity. They were not. Wycliffe and SIL were, and still are, two distinct organizations, each with its own board, president and agenda, Wycliffe at home and SIL on the field. The members who wrote the proposals did acknowledge the importance of SIL's scientific linguistic contributions to Bible translation, but failed to grasp how SIL and Wycliffe differ in scope.

In all fairness to the early Peru membership, it should be said that the question they raised about SIL and Wycliffe was an issue that was to be debated among the larger membership for the next several decades. In 1980, and then again in 2000, Dr. Ben Elson, former Executive Director of Wycliffe, wrote papers explaining the nature of SIL that would have benefitted the early Peru membership. Ben admitted that when he joined in the early forties, he puzzled over the nature of SIL and Wycliffe. Wrote Ben:

> For years I did not fully understand SIL. I assumed it to be a linguistic organization whose members also engaged in Bible translation and literacy. This is true up to a point, and most of our

members understand this aspect of the organization. I have now come to understand what our founder has been trying to tell us all along, namely, that *SIL is a nonreligious organization that relates to governments and academic organizations.* This means SIL's reporting relationship is to an agency within the host government. This also means the decision-makers in the host government are always informed about SIL's goals of translation and literacy. In Peru and Mexico, SIL has formal contracts with governmental agencies. (In some countries SIL's contracts are with universities.) In the early years in Mexico the president of the country was the honorary chairman of SIL's local sponsoring committee. As Bible translations were completed we presented copies to our friends in the government along with copies of primers, dictionaries and other linguistic and literacy materials. To suggest that SIL was in any way duplicitous was incorrect. The governments in Peru and Mexico knew from the beginning what SIL was doing. Therefore, it is not true that we as an organization were lying to the government or to our constituents.

Unfortunately, the Peru membership in April 1948 did not have the benefit of Ben Elson's clear presentation on the nature of SIL. While this tempest of ethics was brewing in Peru, Cam and Elaine (who was eight months pregnant) in far-off Mexico needed time to think about these problems and to prepare for the birth of their second child. The little family left Mexico City for the town of Pátzcuaro in the West central state of Michoacán as the invited guests of Cam's good friend Lázaro Cárdenas, the former president of Mexico. Called *Quinta Eréndira*, the Cárdenas home (modest for a former president) sat on top of a hill with a commanding view of the beautiful thirty-three-mile-long Lake Pátzcuaro, where local fishermen ply the waters in dugout canoes and fish with picturesque butterfly nets. In every letter Cam wrote from this idyllic spot, he made some comment about the estate's profusion of vines, flower gardens and fine orchards. He ended an April 27 letter to a member with the following:

> Elaine and I are living at present at General Cárdenas' home on Lake Pátzcuaro, while waiting for the stork to arrive in a few days. It's a beautiful spot. One veranda looks out over the lake with its

various islands, and the other faces the garden and orchard. The place is a mass of blooms, with so many rose bushes, jacarandas and bougainvilleas. We are asking the Lord to give it to SIL for a translation center, but do not know what Cárdenas' decision will be.

In the midst of Cam's uncertainty about his future as general director, the natural beauty of *Quinta Eréndira* became for him a physical and spiritual oasis. When Evelyn Pike, Cam's niece, learned that Uncle Cam had threatened to resign over the "revolt" in Peru she wrote him a letter. It was dated May 14, 1948, nine days after the birth of the Townsends' second daughter, Joy Amalia. The letter was extraordinary for its candor and clear understanding of what Cam himself believed was Wycliffe's unique ethos:

> I know you are concerned about the problems that have arisen in SIL. As I see it these are growing pains coming from the natural development of a democratic organization, the machinery of which you set up at the beginning. I remember the business meetings we had in Mexico when there wasn't much interest in conducting business until we had heard directly from you. Since that time your program of training and developing leadership has come a long way. That, together with the strong democratic principles instilled in each one of us, has been a major strength of the group.
>
> With our democratic principles have come advantages and disadvantages. In democracies the leadership has to take time to explain issues and major problems. Members want to ask questions and have issues clarified in order to vote intelligently. On the other hand, when the authority is vested at the top, the ruling person can make decisions without consultation. And you never, ever wanted that for SIL or Wycliffe.
>
> Therefore, under our present organizational structure, when someone challenges the status quo, it doesn't for a moment mean they have lost confidence in or distrust your leadership. Democracies trust their leaders, but don't ascribe infallibility to them.
>
> At the same time, you are a man of God; you are like a father to us, you are an example of this new way to get the Word to those who have never heard. Above all else you have been used of the

Lord in finding His place of service for us! Those varying opinions from Peru aren't a matter of distrust. There isn't anyone in the group who inspires us or in whom we have as much confidence in their leadership as we do you. Difference of opinion isn't a sign of lack of confidence. The more strong men you have and the more experience they get, the more there will be differences of opinion on issues.

We were surprised to learn that our sister group in Peru voted not to attend functions where liquor is served. This seems to us here in Mexico to be quite unscriptural. Jesus certainly did not feel uncomfortable at such parties. While we say that the majority rules, it seems that the majority is not always right. I can imagine how grieved you are to see that the majority vote has worked to decide policies that you believe to be unwise.

I know the Peru vote is distressing to you, but I think you have taken the vote personally, more than you have a right to. This isn't your problem; it's the Lord's. This is His work. I am convinced that in God's time He will deliver you out of this trouble and you will be vindicated. How often have you told us if there is a job to do with little or much, we do all we can to do it? And Uncle Cam, those young people in Peru need you. Ken and I thank God continually for Elaine, Grace, and now Joy on your behalf. They are your haven and refuge. You need them and they need you and the group needs you. Even though it will be an uphill battle, you can't stop now. The enemy of our souls is kicking harder and harder, the farther we go into his territory. You can't say no to the Lord, you can't say no to Wycliffe and you can't for your own self, do anything but keep going.

Unknown to Evelyn, others in the SIL and Wycliffe leadership expressed similar views about the natural evolution of this experiment in mission democracy. Evelyn had wisely pointed out that since Wycliffe was drawing people from a variety of theological and cultural presuppositions the future dynamics of the group would change. Cam of course, did not readily accept this idea. In a letter to Ken Watters (who would one day succeed William Nyman as treasurer), then, one of the outspoken opponents of some of the Townsend policies, Cam wrote:

I was happy that Dick Pittman was able to take my place at the Peru conference. Because I feel so strongly about the special policies and methods God has led us to follow in the development of the SIL and Wycliffe work, it would have been hard for me to hear them criticized so severely. Those of you who were not with us at the beginning in Mexico to see the special way God guided and blessed us cannot understand, and therefore, I do not blame you for your attitudes.

What will be the outcome of so many diverse opinions within the group is hard to say. I am sure, however, that He who has begun a good work in Peru will see it through. A verse that has been a great comfort to me since reading the notes of the Peruvian conference has been Luke 1:45, "And blessed is she that believed: for there shall be a performance of those things, which were told her from the Lord" (KJV) That is my confidence and anchor as I see what had promised to be one of the most marvelous advances in the history of modern missions placed in great jeopardy. With Gideon's band I have no doubt that we can complete the evangelization of the tribes that remain, even when we are working behind closed doors. However, with a divided group ready to criticize some of our most basic policies it will be impossible to advance as quickly as I had hoped.

I say this not to criticize anyone in Peru. You need to know I have the highest admiration for you all. I also know how sincere and consecrated you are. Know also, that I too, would have been critical if I had not seen first-hand God's remarkable guidance upon our work in Mexico during each of our beginning steps of faith.

I also know that it takes a lot of faith for new recruits to trust their general when he leads them over strange new paths. I also know for an army to succeed it must have a general and soldiers who have the necessary faith to follow their leader. When that faith and trust is lacking, it is better to have a new general and I am praying very much about this. If Dick [Pittman] were not so busy with responsibilities in directing the SIL School in Canada and the activities of our large work in Mexico, I would like to see him take over the leadership in Peru. God will guide.

On May 5, the day Cam and Elaine's second daughter Joy was born, Dick Pittman wrote Cam and urged him to return to Peru as soon as possible. He wanted Cam to speak face-to-face with the group, rather than to try and work out the policy problems through correspondence. The reason, wrote Dick, was that "none of us, no matter how hard we try, can put into a letter the loving tone and affectionate assurance necessary to win people over on a delicate point." And then, as Evelyn had done in her letter, Dick wrote:

> In spite of the vote taken at the Peru conference, I am confident that once you are back on the field folks will rally to your leadership. Also, I do not believe the divisions of opinion in Peru are any greater than those we had at various times in Mexico. Differences of opinion are entirely normal, even among spiritual Christians. One of the greatest proofs of Christianity is the fact the Lord does not obliterate our differences of opinion, but rather gives us grace and strength to work together in love and fellowship in spite of our differences.

Cam sent a copy of Dick's letter to his friend, board member William Nyman with a hastily scribbled note appended at the top which said he agreed with Dick's assessment that he should not try to explain or impose Wycliffe policy on the Peru members via correspondence. But going back to Peru was out of the question until the MAF and JAARS question could be settled—in his favor. On May 25, 1948 Cam sent a lengthy four-page, single-spaced, reply (without paragraph breaks) to answer Evelyn Pike's May 14 letter:

> Your good letter was greatly appreciated. I am confident the current problems in Peru will be resolved in the end. But for the moment, I am not sure when and how they will be resolved. There have been a number of crises in my life and though they were hard to endure at the time, I praise God for them now. Invariably He used them for the furtherance of His work. Over the years I have had, at times, to disagree with the majority of our workers on certain issues. I have never enjoyed doing this. It hasn't been easy, but you can be sure I did not do so unless I was certain of my ground.

The situation in Peru puzzles me. I cannot understand how it happened. No one ever expressed any disagreement with my methods while I was there. In fact, until Sylvester Dirks wrote me I thought there was nothing but sweet peace and harmony with my methods. Yet at their conference they passed several resolutions that are diametrically opposed to the way the Lord has led me all the years I have worked behind closed doors. I was amazed at the resolution not to attend government functions where liquor was being served. The first man I ever won to the Lord [in Guatemala] was drinking in a beer garden. That was over thirty years ago. Ever since, I have gone into places where "publicans and sinners" have congregated and have always felt that by so doing I was following the Lord's example.

After reading the minutes of the Peru conference I realized we should have a more thorough period of orientation in Mexico before new members are assigned to a new field or given positions of authority on the field. I really blame myself for not getting back to Peru sooner, and for urging the new workers to go to the field quickly.

Regarding the aviation set-up as it now exists, I cannot go back unless our program is under the control of the Institute [SIL]. I see no other solution to the problem. This is true whether Dick or I direct our work there. I believe that a double leadership role will sooner or later bring administrative problems that will undermine our unique cooperative role with the government. We must have unified direction in all departments of the work. I am convinced that once organized, our JAARS aviation and radio program can be just as capable and efficient as our linguistic department. We have workers not only at the jungle base waiting to be allocated but we have workers in dangerous places in the jungle already, like Titus and Florence Nickel and their baby whose lives are in danger unless we can provide them with aviation and radio service.

Regarding our democratic principles, let me say I am in favor of them when the workers have been trained and have had field experience. There are three men on the Peru executive committee who have not done any tribal work, yet they are my bosses. It seems to me that whoever leads future advances into new countries should not be so handicapped. Would it not be wise for a new man in a new field to work under an experienced director for the first five years before being given a position of responsible leadership? In critical situations like we have in Peru, I like to think of myself as the quarterback on a well-trained football team. I call the signals, and throw the ball to the players who enthusiastically carry out their assignments. Every team has to have a quarterback. It isn't that the quarterback is infallible, but simply that he does his best. Outside of Peru I have turned over most of my leadership responsibilities to your husband [Ken Pike]. I no longer have sufficient energy for both Mexico and South America. I prefer to go where I am needed the most. If the board chooses to place its confidence in me, I shall be glad to attempt to rally the Peruvian workers around me and to advance the work in Peru just as soon as God enables us to organize a fully efficient and adequate aviation and radio department that will be second to none. If, however, I fail to convince the board of my vision for Peru and they order me to attempt to carry on subject to the constraints imposed by MAF, I will keep trying to convince them of my position. The only thing remaining now is for me to look to God for His will to be done. Thanks for your loving letter. I appreciate your prayers and your deep interest in the problems that have been weighing heavily upon my heart. I cannot tell you how much Elaine means to me. She is a real partner and I count a great deal on her advice, though she never becomes irritated when I don't follow it. We stand fast in the promise of Luke 1:45 for you and the group.

In the midst of his concern over the way some in the Peru Branch were taking exception to his policies Cam's spirits were frequently heartened by a translator's progress report. Such letters would once again put him in touch with the real reason for working in Peru. One such report came from Esther Matteson working with the Piro people:

I am busy taking down pages of tribal stories, discussions about how the Piros plant their fields, home life and family histories. All of this material will be most important in producing a translation that will sound natural to the way Piros speak.

Chapter Five
Dreams Become Reality

In 1948 worldwide political upset was the order of the day. Harry Truman confounded political pundits by being elected to a full term as U. S. President, defeating favorite challenger Thomas Dewey. Queen Wilhelmina of the Netherlands abdicated and was succeeded by daughter Julianna. David Ben-Gurion became provisional Prime Minister of the newly proclaimed state of Israel. And on May 21, 1948 after eighteen months of lobbying for the right to develop and direct an in-house aviation and radio department, the Wycliffe Board finally gave Cameron Townsend a green light to promote JAARS as the new service arm of the Summer Institute of Linguistics.

What is remarkable about the May 21 board meeting is the reason for the board's reversal of its longstanding and adamant position against ending Wycliffe's relationship with MAF. As late as April 15 (after the April 13 meeting) board member William Nyman wrote Cam to say:

> Cam, I did all I could to get the men to see your side of the MAF difficulties. I could not get even one member to see the advisability of severing our MAF contract in favor of JAARS serving our SIL program in Peru. Remembering you daily in prayer, and trusting

that this issue between MAF and you can soon be worked out, *I am with you all the way.*

Cameron Townsend was not an autocrat. He firmly believed in the democratic process and the free expression of ideas by Wycliffe and SIL members. Yet those who knew him best were aware that when Cam felt strongly that an issue or a program was critical to the development of SIL, he exhibited a dogged determination to motivate people to see his point of view. Years later in an interview with James Hefley who, with his wife Marti, authored the 1976 biography *Uncle Cam,* Cam revealed how he remembered the board's voting record:

> MAF wanted to be governed by home rule in the U.S. I would not agree. I said field personnel must make decisions on the field. I wanted more than one plane. MAF said no, we need to economize, and one plane is all you need. I said I would not be responsible for sending women and children into isolated jungle areas unless we had our own air service support that we could develop according to our own specific needs.
>
> When it came time for the board to vote to establish JAARS, there were three men who wanted to continue with MAF. But when the vote was taken, those three, Ken Pike, Gene Nida and Dawson Trotman, sided with William Nyman, Dick Pittman, and myself, because they said they wanted unity and wanted to side with me in this venture. [While some board members had their doubts, the May 21 minutes reveal that the board's decision was unanimous and JAARS came into being.]

One of the voices that may have influenced the board to follow Cam's leadership was that of George Cowan. Just a month before the May 21 meeting George wrote William Nyman:

> Townsend wants service to the translators in the field regardless of cost. He believes any economy that holds up service is poor economy. MAF gives more weight to economy than does Mr. Townsend. I know if the agreement between MAF and SIL is renewed as proposed by the current MAF leader, Mr. Townsend will not agree. He

will step out of the picture and allow someone else to take over the work in Peru.

However, I recently came across an MAF publication entitled *Wings for Mission*, which cites three different plans set up by MAF to work with various mission groups. Plan 2, says MAF, will, if desired, furnish pilots [as they did with Betty Greene] and a mission can own and operate their own aviation equipment and program, the pilot being entirely under the jurisdiction of the mission. Under plan 2 MAF is simply a recruiting office for experienced pilots for missions. MAF may also take an active part in supporting such a pilot with no strings attached and the pilot does whatever the mission program calls for.

Cam was aware of MAF's plan 2. On June 2, 1947 Charles Mellis, Secretary-Treasurer of MAF, wrote Cam a lengthy letter in which he adamantly said, "We would *never* want you to change to plan 2." Mellis added:

I assure you that it would take extremely extenuating circumstances to cause us to walk away and leave a program that we have started.

By May of 1948, the "circumstances" were indeed "extenuating," and some in MAF leadership seemed to have softened their position. In a letter to Larry Montgomery, in which he discussed at length why it was absolutely necessary for SIL in Peru to have the JAARS program, Cam said:

I believe it would be in the best interests of MAF as well as our own organization for us to change to plan 2 [in Peru]. This would mean we would not have to sever our relationship with MAF. They would then be able to do a better job in Mexico and we would be free to concentrate on Peru as well as on promotion in the homeland. We would still welcome all the help and counsel that MAF might give us, and would be just as glad to welcome help and counsel from other groups of Christian aviators.

On May 27, 1948 Cam wrote Larry Montgomery, Don Stark and Bob
Schneider, Cam's deputy director in Peru, to tell them the good news:
"The Board of Directors has just advised me of the action taken at their
meeting on May 21 whereby the leadership of our Peruvian aviation
and radio communication program is to be my responsibility beginning
the first of June."

A jubilant Cameron Townsend immediately gave instructions for
Larry to take charge of aviation, to sever his formal relationship with
MAF and become a "Wycliffite." Don Stark was to head up radio com-
munications. Bob Schneider would be Cam's representative on the field
until Cam returned to Peru and assumed his duties as coordinator,
counselor and director of all non-technical aspects of jungle aviation
and Cam instructed Bob to begin preparing maps of Peru showing the
various tribal locations, flying routes and estimated flight times for the
Amauta to reach these places. Cam wanted the distance logged between
the base and each jungle location. He also wanted the maps to pinpoint
each gasoline supply storage area and to indicate the availability of mechanics at the struggling SIL repair shop. He asked that copies of these
materials be sent to each member of the Wycliffe board of directors, and
to each member of the recently formed U.S. JAARS committee.

Cam further asked Bob to prepare other materials for full print and
photo coverage in the upcoming issue of Wycliffe's *Translation* magazine. He wanted as many people as possible to know about this new
challenge in Peru. And last, but by no means least, he asked that a
prayer calendar be printed listing the names and locations of all
Wycliffe members. He added that because of limited finances, all this
should be mimeographed, not printed. Promotion of the JAARS program and finances for airplanes and equipment were now Cam's number one concern. Just days after the board's landmark decision, and with
a near-empty bank account, Cam began making plans to order tools and
equipment for a first-class aviation repair shop. He wanted this in place
by October, in time for the arrival of Louis Rankin, an airframe and engine mechanic who had logged over three hundred flight hours. Louis,
along with Larry Montgomery, was scheduled soon to ferry another
Grumman Duck #J2F-236 purchased for $800, from Quito, Ecuador, to
Peru.

While Cam believed that he, along with the membership, should rely
on God alone to supply temporal needs, he also recognized a legitimate

dichotomy in the question of finances. Just as there are both divine and human agencies at work in the process of personal salvation, Cam believed God would prompt people to become financial partners if they were given information and the opportunity to choose. To longtime friend Clarence Erickson, pastor of the Chicago Gospel Tabernacle, Cam wrote about his belief that divine and human action are intertwined:

> I can't tell you what a relief our board's decision has been to me. My heart was desperately burdened over the fact that we had new recruits waiting to be allocated and women and children already allocated in extremely inaccessible places but with such irregular aviation service. It was just too dangerous to let the advance continue. I believe the Lord was trying to show us that we should build our own aviation and radio service. We have been saving money to buy a Stinson Voyager airplane for Peru but only a little over $3,000 has come in and there is no money for a workshop and other essential equipment.
>
> But now that the Wycliffe Board has followed my urgent advice and decided to build up our own aviation and radio department, I believe God is going to work and enable us to do the right thing. Our hope and confidence are in Him. He is able. He has given us many talented linguists so that the linguistic department of Wycliffe is considered to be most outstanding and He can do the same for our aviation program. I shall not be satisfied until our JAARS aeronautical department in Peru ranks just as high as our linguistic department. The same God who has given us Bible translators can also give us the necessary pilots, mechanics and radio personnel. In Peru we have an aviator, Larry Montgomery who is tops. I could wish that it might be your [Chicago Gospel] Tabernacle that would take him and his wife on for support. I do know how wide your interests are already. We also have another young man, Jim Price, worthy of support. He will help install and maintain radio transmitters and receivers in all the stations. We need to have daily radio contact with each of the workers when they are in their jungle allocations. I know God will provide the needed workers for Peru and they will be good men and women I am sure. Recently a most talented man wanted to join us in Peru and was even promised some support, but he was used to a high salary, and so he de-

clined. He found it too hard to live by faith . . . . I have written at such length because you have been a real partner to me and I owe this letter to you.

Pastor Erickson responded by providing partial support for Larry Montgomery. Encouraged by this response, and believing the churches in America needed to be better informed of the needs on the field, Cam, on June 12, 1948 wrote a carefully worded letter about the JAARS program to thirty-five of his most influential friends and supporters. These friends included Henrietta Mears at First Presbyterian Church of Hollywood, California, Dr. Lewis Sperry Chafer of Dallas Theological Seminary, his old friend John Brown of John Brown Schools, Rev. Oswald J. Smith of The People's Church in Toronto and Charles Fuller of the Old-Fashioned Revival Hour. Part of the first paragraph of the two-page letter reads:

> Friends are made for sharing one's needs and so I am taking the privilege of writing to you about a special one. Our work among the tribes of Amazonia is absolutely dependent upon aviation and radio communication. Our advance in the jungles of Peru was coming to a standstill... Women and children of our fine [organization] were in danger because we lacked adequate aviation personnel and equipment.

Then followed an explanation of why JAARS needed the backing of people in the homeland, plus a list of twelve items Cam considered "immediate needs." These included a hangar and repair shop, a four-wheel-drive truck, housing for pilots and their families, financial support for two pilots, a four- or five-place airplane on floats, radio transmitters, a small launch to tow the planes, and much more. At the end of each letter was a personal paragraph like the one he wrote to Henrietta Mears:

> Please give my regards to my old classmate, Louie Evans [who was to became the pastor of the Hollywood Presbyterian Church] and share this letter with him. Remember us to your sister. We are often reminded of your visit and we do not forget your wonderful help.

May God give you continuous blessing in your ministry among the young people.[1] Yours in Romans 15: 20 and 30.

Cam's letter illustrates another in-house dilemma. The early SIL and Wycliffe membership had categorically insisted that its members never publicly solicit money for their own *personal* support, not even in their personal prayer or newsletters. Cam repeatedly cited the faith of Hudson Taylor and George Mueller as models, who looked to God alone to supply their temporal needs. While a member could, when asked, fully disclose the nature and needs of his or her ministry, writing a letter similar to Cam's might be considered by some to be in "poor taste."

Cam would counter that he was not outside the parameters of good taste, since he was not asking for personal support. And he was indeed trusting God to work on behalf of JAARS. He wrote William Nyman to tell him he would not return to Peru until God had supplied half of the JAARS budget of $40,000.

If we examine Cam's correspondence immediately after the board's unanimous May 21, 1948 vote to support him as general director and approve his request for JAARS to replace MAF in Peru, we notice a great relief and joy in his letters. He is consistent in his claim that JAARS was not only one answer to what he called the "Peru problem," it was the *only* answer. However, aware that Cam's tone could sometimes exceed reality, Dick Pittman wrote him a cautionary letter:

> It is my earnest hope and prayer that this action taken by the board [to form JAARS] which I believe is from the Lord, will clear the decks for real progress in the work in Peru. It is my intention to support your program in every way possible. It is also my earnest hope that you will seek to use MAF to the fullest extent possible in all matters technical. I hope there will be a good liaison between MAF and Larry [of SIL]. *I also strongly urge that there may be no occasion, either in their publicity or yours, to cast an unfavorable light on MAF.*[2]

For the next four months, from June until November 1948, Cam waited, often not too patiently, for what he hoped would be positive responses to his letters. One of the first of these responses came from Pastor Oswald Smith:

I wish I could cooperate in a tangible way in response to your appeal for equipment but we are now committed to the support of personnel. All I can do is to make your needs known.

From Torrey Johnson, head of Youth for Christ:

How I do wish I had the time at the moment to be of some help. But with our conference at Winona Lake and our world conference in Europe it is impossible for me to make any more commitments. However, you can be assured of my continued interest and prayer for the work.

After receiving several such responses, Cam vented his frustration in a letter to Bill Wyatt, Wycliffe's representative in Chicago:

It seems it is easier to get people interested in maintaining work that is already started, especially in the homeland, than to get them burdened about people who do not have a single chance to know that Christ can save them. I have a friend in California who once was able to give large sums of money to Christian work. Practically all of his money went to promoting work in Orange County, which is one of the most thoroughly evangelized areas in the world. As far as I know he gave nothing to pioneer missionary work. He now sees his mistake but can no longer give.

As Cam continued his letter to Wyatt we get an interesting insight into how he felt about funding priorities in the American church:

It is startling to realize that for the price of a good pipe organ we could establish our aviation and radio communication program in the jungles of Peru.

Such a sum of money would allow us to efficiently service the needs of ten to fifteen translation teams. However, most large churches would rather spend money on a pipe organ[3] for their own use rather than reach fifteen tribal peoples. Please do not read discouragement into this letter. To the contrary, God gives sweet peace and I have no doubt whatever that He is going to supply the needs which confront us.

On the very day Cam sent this letter to Bill Wyatt, Dawson Trotman wrote to Cam expressing his feelings about the letters Cam had sent out on behalf of JAARS. Part of Trotman's letter said he wished he could be of greater help to Cam and to the JAARS committee:

> Regarding the letter you have written to key people in the United States, I am convinced that nothing short of a special miracle of the Lord will permit you to see your desires, i.e., your statement that you want to have "at least half of the JAARS budget in sight before going back to Peru." You say you dread the job. I do understand what you mean, but GOD will give you joy in it. I know you well enough to know you are willing to tackle the toughest of jobs. Remember II Chronicles 20:15b: "...Thus saith the Lord unto you, be not afraid nor dismayed by reason of this great multitude; for the battle is not yours, but God's."

He then added that in his view, people on the JAARS committee were not very strong. On July 8, Cam sent a report to the JAARS committee and composed it as a rebuttal to Trotman's letter without naming the source:

> A friend wrote me recently and said, "I realize the JAARS committee is not very strong." My friend was looking with the wrong eyesight. Often God selects the weak instruments in preference to the strong! I have seen this over and over in our Wycliffe movement.
>
> The vital issue is not strength, but heart. "The eyes of the Lord run to and fro throughout the whole earth to show himself strong in behalf of those whose heart is perfect toward him" (II Chronicles 16:9). God told Gideon in Judges 7:2 and 3, "lest Israel vaunt themselves against me, saying, Mine own hand hath saved me. . . . Whoever is fearful and afraid, let him depart." Our committee is composed of men whose hearts God has touched, men who are not afraid of the magnitude of the task. I believe we have a Gideon's band in our current JAARS committee. This being the case, we need only to trust God and press on in the battle. He will get more glory for Himself working through a "weak committee" than from one that takes pride in its own strength.

The same friend who wrote about our "lack of strength" added that only a special miracle of the Lord would permit us to see my desire: at least half our budget in sight by the time I return to Peru. This is true, it will take a miracle, and I praise God for what I wrote because it presents in a definite way a special challenge to our God. The history of our Wycliffe Bible Translators movement is a chain of special miracles. The day we crossed the border into Mexico in 1936 with eight unsupported new recruits, a couple in El Paso sent $1,500 to our U.S. office. The Lord opened the door in a special way and then made *special* provisions for our *special* needs. The same will happen now as we do our best and expect God to do the rest.

On July 29, after a series of negative responses and postponements such as, "We haven't forgotten you, but we need to bring your request before our mission board," Cam received his first bit of encouragement. The letter came from Mr. J.D. Hall of the Colportage Division of the Moody Bible Institute in Chicago:

> Your recent letters are exceedingly interesting. I rejoice and praise God with you that there are over three hundred students attending your linguistic schools in the U.S. and Canada, and that you believe fifty or so will become Wycliffe Bible translators. The fact that so many young people are offering their lives for translation work and many others seriously considering it is further evidence that the Lord has wonderfully led you in the Wycliffe program. He who has begun a good work will see you through. You have made great strides since my son and I visited your little group of six in the farmhouse in Arkansas in 1934. May the Lord lead you on to great things in these last perilous days. It gives me real joy to send you this check for a thousand dollars. It won't go far in your great program, but at least it is a vote in the right direction.

When Cam sent the check to Wycliffe treasurer William Nyman, he wrote simply, "You can well imagine the joy that it brought to my heart."

For the next four months Cam dealt with a variety of problems in the U.S., Mexico and Peru—including an infestation of poisonous snakes in the living quarters of the Aguaytia group house in Peru. Dr. Altig, SIL's first medical doctor, wrote:

> We enjoy volleyball three days a week, but no swimming. There are stingrays and snakes in the water. Until now we have seen few snakes up here. But now we see some every day. Yesterday just after Gloria and others had taken a shower in our quarters shower, Beth entered and heard a noise under the board on which we stand while showering. She looked down and saw a small snake there. Titus, our language helper, went in and killed it. He said it was poisonous. He saw a big one outside on the hill near your house but it got away before he could fetch his gun.

When Cam and his family were in Mexico, Cam helped to repair a lightning-damaged roof during a visit to the Aztec village of Tetelcingo where he once worked. Not only did he help fix the roof, but he also comforted five local families who had lost male members in a series of murders. One of the murdered men had been an old personal friend.

Finally, there was the problem of Cam's car catching on fire. Elaine explained how it happened in a letter to a friend:

> Cam was on his way back from Mexico City (we are spending a month or so in Tetelcingo) and was bringing some bottles of poison to kill the cutter ants that destroy the orange trees and other plants. When he was climbing a steep grade, somehow one of the bottles fell over and broke. Cam opened the trunk to throw out the liquid, when some of it fell on the hot exhaust pipe, which set the rear of the car on fire. It was exceedingly difficult for him to combat the flames because of the poisonous fumes. But finally with the help of some passers-by and some women who lived in the area, who brought water, the blaze was extinguished without too much damage. Cam's hands, were burned rather badly however. They are now healing. We thank the Lord also that He protected our baby Joy. One day I was getting a diaper out of the closet and found a big black scorpion hidden away in the folds of the cloth. I was grateful the Lord let me find this. Scorpion stings are often fatal to babies.

Soon afterward, Cam received a letter from a close friend, written on November 16, that helped ease the stress and uncertainty of the previous months. The letter read, in part:

> I presented your case concerning the need for a light airplane to the members of my father's trust and they asked me to send you the enclosed check, which may enable you to make your dreams become a reality. There are no strings attached to the gift. Use it as you think best. We would appreciate no publicity on this gift. The trust prefers to stay pretty well in the background in these matters.

The check was for ten thousand dollars!

Notes

1   It is worth noting that Henrietta Mears, Director of Christian Education at Hollywood Presbyterian Church, was one of the most remarkable and influential Christian educators of the last half of the twentieth century. She founded Gospel Light Publications and Forest Home Christian Conference Center in Southern California. Her weekly Bible study for collegians attracted hundreds of young men and women. Many outstanding Christian leaders, including Bill Bright, founder of Campus Crusade, and Billy Graham remember Miss Mears as one of the most positive influences in their spiritual formation and development.

2   While Cam wanted his own air support in Peru, he, the board and the SIL and WBT membership in no way wanted to create tension between MAF and JAARS. And, in fact, that never happened. For over fifty years the two organizations have enjoyed a warm, supportive, and congenial professional relationship.

3   Cam Townsend was noted for his conservative position on church music. On one occasion during an offertory when the organist indulged in some improvisational flourishes, Cam leaned over and said to Elaine, "I wish he would practice his scales at home."

Trusses are painstakingly moved into place with minimal equipment for handling such large units, to form the base for the roof of the new hangar desperately needed at Yarinacocha to afford a safe, dry and cooler place from which to work on the aircraft so vital to SIL's operation in the jungle.

Chapter Six

"I've Come to Buy My Trusses"

Now to him who is able to do immeasurably more than all we ask or imagine, according to his power that is at work within us (Ephesians 3:20).

With their two infant daughters, Grace and Joy, Cam and Elaine Townsend had moved fourteen times in eleven months! In November 1948 they were in Mexico anticipating their return to Peru by Christmas. In spite of his family's many domestic changes and the increased complexity of his responsibilities, including growing opposition by the dominant church to SIL's presence in Mexico, Cam wrote a jubilant Christmas letter to friends and supporters:

> Last week we received a wonderful Christmas present from our Lord that will be of great benefit for the Jungle tribes of Peru. The present was designated for Wycliffe's aviation and radio communication program. Six months ago I wrote some friends that I was praying that at least half of our jungle aviation and radio budget (from $40,000 to $50,000) would be "in sight" by the time I returned to Peru. At the time it seemed impossible. On June 28, I received a response to that letter from a friend who said, *I am convinced that*

anything short of a special miracle of the Lord will not permit you to see your desire. He was right; we did indeed need a special miracle. In November the Lord gave us that miracle in the form of a large unexpected monetary gift [in addition to the earlier gift of $10,000]. That gift provided half of the aviation budget. It would not surprise me if the Lord sent in part of the second half of the budget by the time we reach Peru. It would be just like Him to perform yet another miracle.

The goal ahead of us is more than we can accomplish alone. If we take the Great Commission literally this must be done: Every tribe in the Peruvian jungle with the Scriptures in their own language. Since aviation, radio, and a well-planned base are necessary to accomplish this, we can expect our Lord to provide and give us the strength and skill to build them.

For its first two and a half years (1946-48), the Peru branch of SIL occupied eight rooms in a run-down former hotel in the town at Aguaytia in the foothills of the Andes. By the beginning of 1948 the group had outgrown the hotel. They were in desperate need of new facilities. The Peru executive committee selected a forty-acre site on the shores of Lake Yarina (*Yarinacocha*), just six miles from the river town of Pucallpa.

At first, Cam was unhappy with the selection. He was concerned that a base with a clinic run by an American doctor would create a point of conflict with the Peruvian doctors in Pucallpa. But as Cam examined the site with its 1,500 feet of lakefront land for a price under four hundred US dollars, he knew it was the right site. Cam saw that God who had the Romans build the roads over which Christianity would spread had specially chosen Yarinacocha for the ministry of SIL in the Peruvian Amazon. Cam wrote about it in the *Wycliffe Chronicle* under the title, "Another Milestone While the Advance Continues":

> In the dim, unknown past our Heavenly Father, knowing beforehand of our needs, caused the Ucayali River to change its course at a certain point, thus permitting its former channel to become a lovely lake.
>
> In a still more distant past, and also with our needs in view, we believe He provided a rise of forty feet above the rest of the lake's low shoreline, to protect us from seasonal flooding. Centuries later,

our Father had a man acquire this attractive site through the testimony of men in New Zealand and New Jersey whose hearts He was going to stir to become pioneer missionaries in the Ucayali River area. In the course of time God worked in the owner's heart and made him willing to sell the property to us.

In recent years He moved officials to construct the one and only automobile road into the heart of the Peruvian jungle to a spot just four miles from the site He was preparing for us, thus giving it accessibility to Lima, Peru's capital city. To increase this accessibility, He had the government make an airport six miles away where commercial airplanes fly twice a week to Lima.

With half of the aviation budget in hand, Cam was now ready to give his attention to the further promotion and construction of the new linguistic and operational center. He had already sent out a number of letters to friends, in which he "hinted" at the need for new living quarters for Peru's SIL workers. To Mr. and Mrs. J.C. Watson of Tulsa, Oklahoma, to the Joseph Woodsums of Glendale, California and to Rev. Clarence W. Jones of Flushing, New York, Cam wrote:

One of the jobs that will demand our attention when we return to Peru is the construction of a new jungle base. The Peruvian government loaned our current base to us, but termites and earthquake damage have left the buildings uninhabitable and we are forced to build our own base. We have chosen a site near the Ucayali River. The Ucayali is the large river that traverses the central part of the Peruvian jungle, flowing from south to north where it joins the Marañón River to form the Amazon. We have to construct living quarters for our service personnel, including the doctor and his family, the nurse, pilots and radio technicians. We also need homes and study buildings for our translators who will come in from their jungle allocations along with their national co-translators to do the hard linguistic research and Bible translation. I would also like to have a farm in connection with the center, plus facilities for our bilingual schools. Of course, we need a hangar and repair shop for the care and repair of our planes, generators and radio transmitters. One of our problems is how to build a $15,000 plant with $5,000. The new Aeronca floatplane cost almost $4,000. We want our cen-

tral base of operations to serve as a jumping-off place for our translators and literacy workers, as well as for our aviation and radio
program. The base will also provide medical care for our own people as well as for needy tribes-people. It will also be a place where
our workers can get the needed rest, relaxation and spiritual re-
freshment after months of living in isolated tribal villages. We are
also in need of a central radio station that will receive daily radio
reports from our translators in their remote jungle allocations. I
know we will solve these problems step by step.

Throughout the weeks of November and the early part of December,
Cam's standard reply to the question, "When are you returning to
Peru?" was, "We hope by Christmas." But then he would add, "When
we can arrange for our passage at half-price." There is no record that he
did in fact get a half-price airfare. We can only assume that he did; his
mailing address as of January 1, 1949 was Box 2492, Lima, Peru. However, before Cam left Mexico for Peru, there were several important
last-minute details to take care of. One was the dedication of daughter
Joy Amalia held on November 28. Always aware of the power of ceremony, Cam took this occasion as an opportunity to publicly express his
personal faith, and to remind people of why he was involved in Bible
translation. Among the eighty guests invited to the reception hall of the
beautiful newly constructed hotel La Posada del Sol in Mexico City
were a variety of distinguished Mexican government officials and educators. Of that Sunday afternoon Cam wrote:

> A long buffet table was beautifully set for eighty people. Through
> stained-glass windows, the almost horizontal rays of the setting
> sun trickled in to vie with the radiance of the stately crystal chande-
> liers. Our little Joy Amalia was to be dedicated to the service of
> God and humanity.[1] The orchestra played, we had a special piano
> and vocal recital. I then spoke and expressed our gratitude to God
> for the gift of our second child and to our friends for their compan-
> ionship and support. I explained we had chosen dedication rather
> than a christening because we wanted Joy to be baptized after she
> had made her own personal decision to follow her Lord and Savior
> Jesus Christ. I write this letter from the Aztec village of Tetelcingo
> where our little home is surrounded by five hundred and

fifty gorgeous poinsettias. Poinsettias remind us to wish you all a
Merry Christmas and a Happy New Year.
   Yours for Christmas-less tribes.

Before Cam and Elaine left for Peru, Jim Truxton of MAF wrote to express how pleased he was that Cam now had enough money to begin
construction on a hangar at the new base at Yarinacocha. He also
wished Cam well with the purchase of the four-place Aeronca Sedan
floatplane. Cam wanted this new, lighter plane to get in and out of small
strips of water along the headwaters of the Amazon and on shallower
rivers. Jim Truxton wrote:

> The burden for seeing the Gospel reach the remote jungle peoples
> of the Amazon is still keenly felt by all of us here at MAF. Our
> prayers certainly do go your way in these days. I must say how-
> ever, that my conviction has not changed. I still believe MAF could
> more effectively accomplish the job if MAF were in the position of
> responsibility for the aviation project. I believe JAARS should have
> the responsibility for promoting and assisting our young organiza-
> tion. But whatever the future holds, I trust both our organizations
> will be united for what is sound, sensible, and God-honoring as we
> go about the development of missionary aviation.

On January 14, 1949, Cam's answer to the Truxton letter showed the au-
thenticity of Cam's diplomatic character. Cam made no reference to past
disagreements, nor did he attempt to justify his position for creating
JAARS. JAARS was now a reality, a reality that, in Cam's opinion, no
longer needed to be defended. Cam's only reference to Truxton's view
that MAF should still be the responsible agent in Peru was: "I believe
the present arrangement between our two organizations is of the Lord
and is a happy one for all concerned."

   On December 30, 1948 a fifty-two-year-old Cameron Townsend,
Elaine, and their children were warmly welcomed by a large company
of SIL members and a prominent Peruvian official with his family at
Lima's international airport. Buoyed by this enthusiastic reception, Cam
recalled how breathtakingly beautiful Lima looked in the golden sunset
as the plane circled the city when he had first arrived four years earlier:

That was a never-to-be-forgotten experience. It seemed like a welcome promise from the Lord of blessing and benediction to reach the Bible-less tribes of the jungle.

Now, with money in hand, an airplane soon-to-be-delivered, three new aviation specialists, pilots Oliver Bryant and Jim Price and mechanic Lester Bancroft, Cam was full of renewed enthusiasm and energy. He was ready to move ahead with his long held vision for Bible translation in Peru supported by Wycliffe's own air transportation arm. The immediate challenge facing the group was the construction of the base at Yarinacocha.

On January 14, 1949 Cam wrote to Earl Wyman:

> We are full of plans here in Peru. Considering the building of the base and the work among the tribes, it makes one want to be quintuplets and be in five places at once. Life in each place would be extremely interesting. I can't imagine work that gives more fun than pioneer missionary work!

In Cam's missionary career, however, there had been two events that seemed to catch him particularly off guard. The untimely death of a trained and gifted translator. In 1941 on the eve of his marriage to Marianna Slocum the handsome and talented Bill Bentley died unexpectedly in his sleep. That occurred in August. The diagnosis was heart failure brought on by complications from a crude treatment for amoebic dysentery. Bill was the first SIL translator to die.

Eight years later, on February 11, 1949, Adelle Cecilia Malmstrom, twenty-four-year-old niece of Cam's first wife Elvira, died suddenly and unexpectedly in Lima just four months after her arrival in Peru. She too, had been taking treatment for amoebic dysentery. In a six-page letter to Adelle's parents, Cam described in detail the circumstances under which their only daughter had died. He said he had been suspicious for some time of the drug that a local physician had prescribed for treatment of dysentery. This, said Cam, may have resulted in complications that caused the young woman to collapse and sink into a coma from which she never recovered. Cam had kept a prayerful vigil over his niece during the hours before her death, even sleeping on the floor of the doctor's office to be with her if she regained consciousness. On February 17, Cam wrote to her pastor, his friend Torrey Johnson:

> You have learned of the homegoing of dear Adelle Malmstrom, just a week ago. She is the first of our SIL personnel to die in Peru. It is very difficult for me to understand why the Lord would permit such a thing when Adelle was so capable and so greatly needed. Surely God has a purpose in all of this. I pray He will use this to point many young people to offer their services in Adelle's place.

Cam ended his letter to Torrey Johnson by informing him that lumber was being cut and supplies were being brought to the lakeside base to begin construction of the hangar and other buildings beginning March first. Cam estimated that it would take about six months to build.

If ever there was an event in the development of the Yarinacocha base that symbolized Cam's dogged faith it was the construction of the airplane hangar. The process evoked the words of 1 Samuel 7:12: "Then Samuel took a stone and set it between Mizpeth and Shen, and called the name of it Ebenezer, saying, Hitherto has the Lord helped us." In an article entitled "How God Has Provided an Answer to Prayer," Cam wrote:

> Our superintendent of aviation told me we needed a hangar fifty feet wide and seventy feet deep, free of supporting pillars and other obstructions. This meant that in order to protect the walls with over-hanging eaves, the trusses would have to be somewhat longer than the fifty feet of the central span. Furthermore, to prevent warping and sagging they would have to be built with seasoned lumber. Steel girders were out of the question, since we only had $1,500 for the project.
>
> When I went to one of several sawmills in the neighboring town of Pucallpa and told the owner I needed seasoned lumber to construct the fifty-foot trusses, he just smiled and said, "There is no such thing as dry lumber in Pucallpa. Just as soon as the logs are sawed we ship the lumber by truck to Lima. If you want seasoned lumber you will have to buy it in Lima. But it might take six months or more to get it delivered to Pucallpa."

I was a bit discouraged and perplexed, but I continued searching. We didn't have the money to buy seasoned lumber in Lima and we couldn't wait six months to have it shipped across the Andes. My only recourse was to pray.

In the meantime, while I was praying and puzzling over what I was going to do, I went to another sawmill to buy some lumber to build a temporary tent-house for my family. I had only three hundred dollars, and was looking for third-class lumber. When I asked the owner of the sawmill where I could get this lumber he pointed to some at the back of the sawmill. As I sorted through the lumber I noticed a palm-leaf shed behind one of the piles of lumber. It was over-grown with weeds and grass. As I pulled away the weeds I discovered to my astonishment some long trusses all cut and stacked in position on top of one another but not nailed. I was almost breathless as I measured them. They were exactly fifty-four feet long. I wondered if there were enough. We needed eight. There were exactly eight all cut out of cedar logs. All were assembled except for the drilled holes for the bolts. It seemed too good to be true. Clearly these trusses "had SIL's name on them!"

As I was praising God for providing the lumber months before we needed it, I thanked the owner for preparing trusses in advance for our hangar. When I asked him how much they were, I was stunned with his answer. "Your hangar?" he said. "No, I want them to expand my sawmill. Can't you see that my machinery is out in the sun and rain? I should have built a building long ago. No, I need the trusses for myself." I tried everything I knew to get him to change his mind, but to no avail. A few days later Elaine and I attended the Inter-American Indian Congress in Cuzco. During the time we were away we prayed daily for the lumber situation. Six weeks later I again went to Pucallpa and spoke to the sawmill owner saying, "I've come to buy my trusses." The owner smiled and said, "All right, you can buy them." I immediately rented a truck in Pucallpa that was large enough to haul the big trusses. They were twelve feet high and fifty-four feet long and weighed over eight hundred pounds. I got them loaded onto the truck as quickly as possible for fear the sawmill owner would change his mind.

After the trusses were safely on their way to our base over the road we had opened into that part of the jungle, I remembered that I hadn't asked the price of the trusses. "Señor Fernández," I said, "I surely do appreciate your kindness in letting us buy these trusses. Now, how much do I owe you?" He quoted me a very low sum that was equivalent to the cost of what green lumber would have been plus the labor of assembly. God does indeed provide!

A postscript to that story appeared in the 1949 in-house *Wycliffe Chronicle*, giving credit to Mr. Ernest Aish, a Christian businessman from New Zealand who had experience in heavy construction. He showed the SIL builders how to safely hoist and set the heavy trusses in place. In the midst of all this happy planning and working Cam received a communiqué that froze his heart. The report stated that on April 30, 1949, the Grumman Duck had flipped over while landing on a narrow muddy strip and was seriously damaged. The passengers were non-SIL members—two men, a woman and her baby.

Note

1   Decades later, Joy married Dave Tuggy, and joined Wycliffe. The Tuggys returned to the same Aztec village of Tetelcingo where Cam and Elaine had once worked. Together they finished translating the New Testament into the Náhuatl language while raising their family of five (three daughters and two sons).

An aerial view of Yarinacocha, SIL's language center near Pucallpa, Peru.

Chapter Seven

Soft Ground and Tall Grass

The news came first as a radio message from Peru's Ministry of Aeronautics. It read simply that on April 30, 1949 about 4:35 P.M. an SIL J2F-236 Grumman Duck had crash-landed on the airstrip in Puerto Inca. There was no word about the condition of the pilots or passengers. Cameron Townsend, in Lima at the time would have to wait 48 hours for a full report of the accident.

The report came from co-pilot Louis Rankin. Louis began his report by explaining that Peru's Air Ministry had asked SIL to transport a woman, her infant child and two government employees to the small town of Puerto Inca on the Pachitea River. Louis said he and pilot Oliver Bryant[1] took off at 3:35 P.M. on April 30 on what was considered a high-risk mercy flight since it would have been difficult for the woman to travel by canoe with her infant child. The four passengers occupied the lower part of the plane. One of the passengers, a Señor Ríos, was a rather large man who could not get his safety belt buckled. The female passenger was fastened securely, and held her baby in her arms. The fourth passenger also wore a safety belt. Before taking off, Oliver and Louis were warned that the airstrip at Puerto Inca was short, narrow, wet and at this time of year, muddy. They were advised to land in the center of the strip.

As they approached Puerto Inca, Oliver circled the field three times. The second time, he came in low and lined up with the runway. On the third approach he landed normally and rolled about six hundred feet down the runway when the field suddenly narrowed and the wheels on the under-carriage of the Duck began to slip in the mud. When Oliver applied the brakes, the plane swerved to the right and the wing struck the high grasses and bushes on the side of the strip. This pulled the plane to the right but the momentum caused it to roll to the left. The plane then nosed down and ground-looped, severely damaging both wings and propeller. The plane came to rest on its right side in soft, muddy ground and tall grass, facing the direction from which it had come.

Louis said he quickly opened his canopy, got out, and checked on Oliver, who was unhurt. Louis made sure the battery switch and gas were turned off, and quickly got the passengers out through the window that was facing up. Except for a few bumps, bruises and scratches no one was hurt.

A day later, with the help of Jim Price, who had been flown to Puerto Inca in the newly acquired Aeronca, Louis and Jim (after deciding the damaged plane could not be repaired) began salvaging the Duck's engine, battery, flight instruments, fittings, cables and other parts. Two of the men then located a raft and began the four- to five-day journey floating the parts down the Pachitea River to Pucallpa. When Cam gave his report to the U.S. JAARS committee, he said:

> We would request your prayers for Ollie that he may not be discouraged over this second misfortune. I believe all this is within the will of God. He has a plan in all this that will further the great cause He has committed to us. Bless His name. Acts 20:24.

Cam was more magnanimous in his support of Oliver than some others on the JAARS committee. They wanted to reassign him since this was now his second aviation accident. The first had occurred a few months before when he failed to set the wheel blocks on the Aeronca while the motor was still running—the plane rolled into a wall. William Nyman, Wycliffe's venerable Secretary-Treasurer, had written Cam to tell him that even with the insurance paying the two-thousand-dollar repair bill,

JAARS lost a year's premium and had to pay ten percent of the repair bill. This left the JAARS bank account at zero.

William Nyman, always a conscientious and careful treasurer, often questioned expenditures for PR publicity on the "home front," and was cautious of top-heavy management. But in a lengthy March 18th letter to Cam from Bill Wyatt, Wycliffe's only full-time public relations worker, we see evidence of the seeds of change being sown. Wyatt began his letter by informing Cam that a gift of sixteen hundred and fifty dollars had been received toward the Adelle Malmstrom Memorial fund, to be used for the construction of a dormitory for single women at the Yarinacocha base.

Wyatt then expressed his concern that Wycliffe was embarrassing itself by producing literature for the Christian public that was outdated and not well presented. He urged Cam to campaign for improved literature for Wycliffe constituents. Then, in defense of his conviction that more money should be invested in publicity, Wyatt expressed feelings that surely must have warmed Cam's heart:

> With regard to the JAARS financial situation, I believe it will require a coordinated effort for a full-time JAARS deputationist, together with key [lay] men in different parts of the country to turn this around. I believe the Lord is looking to Wycliffe's to do for the world what the Church in nineteen centuries has failed to do. The rate of Wycliffe's progress in recent years should be an encouragement to all of us, namely, to fulfill the desire of His heart, which was His final word to us, "to preach the gospel to all the nations." Paul's speech before Agrippa in Acts 26: 20 should be our aim. I have had a burning desire to do my very best for the cause of Christ in pioneer lands. If my enthusiasm should run ahead of my good judgment and if I have been too critical I ask your forgiveness; I don't mean to be. I just love Wycliffe and all it stands for.

Cam responded almost immediately to the Wyatt letter urging William Nyman to find ways to produce more up-to-date literature. Cam strongly favored print media, and wanted as many people as possible to write articles and books about the work of Wycliffe. Additionally he was always looking for practical ways to involve friends and supporters in a field experience. He wanted as many people as possible to understand the nature and role of Bible translation in the overall mission of the Church. To this end, in his letters Cam was continually extending warm invitations to pastors, laity, business executives, and just plain folks to come and see for themselves what SIL was doing in Mexico and Peru. Over the years hundreds of people accepted Cam's invitation and visited the fields to experience first-hand the ministry of SIL.

One of these visitors was Cam's long-time friend Henry Crowell, executive vice president of Moody Bible Institute and trustee of his parents' foundation. In March of 1949, Crowell, along with Paul Robinson of Moody Aviation, spent two weeks visiting various jungle locations in Mexico and Peru. Their time in Mexico included a trip to Jungle Camp and a visit to the then-isolated Lacandón people. The visitors endured long, sweaty hikes through the jungle and bumpy mule rides. In Peru, they feasted on the liver of a land-turtle: Henry Crowell declared it "delicious." Crowell and Robinson made themselves useful by repairing a translator's broken typewriter and gasoline stove. They also visited translators Esther Matteson, Doris Cox and Lorrie Anderson on the Urubamba River, working with the Piro[2] people. After their visit, Cam wrote a newsletter that echoed the Apostle Paul's Macedonian call:

> Such visits to the field by leaders in the homeland are highly desirable. They encourage our members, bring fresh ideas and give the visitors a new vision of the need and opportunity for missions they could not get from a verbal or written report. We believe God is going to use the Crowell and Robinson visit to interest many young people to join our pioneer effort to bring God's Word to Bible-less tribes. We need a hundred new recruits this year. There are open doors all around us, but no one to enter them. Do come over, young people, and help us. It will be the greatest day in our lives when the last of the many thousands of people groups receive God's Word in their own language.

Whenever Cam began to push for more members to step through the doors that were opening to SIL, it appeared to some of the board members, including Cam's nephew-in-law Ken Pike, that Cam's reach exceeded his grasp. In mid-June 1949, Cam and Elaine, together with SIL members Gloria Gray and Mary Hinson, made a two-day journey to the city of Cuzco. Located in the southern Andes at an elevation of over nine thousand feet, Cuzco was once the capital of the powerful Inca Empire. It was the place where the four parts of the empire came together. So strategic was this ancient city that the Quechua-speaking people called it the navel, or center. None of this history was lost on the organizers of the Inter-American Indian Congress, who chose Cuzco as the site for their second annual congress, held from June 24 to July 4, 1949. After only three years in Peru, Cameron Townsend was chosen to be one of the official members of the Peruvian delegation to the International Congress. In his report to the group Cam wrote:

> Yesterday (June 27 or 28) was a great day for our Institute. The educational section of the Congress adopted a resolution expressing the admiration of the Congress for the work our Institute is doing. It was carried unanimously although the Ecuadorian delegate got to his feet before the vote was taken to say that there were probably other institutions that were doing the same type of work and if the Congress applauded one, it should applaud all. The Mexican delegate, Dr. Emmanuel Palacios, who had written and sponsored the resolution, replied that as far as he knew there was no other organization carrying out on a continental scale the type of work we were doing.
>
> Our American delegate, Commissioner Nickels, knowing the motion was coming to the floor, asked me to attend the educational session as his interpreter. After the resolution was passed I spoke briefly in appreciation of the resolution and assured the group that it would encourage us to go forward with new zeal toward the completion of the task. After I sat down the Ecuadorian delegate (the one who had raised the question about other institutes) jumped to his feet and said he would like for us (SIL) to extend our work to include Ecuador. Then the Paraguayan delegate invited us to come to his country. Then the president of the session, a delegate from Venezuela said he was anxious for us to begin work there as well. Previously one of the Bolivian delegates, the director of Rural Education, had extended an invitation for us to work in Bolivia also. So now we are confronted with many more "open doors" than we can enter. I ask for your prayers that it will not be necessary to turn a deaf ear to these Macedonian calls. In addition, there were overtures for an SIL presence in New Guinea, and Panama.

For several years, Cam and Ken Pike had been corresponding with Robert Story, Home Director for Unevangelized Fields Mission, headquartered in Melbourne, Australia. Story requested SIL to begin a linguistic

school to train Bible translators interested in the ethnic languages of the vast South Pacific area. Covering over 3,000,000 square miles, the South Pacific includes Australia, New Zealand, the eastern end of the island of Papua New Guinea and several hundred smaller islands, including the Solomon Islands, Fiji, Vanuatu and the islands of Micronesia. After considerable deliberation as to who might direct the course and who would sponsor the school, Ken Pike, with his wife Evelyn, made arrangements to begin an SIL linguistic institute in Melbourne in January 1950, under the sponsorship of the Interdenominational Missionary Fellowship of Victoria, Australia.

On August 20, 1949, at the end of a long letter to Cam about his upcoming assignment to Australia, Ken cautioned Cam about the dangers of SIL growing too fast, urging him to be

Henry C. Crowell was used by God as an enormous encouragement to Cameron Townsend, especially in the early days of building Yarinacocha in the Peruvian jungle and in developing a safe, serious flying program in Peru's Amazonia, largely unchartered in the 1940s and 1950s. Through his father's trust fund Crowell directed significant gifts to specific projects for both programs.

aware of political bias against an American presence in certain countries, and reminding him of the vital need for SIL to have competent people with masters' degrees and Ph.D.s who could teach advanced courses in linguistics, anthropology and related subjects:

It seems to me to be out of the question to plan for new advances. We need more people who have had thorough linguistic training at home with their Ph.D. before we can offer our services [to foreign governments and their educational departments]. It seems to me, therefore, to be out of the question to plan for an advance into New Guinea in the foreseeable future, since we lack both funds and personnel.

Ken Pike wasn't the only person to offer an opinion about the critical need for more candidates. Otis Leal, in his role as Deputy Director of SIL (and later as Candidate Secretary), was also calling for more personnel. However, unlike Ken Pike, who favored people with advanced degrees, or Gene Nida, who once pushed to accept only seminary-trained candidates, Otis had a less restrictive view. In a letter dated May 7, 1949, he wrote Cam the following:

> I've been thinking about why we haven't been receiving as many candidates as we need or would like. First, it seems we are rejecting more candidates than ever before on the grounds of immaturity, or not having enough formal education. When we reject such a person we have no program in place for follow-up, keeping in touch or trying to renew their interest in our pioneer work. Second, I think there has been too much emphasis on demanding that a candidate know what country he or she wants to serve in before they come to SIL or before they apply for membership. There are many who come to SIL believing the Lord will use the SIL experience as a way to help them decide on a particular field. Third, I wonder if in our attempt not to proselytize people who come to SIL, or compete with other mission boards, we haven't leaned over backwards and failed to challenge the unaffiliated student with the opportunity of working with Wycliffe and SIL. And fourth, I wonder if our emphasis on linguistics has been so strong that we have frightened people out of applying because they feel that Wycliffe is for linguistic geniuses only.[3]

In 1949 and 1950, the world of SIL and Wycliffe was growing more and more complex. As General Director of Wycliffe and SIL, and Director of SIL in Peru, Cam wore a variety of hats. He was an administrator, a public relations diplomat, a private counselor, and the author of several books. It was Cam's responsibility to lead, help form policy, and provide vision, inspiration and support to the growing number of members. He was in demand as a deputation/recruitment speaker, lecturer, interpreter of Wycliffe principles, as well as a fund-raiser for new programs. And, as he did in Cuzco, Cam functioned as chief diplomat and elder statesman for SIL in Peru and Mexico. Such demands would have put many men psychologically and physically out of touch with the problems and concerns of the SIL members. But Cameron Townsend was unusually determined to remain connected to the membership. Throughout his life, no matter how heavy his schedule (which included thousands of letters[4] to an ever-expanding constituency), he maintained an open-door policy and never seemed too busy to take an interest in a member's smallest concern. In a letter to Otis Leal concerning a series of financial matters, Cam clearly demonstrated he hadn't lost his touch with the needs of individual members.

Some members were concerned about the high cost of living. Cam had asked for, but not received, a cost-of-living comparison between Mexico and Peru. In what seems like a frustrated letter, he rattled off the prices of everything from evaporated milk (seven cents), to canned tuna fish (twelve cents), to bus and taxi fares:

> When I suggested that we charge each member 40 cents, rather than the customary 25 cents as a way to defray the cost of entertaining the Minister of Education at a special luncheon where the members would eat with us, two members said that was more than they could afford. I reminded them that to eat bacon and eggs at a tearoom in Lima costs about that amount. They said, "We never go to tea rooms because we can't afford it." It seems to me that our workers should get enough personal support that would allow them at least once a month or so to go out and splurge and have a meal in a nice place. When our workers cannot afford to spend as much as 40 or 50 cents on a meal once in a while, it gives the appearance that we are downright parsimonious.

While Cam certainly was not stingy, he was frugal. In a letter to William and Etta Nyman on July 14, Cam related how he had rescheduled a direct flight to Chicago: "By flying tourist class on Panagra Airlines via Balboa, Panama, and Miami I can save twenty-nine dollars."

Cam told his close friends about the tent house he was building for his family at Yarinacocha for $300:

> I've built a tent-house, 24'x16' with a wood floor and a part canvas and part metal roof. The walls are of mosquito netting. (The mosquitoes and chiggers are very bad.) I put up a chicken wire fence around the house to keep our kiddies in and the wild jungle creatures out. We will be crowded, but happy. Now for some big news. We are expecting an addition to our family in about five months from today. He or she will be a jungle baby since we plan to stay in the jungle until January.

Besides wanting to be at Yarinacocha in December for the birth of their third child, Cam also wished to be present for the arrival of photographer and film producer Dr. Irwin Moon, of the film division of the Moody Institute of Science. Irwin Moon and his colleagues had produced a series of award-winning films entitled *Sermons from Science*. In the late forties and early fifties, these were shown throughout the United States and Canada to overflow crowds. For months Cam had been in correspondence to arrange a time when Dr. Moon could fly to Mexico and Peru to film the work of SIL. On October 30, 1949, Moon arrived at Yarinacocha[5] to begin work on a film that would become one of the most influential and important recruiting tools Wycliffe ever had. At a cost of $5,000 came Wycliffe's first film "O For a Thousand Tongues."[6]

The premiere showing took place on July 30, 1950 at Charles Fuller's *Old Fashioned Revival Hour*, held at the Long Beach Municipal auditorium. For hundreds of people, including this author (an estimated four to five thousand attended the premiere), "O For a Thousand Tongues" became a pivotal influence in the decision to become a member of Wycliffe and SIL. And, contrary to William Nyman's prediction, the film more than paid for itself.

Notes

1   Like many of the pilots who joined JAARS in the late forties and early fifties, Oliver Bryant had come out of the U.S. military and had seen active duty in World War II.

2   The Piro are now known as the Yine people. On April 21, 1949, Esther Matteson scribbled a note on the bottom of a typewritten newsletter sent to Cam: "My co-translator Gishonki just this minute surprised me by coming in to translate. So the Gospel of Mark in Piro begins at 9:00 A.M, April 21, 1949! Praise God!" In 1960, the Piro (Yine) became the first people group to receive the translation of the New Testament in their own language through the work of SIL in Peru. There are now congregations in most of the Yine villages. As of this writing, a Yine New Testament revision is completed and distributed.

3   Otis Leal wasn't suggesting that SIL and Wycliffe lower their academic standards for admission. He supported Ken Pike's urgent call for selected members to get advanced degrees. And there were a number of people in the academic "pipeline." Rather, Otis wanted potential candidates to know that anyone with a good "B" average, a strong spiritual commitment to Christ and motivation toward Bible translation could become a competent linguist and Bible translator. In fact, members who had graduated from Bible colleges and institutes were doing much of the best work. Further, Otis wanted it understood that there were a variety of supporting roles within the group that could be filled by people who did not have academic expertise.

4   The Townsend archives include over 47,000 documents and 4,500 photos.

5   In Mexico Dr. Irwin Moon filmed Jungle Campers, as well as the Tzeltal and Lacondón people.

6   Cam and Elaine spent five months editing the footage and writing the narration for the finished project.

Chapter Eight

Sudden Squalls

Before mid-century, much of the tropical rain forest of Peru's eastern Amazon basin was relatively unspoiled by oil developers, rubber hunters and over-zealous logging enterprises. All this would change during the decades of the sixties and seventies, when new road building brought a dramatic encroachment by farmers and cattle ranchers, resulting in escalating deforestation.

In 1950 Yarinachocha was still a tangle of thick jungle greenery, rich with bird, animal, and insect life. In early January of 1950, Cam answered the dozens of congratulatory letters he and Elaine received on the birth of their third daughter, Elainadel, who entered the world on December 28, 1949. To his friend Andrew Wyzenbeck of Chicago, on January 17, 1950, Cam wrote:

> I wish you could visit us at our new base in eastern Peru. We are on the shores of a beautiful lake where our gang goes swimming every day. Huge freshwater porpoises play constantly in the lake's normally tranquil waters. There is dense jungle growth all around except where we have cleared it for our buildings. This is an ideal spot for our amphibious operations. We now have a hangar with a ramp leading to the water's edge. There is also an administration

building, and the Adelle Malmstrom Memorial building as well as several individual homes. It has been a time of constant building since last spring. Most of the structures are cedar, or brick and cement, with aluminum roofing. However, I am writing this from under a palm leaf-roof and it is certainly delightful.

What weren't quite as delightful were the annoying mosquitoes and "no-see-um" biting midget chiggers that cause insidious itches, the spiders and cockroaches, and the hordes of cutter and army ants. Also lurking in the shadows near the lake were snakes—boa-constrictors and bushmasters. Over all this was a mantle of stifling, super-humid heat. Cam occasionally allowed himself to allude to such discomforts in letters to longtime friends.

The lake Cam described in such glowing terms also had a dark and menacing side. Several people were to suffer serious wounds to their ankles or calves when the vicious spines on the tail of a bottom-dwelling stingray jabbed at them as they waded along the shallow shoreline. The lake is notorious for its fluctuating seasonal levels. In March 1950, it rose abnormally and put the hangar floor under a foot of water. The lake also has a reputation for sudden squalls. To a friend in Pasadena, California, Cam related the following incident:

> We have about a dozen national men cutting down trees, and digging foundation holes for our buildings. They are amazingly energetic workers, starting at seven in the morning and working straight through till three in the afternoon without a break, even for a meal. All twelve of them come to work in canoes. Yesterday one of the boatloads that had left our base shortly after quitting time was caught in a sudden squall. As the fellows attempted to cross the lake their canoe was upset and filled with water. Fortunately the men escaped drowning. We took them, along with other men who were soaked to the skin, to the little jungle shanty we call home. To warm them up Elaine treated them to hot lemonade and bread. When the rain stopped the group made another try for home. However, the wind was still blowing hard and two of the canoes were again swamped and sank below the surface, though not to the bottom. With the aid of an inflated inner tube we rescued the men who were clinging to the submerged canoe.

While Cam was inconvenienced by abnormal weather and sudden squalls on the lake, his real concerns were the several organizational "storm depressions" that had begun to form several years before. The most recent one centered around Jim Price. Tall, muscular, with perennially disheveled hair, Jim had spent six months in Peru in 1949 with his wife Anita, working as guest helpers. Growing up on a cattle ranch near Watsonville, California, Jim had developed into a competent and self-assured jack-of-all-trades. Also, he had honed his skills as a pilot while herding cattle from the cockpit of his small plane. After becoming acquainted with SIL's ministry Jim and Anita applied for membership. And, like all those who were interested in joining Wycliffe and SIL, they were required to spend a summer studying linguistics and field-related subjects at the SIL course then offered at the University of Oklahoma at Norman.

During the months Jim was in Peru, he had impressed Cam with his unpretentious workman's common sense. Cam urged the SIL staff and candidates committee to expedite the Prices' application and to send Jim and Anita back to Peru as soon as possible. Cam's oft-repeated request was:

> We need Jim urgently. He should come back to us as soon as possible. Our aircraft maintenance expert Lester Bancroft is simply swamped with mechanical work. Jim is just the kind of man we need in Peru.

On August 20, 1949 Ben Elson, writing on behalf of the SIL Staff Committee, told Cam that the board of directors, after six hours of discussion recommended not accepting Jim Price for membership. Ben added that the board had not yet taken formal action, since not all the members were present. The stated reason was:

> It is the general consensus of the staff that we do not accept persons of a Pentecostal persuasion, who believe in speaking in tongues as evidence of the baptism (or manifestation of the indwelling) of the Holy Spirit in the present age, and in physical healing in the atonement on the same basis as salvation.

Jim and Anita were broken-hearted. On August 28, Jim wrote Cam that he simply could not understand how this happened. The following is an excerpt from Jim's letter:

> When you told me in Peru you were wholeheartedly in favor of my joining, I assumed the staff at SIL would also be of the same mind. My regret is that the experiences and the contacts I have made over these past two years as well as the money spent could have been better reserved for someone who would be acceptable to the group. Even so, I greatly appreciate the opportunity I had in a small way to take part in pioneer mission work. I know of no other group that could possibly have needed a brick hauler, jungle clearer, and general flunky. At the end of the SIL course in Norman, Oklahoma, some of the staff, which had assumed we were "in," could not understand why we were not accepted. We had been given to understand the staff was in agreement on the matter of our doctrinal position. Perhaps we will have to wait until we get to heaven where we will all live and work together as one in Christ. Until that time I can only say that I have greatly enjoyed working with those I came to know and love in the fellowship of co-workers in the service of Christ our Lord in Peru.

This was only one of several letters Cam received expressing disappointment over the rejection of Jim and Anita Price. Long-time friend John Twentyman who, with his wife Isabel, had joined SIL and worked in Mexico for several months in 1936, was one of the most outspoken. On August 25, 1949, he wrote:

> To answer your question about Pentecostals here in Peru, we have closely observed such co-workers during our four and a half years here. I notice they are doing a real work for the Lord. I would say the people in the Assemblies of God and other Pentecostals are among the most spiritually alive people I have ever met. One cannot but concede that God is blessing them and their work.
>
> I want to urge you to be extremely careful in excluding those of Pentecostal background from the SIL movement. By so doing you may grieve the Holy Spirit, which would indeed be tragic. Beware

of what you do, lest "haply you be found fighting *against* God," and not *for* Him!

Cam agreed wholeheartedly with Twentyman's letter. In fact, he had been lobbying for Jim Price's acceptance long before Jim wrote. Three days after receiving Ben Elson's letter, Cam wrote board member William Nyman:

> Except for Jim Price's help at the start, I have had to do practically all the construction work on our little house with my own hands. I have put in long hours on this project while my younger colleagues were playing volleyball or going swimming. Jim would have helped me in so many ways if we had him here. He is just the kind of fellow we need for all-around service at the base. He is so capable, humble, amiable and inoffensive in every respect. In one way I am sorry I tried to please Ken Pike and the staff by sending Jim back to take the SIL course. But in another way I am glad because it has paved the way for a great victory for Wycliffe principles as I envisioned them at the beginning, but from which the staff has slipped. I was deeply disturbed when I read this recommendation against Assembly of God people and others who believe in healing. But God gave me the assurance that He is going to overrule this sectarianism and permit me to continue to truthfully tell government officials that we are nonsectarian, as I have been telling them for fifteen years. God assures me that He will help us carry out this resolve without losing any members. Praise the Lord! We'll continue united on the fundamentals without worrying about non-essentials until every available force is harnessed to give the Word to every tribe on the face of the earth.

Then, on September 14, 1949, Cam sent a hastily-composed telegram to Mr. and Mrs. James Price, Montevista School, Watsonville, California:

> Wycliffe regrets hardship caused you. If you can forgive us, we would welcome you for Peruvian assignment. Please answer earliest convenience, Lovingly, Uncle Cam.

Cameron Townsend's lobbying had paid off. In another letter, also written on September 14, he explained in greater detail why the board had opposed Jim's becoming a member. Cam ended his letter with: "Loving you, and rejoicing that we shall be working together in Peru, I remain yours in Romans 15:20."

As he did in the Jim Price situation, Cam often won difficult, troublesome, and frustrating battles through persistence in debate and his indomitable personality. The board also held Cam's many years of experience and his spiritual sensitivity in high regard, and was often willing to reconsider its position.

However, not all of those involved were as easily persuaded by Cam's quiet logic and force of personality. One of these was Eugene Nida, who, while a member of SIL, was partially released to work with the American Bible Society as their Translation Secretary. The agreement was for Nida to devote three-quarters of his time to the ABS and one-quarter to SIL. Not wanting to lose Nida after his assignment with the Tarahumara people in northern Mexico was cut short in 1936 due to poor health Cam had secured the position for him with ABS. Cam was relying on Nida, a brilliant scholar and linguist, along with Ken Pike and other promising linguists, to bring about his 1935 prediction that "in fifteen years the scientific [linguistic] world will sit up and take notice of SIL's pioneering linguistic and scholarly research." That prediction had indeed come true.

By 1950, the University of Oklahoma authorized SIL to include on its letterheads "Affiliated with the University of Oklahoma." Dr. George Cross, president of the university, commended Pike for his published monographs and linguistic papers, which were appearing in the prestigious *International Journal of American Linguistics*. And Dr. Charles Fries, head of the English Department at the University of Michigan, wrote Cam to tell him he thought SIL "was carrying out the most significant linguistic work of the present decade."

Nida, too, was making his mark as a published scholar. However, while Nida fully endorsed SIL's ideal of providing the scriptures to those without them in their own languages, he included a caveat. His concerns mirrored the ABS criteria for accepting a newly translated New Testament for publication. In general, the ABS position stated that there had to be "Christian constituency," permanency of personnel, and a constructively oriented program" [i.e., an ongoing literacy program].

A further stipulation was that the Society would not publish a New Testament when the translation work was done primarily by a single expatriate translator, assisted by only one national co-translator.

At issue in 1950 was Cam's desire to have the Mixteco[1] New Testament, translated by Ken Pike and Don Stark with Angel Merceias as the national co-translator, published as soon as possible. However, the Mixteco translation did not meet the criteria spelled out by Nida. At best, there were only a dozen or so believers and not many of them knew how to read. In spite of his awareness of this issue, Cam wrote to George and Florrie Cowan, encouraging them to complete their Mazateco New Testament as soon as possible:

> I realize that Dr. Nida puts great emphasis on the need for preparing readers before the translation is published. The result is to put reading campaigns ahead of the translation itself. Ideally, literacy and translation should go hand in hand. It is interesting to notice however, that early translations were often made for communities that had few readers. I personally would be willing to prepare a translation even if it were only for a few national leaders. It is my firm belief that the Scriptures in the ethnic language are the best agent for evangelism. George, I know you have many demands on your time, but I urge you and your team [Florrie and Eunice Pike] to prepare a complete New Testament as soon as possible. If you don't, you may find interruptions so numerous that it will be virtually impossible to complete the translation.

Here was a major philosophical and practical difference between Nida, the American Bible Society, and Cameron Townsend. Townsend believed passionately and unreservedly that SIL's major responsibility was to "prepare God's Word in the vernacular languages for all ethnic peoples that do not yet have the New Testament Scriptures." This was to be SIL's policy no matter how small the ethnic minority or the number of people who had learned to read prior to the publication of the New Testament.

Nida was equally firm in his insistence that he and the ABS had a certain obligation to allocate their funds in projects that would make the investment worthwhile in terms of actual readers. Cam, on the other hand countered that enough people would be saved even in a small tribe through having the Word in their own tongue to make the expense, as well as the effort, worthwhile. He reiterated that the ABS reasoning would automatically cut off many tribes in Mexico, since most ethnic groups had populations of only five thousand to twenty thousand. Cam also said that from his experience, people would be motivated to learn to read in order to discover what God had to say to them. He cited examples from his days in Guatemala working among the Cakchiquel people, a group in which people learned to read with only the help of a neighbor.

Nida, however, remained uncompromising in his position—ABS would not underwrite the expense of publishing the New Testament for the Mixteco people. The one concession Nida did make was to suggest that Cam might find some other source of funding for the Mixteco translation.[2] Long before computers and desktop publishing came into use, Cam ended a January 9, 1950 letter to Nida :as follows:

> With cheaper methods of publishing and more people interested in contributing toward the expense, it will be perfectly possible to give the New Testament to tribes where the chances for large sales are even smaller than in the case of the San Miguel Mixtecos. That being the case let us plan to translate and publish for all the tribes even where few know how to read, and few as yet have believed. Inevitably both readers and believers will result. "My Word," says the Lord, "will not return to me void." There are enough stateside donors who believe that promise, who will to provide the American Bible Society and the Wycliffe Bible Translators with ...support to enable us to give at least the New Testament to every tribe. Yours in Romans 15:20.

Meanwhile, in Peru's Amazonia, the sudden rain squalls that sometimes hampered construction at Yarinacocha could have more serious implications for translation teams living in isolation along one of eastern Peru's smaller jungle rivers. In March of 1950, Dale Kietzman, his pregnant wife, Harriet, and their seven-month-old daughter Ruth, were living among the semi-nomadic Amachuaca people on the Sepahua River. Dale was starting translation work, when he came down with a serious case of undulant fever. The following is Harriet's account of how they almost didn't make it to safety:

Shortly after we arrived in the village Dale began to run a low-grade fever. We were not too concerned, thinking it would pass and we could remain in the village. However, after two weeks Dale, still running a fever, became extremely sick. When we radioed the base for advice about Dale's fever, Dr. Altig advised us to return to the Yarinacocha base, and arranged for the SIL plane to bring us in.

At this point, circumstances began to work against the Kietzmans. Transportation posed an immediate problem. The Sepahua River was too narrow and too full of debris for an SIL plane to land and evacuate the little party, and there was no large canoe available to them. In place of a canoe, the Amachuaca people made a balsa wood raft and paddles for the Kietzmans. The night before they were to leave, Harriet wrote:

> We experienced a tropical rainstorm that turned the Sepahua River into a raging torrent. The river rose twenty feet above normal, took our raft away with it, then continued to rise until it was forty feet above its normal level! [Rivers can rise very rapidly, as much as thirty feet in twenty-four hours.] We waited several days for the river to recede while another raft was lashed together. When the raft was ready for our downriver trip we radioed for Larry Montgomery to pick us up at the confluence of the Sepahua and Ucayali Rivers at a mission station on the Ucayali. Since the raft was smaller than we had planned we could only take one Indian couple (a man and wife) to act as paddlers.
>
> When we began our early morning trip we noticed the swollen river had cut a series of new channels. The riverbanks were caved in on both sides and huge trees had fallen and stretched more than half way across the river. About three hours into our approximately six-hour trip, we came to a place where the river was almost blocked by fallen trees. Although our paddlers paddled as fast as they could, the swirling current was too strong and we were carried backwards into a floating tree. At first we expected nothing more than a hefty beating from the tree branches. But the treacherously strong current forced the leading edge of the raft down and under one of the large tree branches, tipping the raft at a precarious angle and sliding all our equipment and food into the river. In a blink of an eye the torrent piled up under the raft and flipped it upside

down. I was holding little Ruth in my left arm and I went down into a maelstrom, all the while trying desperately to reach up through the tree branches to grab the raft with my free hand.

The next few horrific minutes would forever remain something of a blur for Harriet. For a long, terrible moment Dale, still weak and feverish, managed to hang on to the raft with no idea what was happening to his wife and child. Harriet was likewise disoriented. She remembers the strong current tossing her around like a rag doll, while she was pushed through a tangle of submerged tree branches; she then surfaced underneath the capsized raft. This makeshift bundle of logs with fever-racked Dale still clinging to it had been swept along and lodged into the branches of another fallen tree a short distance downstream. This was a miracle—without the raft the Kietzmans would have been utterly stranded. The two Amachacua paddlers, who had tumbled downstream to the opposite side of the river, were miraculously unhurt. Harriet and baby Ruth endured the entire ordeal without a whimper. Harriet, however, had lost her shoes.

Dripping wet and exhausted, the little group made it to the safety of a nearby sandbar. The upturned raft had dumped all their equipment. Cameras, typewriter, clothing, portable stove, a pail containing bottles and supplies for the baby, food for the trip, and paddles all had been lost in the river. Dale managed to find a gallon thermos of water and one of the baby's bottles floating under the raft. Unfortunately it was one she had recently emptied. Nevertheless Harriet was able to pacify her with the thermos water. They also found some wild jungle fruit, which little Ruth ate eagerly.

Before starting out on the trip, the two paddlers had stuck a machete and an ax into one of the balsa logs of the raft. These had remained fast. The paddlers retrieved them and spent the rest of the day chopping the raft free from the tangle of tree branches and fashioning two new paddles. In the late afternoon, Dale and Harriet heard and saw the SIL plane flying overhead. Larry was following the zigzag river in an attempt to see why the Kietzman party hadn't met their scheduled rendezvous. But no amount of waving caught the attention of Larry or his co-pilot.

That night, under a clear sky and a bright, full tropical moon, the bedraggled Dale, Harriet, and baby Ruth, along with their two

Amachacua paddlers, tried to ignore the rumblings of their empty stomachs, stretched out on a canvas tarp they had salvaged, and made a fitful attempt to sleep. Some time before midnight, when the moon was almost as bright as day, Dale woke up from his fevered sleep just in time to see a large vampire bat stalking baby Ruth. He and Harriet quickly drove it off. They knew that vampire bats can extract large amounts of blood from their prey. After breathing a prayer of thanks to the Lord, they remained awake for the rest of the night.

The following day the little party made their way down the river on the upside-down raft without further incident. They arrived at noon to find the SIL plane waiting for them. Lucille, wife of Dr. Altig, was the first to greet the Kietzmans when they arrived at Yarinacocha. Later, she wrote Cam and Elaine about the Keitzmans' near-death rafting experience:

> Harriet got out of the plane obviously pregnant, shoeless and badly sunburned as was baby Ruthie. Dale is now under the doctor's care but is still having high fevers and is very weak. They certainly have had their share of trials, but we praise the Lord for His protection. Little Ruthie is just darling and laughs a lot.

On July 10, 1950, Bob Schneider wrote Cam to tell him that Harriet had, on July 9, also delivered an eight-pound six-ounce baby boy, John Mark. Both were doing just fine.

Notes

1   This was Wycliffe's first New Testament translated for an ethnic people in Mexico.

2   The American Bible Society did agree to fund the publication of a New Testament for the relatively small Yine group of Peru (previously known as the Piro) as well as a number of New Testaments in Mexico. These included the Totonac, Tzeltal and Mezquital Otomí. Each of these people groups had a modest number of believers and readers in place upon the arrival of the printed New Testaments. In later years, the World Home Bible League (now known as "The League") was responsible for funding the publication of the majority of translated New Testaments in Mexico and elsewhere.

JAARS plane flying over dense, impenetrable jungle. This is a graphic display of the enormous problem that Cameron Townsend and the Peru SIL group faced as he set out to reach isolated tribes in Peru.

Chapter Nine

Advance in a New Direction

Cam's September 15, 1950 yearly progress report to the group in Peru was jubilant. He began by saying he believed there was greater harmony and unity in the group than ever before. This was, in part, an attempt to offset unhappy rumblings about the way Cam had allocated funds for houses to be built for JAARS personnel. A number of the Peru group were irritated when they learned the pilots and mechanics were getting what they considered preferential treatment. They complained it was against basic Wycliffe policy to allocate money for one and not for everyone.

So eager was Cam to promote JAARS and to attract pilots and mechanics to come to Peru that in his idealism and occasional naiveté, he said, "Surely no mature group member would begrudge, complain or be jealous because pilots, who are so necessary to the success of tribal work, would have monies allocated for their private residences." Besides, Cam argued, money had been designated for such purposes.

At issue was an ongoing concern over many members' low financial support. Ken Pike had argued in lengthy letters to Cam that, while he was not against Cam's vigorous campaign to make the need for projects known, he was concerned that people who gave money designated to projects might forget or neglect to support individual workers. Cam responded to this criticism in an open letter that said in part:

> I was grieved when one of our members [Pike] intimated that projects like JAARS, and raising money for new airplanes, drained away money from our workers' support. The facts show the exact opposite.[1] I feel that every member should be just as interested in the promotion of our essential projects as in securing their own personal support.
>
> Some of the decisions I have had to make regarding the use of funds have been difficult, but in most cases expenditures have been in line with the recommendation of qualified advisors. I have been careful to report such matters to Mr. Nyman [our Secretary-Treasurer] and to our main JAARS coordinator explaining the problem to them. As far as I know, the board continues to have confidence in my judgment as to how such monies should be spent. I invite those who criticize to speak to me directly. Finally, please don't limit your burden and faith to supplying only the needs in your immediate circle, but branch out in faith and trust, to the whole outreach of our worldwide program.

Ken Pike did not agree with the logic of Cam's argument and continued to express his concern about members' low support. He did keep in mind that Cam had spoken out on behalf of Ken's own project, the publication of the Mixteco New Testament. Though Ken and Cam had presented forceful arguments in favor of publishing a New Testament for an ethnic group with a limited number of readers, Eugene Nida had held firm against using the American Bible Society's money for funding such an edition. Nida had urged Cam to find private funding for the Mixteco New Testament, which is precisely what he did.

In April, Cam was invited to speak at the People's Church in Toronto Canada. During his presentation, Cam spoke about Wycliffe's commitment to provide the Word of God as extensively as possible to both small and larger tribal groups that had never had the Scriptures in their own language. Cam emphasized reasons why the entire New Testament needed to be made available to a fledgling church:

Just think of the problems of building a strong self-supporting, self-directing church without the Prison Epistles, instructions concerning elders, and such important passages as the Lord's prayer, the beatitudes, the second coming, the annunciation and birth of our Lord, the fruits of the Spirit, the armor of God and the heroes of the faith. How can churches grow without the entire and complete New Testament?

Mariana Slocum, translator, and the two main co-translators, Juan López Mucha and Domingo López Mucha, examine the newly arrived highland Tzeltal New Testament translation which they helped translate. August 5, 1956.

Cam then spoke about the philosophical publishing differences between the ABS and SIL. He specifically mentioned the reasons why the Mixteco New Testament needed to be published with all possible haste:

It seems clearly evident to us that new Mixteco believers and others cannot grow into a trained position of leadership, nor attain the strong Christian enlightened character necessary for leadership unless they have access to the Word of God, which is profitable to them in all spheres of their life. It seems essential that the few present leaders among the Mixtecos have the whole New Testament now so they will be absorbing its precepts in preparation for the care of new believers, which we expect to see in the near future.

While he didn't mention it specifically, Cam knew that, historically, whenever there was persecution among a company of new believers, those with the Scriptures available to them in their own language were able to read and memorize major passages of Scripture and had a much greater chance of withstanding persecution. In some cases, local congregations grew in numbers in spite of the persecution.

Among those who heard Cam speak that Sunday afternoon at People's Church, Toronto, was Jack McAlister, a pastor from Prince Albert,

Saskatchewan who had recently launched a tract society. When the meeting concluded, Jack was one of the first to shake Cam's hand and ask if they could meet to discuss the problem of how to finance the Mixteco New Testament. In a handwritten note to Ken Pike dated April 7, 1950, Cam wrote:

> It was good to talk to you yesterday but gooder [sic] to be able to write to you today. Rev. Jack McAlister, director of a new tract society, Tract Club of the Air, has promised a thousand dollars toward the publishing of the Mixteco New Testament. I told him by doing the typing ourselves on a Varityper I thought we could publish five hundred to eight hundred copies of the N.T. on an offset press.

Jack McAlister was as good as his word. On January 18, 1951 Ken Pike sent Rev. McAlister a copy of the complete typed manuscript. Pike sent the camera-ready pages to a printing company. Five months later, on June 1, 1951, with Ken Pike, Donald Stark, and co-translator Angel Mercías present, the first published New Testament translated by an SIL team was dedicated in the Mixteco dialect of San Miguel el Grande, Oaxaca, Mexico.

The phrase "new birth" is an apt metaphor used by Jesus to describe the change in those who commit to follow Him in faith. By its very nature, birthing is dangerous, difficult, painful, and joyful. In August of 1950, Cam received a letter from Mr. S.E. Slocum, father of Wycliffe member Marianna Slocum that spoke of this very metaphor. Marianna, with her co-worker Florence Gerdel, a nurse, worked among the Tzeltal people in the mountains of the state of Chiapas in southern Mexico. The Tzeltals were one of the ethnic groups featured in Irwin Moon's film "O For a Thousand Tongues." When Moon learned of Marianna's story, including how her fiancé Bill Bentley had suddenly died a week before their wedding date, Moon decided to make a film called "The Bill Bentley Story." Part of Mr. Slocum's letter had to do with the arrangements for a premiere showing of the film in Ardmore, Pennsylvania. He went on to tell Cam of some of the difficulties and joys of "new birth" among the Tzeltal people:

> I must tell you there is much persecution against the Tzeltal believers. Many are in danger of their lives. The threat is especially strong

from the merchants whose sale of liquor has fallen off. Yet in spite of such threats, and as a result of the persecution, the number of Indians attending Sunday services has increased. Even during the rainy season when the trails are impassable, there are over a hundred who come for worship service, and on the sunniest day over three hundred come. After one bad persecution threat over six hundred and fifty attended. One of the leaders in the Tzeltal congregation is a man called Juan López Mucha. He speaks almost no Spanish, and has had no outside spiritual influence other than from the Scriptures Marianna has translated into the Tzeltal language. Each week before Juan Mucha is to preach, he and Marianna read through the passage of Scripture he has chosen to use for his Sunday message. Marianna tells me she is constantly amazed at the man's spiritual discernment and insights, and goes so far as to say that this unlettered man is one of the most intelligent men she has ever known.

About three months before receiving Slocum's letter, Cam received what he deemed one of the most precious letters of his career. It came from the same Juan López Mucha, written in Tzeltal and translated into English by Marianna Slocum. When Cam opened the letter, he found enclosed a much-worn fifty-peso bill (the equivalent at the time of about five American dollars). The letter read:

Very esteemed Brother:

Very much I greet your heart in the Name of our Lord God living in heaven. We are brethren in the Lord. Therefore I greet your heart in the name of our Lord Jesus Christ. We thank God for saving us. Our hearts are glad because we have heard the Word of God. We are from [the village of] Corralito. Marianna is here where we live; she is the one who explains the Word of God to us. We love Marianna and Florence very much.

Every Sunday we gather together to sing. Our hearts are full of joy, all men, women, children and us. Therefore I send you this little letter. Thank you for sending your servants here to us. And thank you for sending them to each tribe. It is because you have love in your hearts for us, so we have love in our hearts for you too. Here is a little gift for you from us, fifty pesos. We thank God that

He loves us so much. Remember us all the time; pray for us all the time. I too will pray for you. Tell all our brethren who are there, greetings to them all, because we love one another in the Lord. This is your greeting from me. (Signed) Juan López Mucha

On May 24, 1950 Cam wrote to thank this Tzeltal leader, greeting him as a highly esteemed and beloved brother. In part the letter read:

We greatly appreciated your greetings and the offering freely given by the brothers and sisters of Corralito to go toward giving the Word of God to all the tribes of the world. We pray that the Lord will multiply your offering just as He multiplied the loaves and fishes for those hungry people who followed him on the shores of Lake Galilee. God bless and repay you for the sacrifice you have made for His blessed name. (Hebrews 6:10: "God is not unjust; he will not forget your work and the love you have shown him as you have helped his people and continue to help them.")

In 1917, during his days as a Bible salesman in Guatemala, Cameron Townsend had spent a night on a mountain ridge with his traveling companion, Francisco Díaz, a Cakchiquel Indian. That night, Francisco challenged Cam to somehow make the story of God's love and the message of salvation available in his own Cakchiquel language. When Cam realized that over half the population of Guatemala did not have access to a single verse of Scripture in their own language, and that their languages had never been reduced to writing, he wrote the following in his journal:

I have come to realize that it is imperative for this need to be surmounted in this generation, and that ethnic peoples be reached with the message of salvation. God has given me youthful vigor, faith and a challenge. Therefore, I have decided to devote my life to the evangelization of Indian peoples.

That challenge became the vision that motivated Cam throughout his life. He was continually reaching out to explore where the next "advance" might be. No sooner had SIL established a presence in Peru than Cam was planning to train a corps of young translators to establish an

SIL presence in Venezuela. But gaining permission from the Venezuelan government to work with their ethnic peoples was proving to be more difficult than he had anticipated. Some of the government officals who earlier had expressed a warm interest in having SIL work in the country were now noncommittal and even denied ever having given the impression that SIL would be welcomed.

In September 1950, Cam sent Bill Nyman, Jr. and his wife Marjorie (Marj) to Caracas to be SIL's unofficial ambassadors to Venezuela. Bill was to enroll in the Central University of Venezuela, make friendly contacts and "scout out the land." On October 6, Bill sent Cam the first of a number of less-than-favorable reports. These reports included information about Article II of the Venezuelan Constitution. This article gave Franciscan missionaries authority over the Indian territories. This meant the Franciscans would have to give permission for SIL to begin work in those areas. Bill also wrote that Dr. Requeña of the Venezuelan Indian Commission told him a rumor had surfaced about SIL's intentions. The rumor was that although SIL was a scientific organization, it would catechize the Indians in its own religious doctrine. Said Bill:

> Immediately after Dr. Requeña returned from the Inter-American Indian Conference, he went to the government and presented the work of SIL and told them of the invitation we had received to enter Venezuela. The government seemed favorably impressed. However, it was while Dr. Requeña was working on plans for us to enter the country that he got wind of the aforementioned rumor. For the ultimate good of our group and the commission, Dr. Requeña suggests we let the matter rest. He then frankly said he did not know how he could be of further help to us. He said the Franciscan law about granting permission to enter the Indian areas was very strong. He said even he had to get permission before journeying into the Indian territories.

For the next several months Bill continued to send lengthy reports to Cam suggesting legitimate reasons why SIL should "give up the Venezuelan plan." Bill cited the continued unfavorable press and resistance from the scientific community to have "any foreign scholars meddling in their domain." Bill had also discovered it was impossible for him to take any courses at the university for credit: "too much red tape for expatriate students to receive credit." Also Bill's letters mentioned the high cost of living. In his February 11, 1951, letter Bill wrote:

> It seems strange that we should consider not advancing into another country based on cost of living. But because costs of housing, transportation, domestic help, food, clothing, repairs are two to three times what they are in the States (and going up), Marj and I have just about reached the conclusion that it would be best to advance this year in another direction.

In an earlier letter, Bill had written at length about the reported open hostility from a number of Indian tribes against intruders into their territory. One of the most notorious examples was the Motilone group, in the state of Zulia on the Colombia-Venezuela border, south of Lake Maracaibo. Bill said he had talked with oil employees who reported that very few people had ever seen a Motilone Indian— they shot their arrows before anyone could spot them. Motilone arrows had killed several oil company employees. Bill concluded his report by saying that it would be "wonderful if SIL workers could go into such territory, the danger notwithstanding, and make friends with the Motilone people."[2]

In typical fashion, exploring every possible angle before conceding a new option, Cam asked Bob Schneider to fly to Caracas in February 1951 to assist Bill in making further government contacts. At the same time, Cam had written to Bill advising him not to "push things."

> While it is true that we (SIL) were invited by two high-ranking government officials and the invitation was published in a Lima newspaper, we had better not try to refresh their minds on the matter. If it is the Lord's will that we enter Venezuela He will have the invitation renewed. On the other hand, it is perfectly all right for you and Bob to let your friends know you are exploring the situation with the intention of coming into the country. It's important that you work through the university and government officers rather than the oil company or mission groups. It is important to make your friends among the Venezuelans.

One of the assignments Cam had given Bob Schneider was to make arrangements for an official ceremony in Caracas to honor the arrival of

JAARS' newest airplane, a twin-engine Catalina (PBY) on a stopover on its way to Peru. The plane was to be advertised as part of SIL's Interamerican Friendship Fleet and was in fact a gift from Mexico to Peru. The plane would be carrying high-level Mexican government officials, including the Mexican ambassador to Peru and Peru's ambassador to Mexico. The group was traveling to Lima for the plane's second dedication ceremony.

The plane was to be called the "Moisés Sáenz." Before his untimely death as a result of pneumonia in November 1941, Sáenz had been Mexico's ambassador to Peru. He was highly regarded for his service to the ethnic peoples of both Mexico and Peru. Cam had met Moisés Sáenz one morning in 1931 while taking a walk along the edge of Lake Atitlán in Guatemala. Cam invited Sáenz to his home, where he shared his vision for the ethnic peoples of Guatemala. After observing Cam's work with the Cakchiquel people, Sáenz invited Cam to do the same thing in Mexico. This "chance meeting" developed into a deep and lasting friendship. When Cam approached a number of longtime Mexican friends to form a committee to honor Moisés Sáenz, he suggested they raise money to buy a goodwill plane. The plane would be used by SIL in Peru for the benefit of the ethnic tribes. The Mexican committee happily raised $10,000.

Meanwhile, Bob Schneider was having no more success than Bill Nyman in stating the case for SIL's desire to work in Venezuela. The Minister of Education was uncharitably harsh in his refusal to hear Bob's presentation. Then, in the midst of Bob's struggles to arrange for the plane ceremony, Cam phoned to tell Bob he had changed his mind about stopping in Venezuela. Cam and the group of dignitaries would fly directly from Mexico City to Lima.

At first Bob was flummoxed. The staff that worked with and loved Cam, all made allowances for his habit of occasionally changing his mind at the last minute. It never seemed to bother Cam that people may have spent considerable energy and time making arrangements, sending out invitations, and preparing a special location, only to be told at the last moment that he felt the Lord leading him in another direction— to cancel whatever it was that had been planned. It would fall to Cal Hibbard, now working as Cam's secretary, to explain why Cam had changed his mind:

The ceremony in Mexico City is set for April 6, [it actually occurred on the 5th]. The president will be here and a host of other dignitaries. Uncle Cam expects to have water from the Amazon River for the actual christening, and possibly a Peruvian Indian gourd.

The president of Mexico is sending his special representative to Peru to take part in the christening ceremony there, so Uncle Cam feels we are forced to go directly to Lima. Therefore it will not be possible to stop over at Caracas as originally planned.

On April 12, Elaine Townsend wrote the following newsletter:

Another miracle has taken place in the history of Wycliffe and SIL. Let me take you back a few months before I tell you about the christening ceremony. In November, during our day of prayer in Mexico City, Cam reminded those of us present "we have not because we ask not." Each of us then told the others what we were trusting God to do for us in 1951. When it came Cam's turn to share, he said he didn't feel he should mention his request except to his wife because the group might think he was crazy.

When we returned to our room Cam told me he was asking God for a Catalina [airplane] for the work in South America. I was amazed. I knew God had answered other big requests, but I thought this was one that was just too impossible. However, I joined him in prayer that if it were God's will it would come to pass. Now, scarcely five months later, God answered that prayer and in a way that we could never have dreamed of. It does indeed behoove us to ASK God for big things.

The ceremony began on April 5th at 8:15 am when the president of the republic [Miguel Alemán] arrived while the marine band played the Mexican national anthem. There were at least one hundred people present. Among them, besides the president, were three ministers from his cabinet: Finance, Education and Commerce. There were five ambassadors, representing the U.S.A., Peru, Venezuela, Bolivia and Mexico and many other distinguished guests. All of the SIL family that could possibly attend was present. The plane looked magnificent. Green, white and red bands were painted around the engines. The tips of the propellers were painted yellow and the nose of the plane dark blue. The Mexican and Peruvian flags were painted on both sides of the plane with the Mexican flag on top on one side, and the Peruvian flag on top on the other.

In blue letters, the name MOISES SAENZ appeared on both sides and just above it in smaller letters the word AMAUTA, which in the Inca language means, *wise man at the service of his people...*

Elaine's letter told about the actual christening by the widow of Moisés Sáenz—unfortunately the water from the Amazon did not come in time— and of the various speeches, including one by Moisés' brother Aarón, one of the wealthiest men in Mexico. Aarón Sáenz would one day give several large monetary gifts toward building a new SIL center in Tlalpan, on the outskirts of Mexico City. Elaine concluded her news-letter by saying:

> Tonight the Peruvian ambassador is having a farewell reception at the Embassy to which we are all invited. The plane leaves for Peru one week from today, the 20th. I know you will be in prayer for the safety of this trip and our entire flying program.

And to Ken Pike, Cam added a P.S. to Elaine's letter:

> Word has come from the Foreign Office in Lima that President Odría and his entire cabinet are to meet us at the airport on Sunday afternoon [the plane left on the following Friday]. We count on your prayers that this great victory may be mightily used of God, not only for Peru but also for other countries as well. The Lord has done exceedingly above what we could possibly have imagined.

Notes

1   A year later, in March 1951, Cam would report that for the first time
     in over a year the group's financial income was up to almost 100% of
     the members' basic quota needs. He then wrote, "Let's be more
     faithful in prayer that our large, rapidly increasing family may have
     enough to live on and to pursue their duties efficiently. God is able,
     but sometimes 'we have not because we ask not'."
2   It would fall to 19-year-old Bruce E. Olson, an independent
     missionary linguist and adventurer, to make the most significant
     contact with the Motilone people in 1961. It was a contact that almost
     cost him his life. See his book *Bruchko* published by Creation House,
     Altamonte Springs, Florida.

Chapter Ten

For Friendship

It took fifteen years (1937-1952), but in February 1952, Cam's long-awaited biography of his friend and Mexico's past president, Lázaro Cárdenas, was finally published. While many in SIL applauded Cam for this achievement, there were those who wondered aloud about the benefit of such a book. Clearly, the book had consumed hundreds of hours of Cam's and other members' time—time that could have been spent in promoting Bible translation or in other activities more directly related to SIL's primary objectives.

What those who criticized Cam failed to understand was that this biography was furthering the work of SIL and was indeed fulfilling Christ's command to "love one's neighbor as one's self." In overt and in less obvious ways, Cam continually strived to build bridges of friendship between individuals and nations. In an early diary Cam wrote that it was his dream to "help people, to teach them to read and write [in their own languages] and thereby help governments." Unfortunately, a great many Christian workers had grown up with the notion that any ministry not directly related to public evangelism was somehow less spiritual and even non-essential to Kingdom work. It would take Christian leaders, like John Stott, Billy Graham, and the Lausanne movement to call the Church back to a partnership between social action and evangelism. This partnership could mean giving a cup of water in Christ's name, a practical kindness shown to a neighbor, working in a soup kitchen or serving as an advocate to the vulnerable and disenfranchised—all "spiritual" activities.

Cam had long held that all people must be taken seriously and treated with dignity. He reasoned that since the Creator loves all people, they have a right to our respect and, if at all possible, our help. This meant everyone, from the garbage collector to the highest cabinet officer in government, should be given a sincere word of encouragement, a tender smile, a warm embrace or a sympathetic listening ear and the warmth of friendship. For this reason, Cam urged SIL members to do what Jesus said we should do in Matthew 7:12, "Ask yourself what you want people to do for you, then seize the initiative and do it for them" [Cam's paraphrase].[1]

And so it was for friendship that Cam labored long and hard to write the biography of his longtime friend, a book entitled *Lázaro Cárdenas, Mexican Democrat*. And it was for friendship that Cam wrote to dozens of magazines, libraries, other media and friends, urging them to review and advertise the book in an effort to make it known to as many people as possible. Some of those media included *The Washington Post* and *The Chicago Tribune*. *The Washington Star* likened Cárdenas to Gandhi. Cam also contacted Marshall Fields' bookstore (they took ten copies), the *Reader's Digest*, Walter Lippman, and dozens of news agencies in the U.S. and Canada.

Cam's longtime friend and founder of Dallas Theological Seminary, Lewis Sperry Chafer, just before he died in August 1952, thanked Cam for the Cárdenas book he had sent. In his letter, Chafer wrote:

> I am amazed at the wonderful thing that God has chosen to do through you. The whole linguistic undertaking is one of the greatest missionary efforts that the world has ever seen. I am proud to be the friend of the one who has done this great piece of work under the hand of God. We need our friends sometimes to tell us how much we have accomplished and I now think I may tell you with all sincerity of the marvelous things God is doing by your hand. What a triumph to win the affection and cooperation of President Cárdenas!

It was also for friendship that Dick Pittman sent a copy of Cam's book to a new friend whom he had met during his 1951 linguistic survey in the Philippines. That new friend was Ramón Magsaysay, the Secretary of Defense of the Philippines.[2] And it was for friendship that Ramón Magsaysay phoned Dick long-distance from the Philippines to personally thank him for the gift of an autographed copy of the Cárdenas biography, saying, "It is a very important book and it will be valuable for my people, if they read it." Almost fifty years after the book was published, Bob Schneider reflected on its influence, saying:

> I got to thinking about the importance of Cam's biography of Lázaro Cárdenas and how it changed the course of the life of the Philippine war hero and president of the Philippines, Ramón Magsaysay. The book also opened the door to SIL's work in Colombia and influenced a number of Latin American leaders.

When Bob reflected on how the book and other media had been "door openers" for SIL's work in other countries, he related how SIL was first invited to work in Ecuador:

Early in 1951, after four years in Peru I wrote a simple report about SIL's work and sent it to one of the indigenous magazines of the Americas. Without fanfare, I told about SIL's purpose and what had transpired during our four years in Peru. The Ecuadorian ambassador to Mexico happened to read the article, and forwarded it to the Ecuadorian ambassador in Washington, D.C., who in turn sent it to Ecuador's President Galo Plaza Lasso in Quito. Since I had mentioned in the article that SIL represented the University of Oklahoma, Ecuador's president contacted University of Oklahoma president Dr. George Cross and mentioned Ecuador's interest in SIL. President Cross then forwarded Plaza's invitation to Mr. Townsend in Lima. The circle was complete when Cam handed me the letter with the remark, "Why don't you go to Quito and sign an agreement with the Ecuadorian Government?"

On July 19, 1952, Bob Schneider, representing SIL, signed an agreement with the government of Ecuador to work with Ecuador's nine ethnic minorities. Ten months later, in May of 1953, under Bob's direction, the first contingent of SIL workers from Peru arrived in Ecuador.

The pace of SIL's expansion accelerated further when on September 25, 1952 Bob's colleague Don Burns signed a similar contract with Guatemala's Minister of Education. Earl Adams became SIL's first team director in Guatemala. On that same date, Turner Blount suggested that SIL begin work among the ethnic minority groups in Canada and Alaska.

In April 1953, twenty new SIL members arrived in Manila to begin language work under the direction of Dr. Dick Pittman. In July of 1953, Ken and Evelyn Pike opened the first SIL linguistic courses in England, at London Bible College. Additionally, negotiations were underway for a cooperative contract with the Bolivian government, which was signed by Cam on August 12, 1954. The first SIL members arrived in Riberalta, Bolivia on June 7, 1955. Harold and Mary Key were the first branch directors. On August 1, 1956, an agreement of cooperation between the National Museum of Brazil and SIL was signed. Dr. Dale Kietzman was selected to be the first director for SIL's work in Brazil.

During those first years of the decade of the fifties, when SIL was experiencing its greatest expansion, the mood in America was, for some, one of anxiety. But Cam appears not to have been among them. To be sure, he and the group were gaining momentum—sometimes faster than there were funds, people and energy to answer the demands for the expanding work. At the same time, there appears to have been no hesitancy on Cam's part to continue pushing forward to enter as many countries as possible, as soon as possible.

Dick Pittman, who shared Cam's fundamental vision for expansion, was nevertheless more restrained in his public comments. In a 1952 answer to a letter from one Frans L. Schalkwijk of the Netherlands, who wanted to know when SIL could begin work in Suriname, Dick said SIL did not contemplate entering that South American country in the near future, since their energies were taken up with the advance in the Philippines. But, said Dick: "SIL has a real burden for all the fields where Bible translation needs to be done and where no one else is doing it."[3]

In the midst of SIL's rapid development Cameron Townsend demonstrated the ability to handle an amazing number of letters, memos, meetings, ideas, personnel issues, public relations problems and events that he was asked to consider, schedule, organize and resolve never collapsing under the weight of his administrative load.

In addition to negotiating high-level government contracts and using his skills as a leading mission statesman, Cam was often asked to answer a number of letters concerned with smaller issues. For example,

Cam received a letter from a supporter halfway around the world lashing out against "liberal" churches and wanting to know if there were any Arminian members in Wycliffe. Then Cam received a letter from an older member who wanted to know what could be done about a taciturn newer member who was "socially inept." The older member wondered why Wycliffe hadn't done a better job of orientation to the policies of SIL. From Peru came a report that the Aeronca airplane was in bad shape after the floats had been damaged from hitting a submerged log. Then came another request to contact a pastor in the U.S. who wanted Cam to present a message at their mission conference. At the same time, Cam was sending memos to the Mexico director to check on the citrus trees in Tetelcingo to see if they were being properly watered. If they weren't, he wanted money taken from his personal account to pay for their care.

But there were times when the demands of being general director did seem overwhelming to Cam and Elaine. After spending September to December 1951 in Chicago working on Wycliffe's second film, "Each in His Own Tongue," Cam, on January 20, 1952, wrote to a friend that he had been "pressured almost beyond the point of endurance." Part of Cam's emotional exhaustion had to do with his family's living conditions. For several months that fall all five of them were squeezed into one room in Elaine's parents' home on Drake Avenue in Chicago. Adding to the discomfort of cramped quarters was the illness of their three preschool children, all of whom came down with measles at the same time!

Desperate for a short vacation, Elaine and Cam decided to take a merchant ship out of New Orleans for the voyage to Guayaquil, Ecuador. From there they would fly to Lima, Peru. Elaine knew Ralph and Vera Borthwick, new Canadian members with two preschool boys, who were also scheduled to take a merchant ship out of New Orleans on their way to Lima, Peru on March 2. On February 25, 1952, Elaine wrote the Borthwicks to ask if they would be willing to give up their reservations in order for Cam and her to have some much-needed rest:

> There is so much waiting for Cam to do when he gets to Peru that I have no idea when he can take another break from the work. At the moment Cam and I are in desperate need of a rest and probably the only way we can get it would be on the boat.

In her letter to the Borthwicks, Elaine admitted it was presumptuous of her to ask them to change their plans and take a later boat, particularly since she had never met them. However, Elaine softened the request by offering to pay the Borthwicks' airfare if waiting until mid-March for another boat was inconvenient. Since passenger space on the boat was limited, Ralph Borthwick accepted her offer and flew to Lima with the older of his two sons. Vera, with their youngest son, traveled with the Townsend family. As it turned out, the Norwegian freighter left not on March 2, but on the 15th. From his correspondence aboard the *M.S. Mosdale* en route to Guayaquil, Ecuador, Cam wrote:

> Leading the SIL advance is exciting, but after working day and night on different assignments in the United States and Mexico, we really did need a rest. We are now getting the most restful vacation we can remember. This, in spite of extremely high seas on the fourth day that sent chairs and tables sliding all over the dining room and caused some unpleasant seasickness.

Curiously, Cam and Elaine did not engage in the usual onboard diversions. Rather, they created their own activity by holding an impromptu social for the captain and seventeen of the crewmembers. Vera Borthwick made fudge and then she sang "I'd rather have Jesus than anything." Cam explained SIL's mission and gave a challenge to the crewmembers to become personally acquainted with Jesus Christ as their Savior and Lord. Elaine reported that there was much interest in Cam's talk.

After the rest aboard ship, and upon his return to Peru, Cam immediately dug into his waiting correspondence with the help of his new personal secretary, Cal Hibbard. (Cal's skill and his commitment to become Cam's secretary was a long-awaited answer to prayer.) One of the many letters Cam answered was on a subject rarely discussed within the group—the question of race.

Cam had received a letter from Dr. P.E. Dinkins, a black brother from Selma, Alabama, who had inquired about taking the SIL course in Canada (then under the direction of Dick Pittman) but then decided not to attend. In the letter, Dr. Dinkins raised the question of racial prejudice. Here is part of Cam's reply:

I was disappointed with your decision not to attend our course in Canada. I note you say that racial prejudice is not much of a problem with you. That is a wonderful attitude. For myself, racial discrimination makes my blood boil. It is not only anti-Christian, but also anti-American. Just now I am staying at the home of ex-president Cárdenas, on beautiful Lake Pátzcuaro. The home has a wonderful garden and just off the veranda there is a monument bearing the faces of Lincoln, Juárez and Martí (the Cuban hero) and an unbroken chain. General Cárdenas admires them greatly, as do we all. How I long for the day when Christ shall return, and we of every race who believe on Him will live together as brothers and sisters. Why should color influence our attitude when it comes to human relationships?

In May 1952, Cam wrote the members of the Wycliffe board to remind them that under no cirmstances must a candidate be rejected on the basis of color or ethnicity. "Before God all men and women are created free and equal." Cam urged the board to put a greater emphasis on encouraging black students to consider Bible translation and linguistics as a mission option.

One of Cameron Townsend's longtime friends, and a supporter of Wycliffe and SIL, was Henry C. Crowell, of the Moody Bible Institute. Crowell was one of the trustees who administered the Crowell Foundation (begun by his father), which had supplied funds for several JAARS projects including a second Aeronca airplane. On May 27, 1952 Crowell wrote Cam to inform him that the foundation was beginning a new ministry to aid gospel workers worldwide. It was to be called Missionary Equipment Service.

Crowell had visited Peru in May of 1949 and was flown to several jungle locations. The JAARS pilots, who always carefully weighed their cargo to determine how much weight was scheduled for the flight, gave Crowell the nickname the "Kilo Kid," as he was rather large. Crowell took this in good humor and thereafter generally signed his letters to Cam as, "Yours sincerely, the Kilo Kid." Because of his friendship and deep respect for Cam, Crowell felt free to occasionally criticize the way Cam was administering SIL or the way the board had decided a particular issue. In the letter telling Cam about the new Missionary Equipment organization, Crowell cautioned Cam against advancing too quickly into new fields:

> Let me give you an observation of missions in general and Wycliffe in particular. It is this, namely, the terrific eagerness to expand into new fields with the gospel. So eager are mission boards to expand that they seldom take time to stand still long enough to evaluate their strengths and weaknesses. While I am as anxious as you are to see SIL expand into new fields, I would hate to build a house higher if the foundation is still wobbly. (And the JAARS foundation is still not strong). The success of JAARS is a most important consideration for your overall success.
>
> There is yet another problem that provokes me about Wycliffe and many other mission organizations as well. It is their lack of support personnel. Most of the recruitment efforts center around so-called "frontline missionaries," those that do linguistics and Bible translation on the field. However, the work you are doing is no different than an army that must employ fifteen to twenty men in the rear to every man or woman in the front. You need bookkeepers, secretaries, mechanics and people to buy and send supplies and medicines to translators living in isolated areas. You should have a staff of people who can write articles and books that can relate the stories of what God is doing on the field to those at home who pray and send money to support those on the field. Well, enough for the lecture. I know you see this need as clearly as I do but there must be some way of making the rest of your organization broaden its thinking along these lines.

Actually, the group was thinking more broadly than Mr. Crowell realized. The foundations of SIL and Wycliffe were growing stronger month by month and year by year. In 1952, there were more than three hundred members, half of whom were support workers. In Mexico and Peru, there were a total of sixty language groups that had full-time SIL workers.

Cam constantly encouraged SIL members to "never lose sight of our responsibility to produce translations." The Mexico branch of SIL established three translation centers located in Mitla, Tetelcingo and Tasquillo. With the exception of Mitla, the centers would, in 1961, be replaced by a state-of-the-art translation center in Ixmiquilpan, Mexico, then under the direction of chief translation consultant John Beekman.[4] The center provided expert consultant help and careful exegetical checking of the biblical text for clear understanding and for the didactical accuracy of translations in process.[5]

The support workers in Peru included radiomen, pilots, mechanics, teachers, a doctor, nurses, builders and others. The Mexico branch, however, had fewer designated support personnel. Their contractual agreement with the government was that all Mexico branch members were to be assigned to a specific tribal area and were required to produce linguistic, anthropological and other publishable materials related to the ethnic minorities. Thus, those who were considered support personnel by SIL were also required to be involved in some way with a language project.

In addition to the growing field programs in 1952, Cam spearheaded a small network of regional offices in the U.S. and Canada. These were the forerunner of the layman-run organization Wycliffe Associates. The principal lay-support groups for Wycliffe in 1952 were the Chicago Committee, the Wheaton Committee and the Moose Jaw Committee in Canada. Working in tandem with these lay-run committees was Wycliffe's U.S. Extension Department under the direction of Bill Wyatt. (Later Harold Key and Dale Kietzman would direct Wycliffe's publicity department.) There were, of course, hundreds of churches and special friends of Wycliffe in the U.S. and Canada that gave substantial amounts of their time, energy and resources to further the work of Wycliffe.

George Cowan, then director of the SIL work in Mexico, reported in April, at a banquet held to honor Cam and Elaine, that a number of people were coming to know the Lord in a half-dozen different ethnic groups in Mexico and Peru.

> We are grateful to the Lord for this evidence of His blessing. But in reality, this is an infinitesimal number compared to those we have not reached. However, in comparison to what was true fifteen years ago, there is much for which to praise the Lord. We also praise the Lord for the complete New Testament in the Mixteco language. This is, after all, what Wycliffe is all about, i.e., giving the written

Word of God to ethnic peoples who as yet do not have it in their own language.

Such reports always gave the membership a general sense of optimism that the group was progressing steadily toward their stated goals. But the events that would occur in Peru in early 1953 would give Cam and others a painful opportunity to consider what God was trying to teach them. Four Roman Catholic bishops, under the leadership of the archbishop, took out full-page ads in two leading Peruvian newspapers, denouncing SIL and advocating that the government expel all SIL workers without delay.

Notes

1   It is this author's conviction that Cameron Townsend would have enthuastically agreed with Dr. Charles Ringma, Professor of Missions and Evangelism at Regent College, Vancouver, Canada in his definition of Mission: "Mission is the whole church, participating as witness and servant, in all of God's activity to bring salvation, healing and wholeness to humanity and the created order." See *CRUX*, XXXVIII, no. 2 (June 2002): 29.

2   Ramón Magsaysay became the third president of the Republic of the Philippines after World War II. In a letter to Dick Pittman he wrote, "The Cárdenas biography guided my decision-making throughout my candidacy for the presidency of the Philippines." On March 17, 1957, Magsaysay and twenty-five of his party were tragically killed in an airplane crash.

3   SIL began work in Suriname in 1966 under the direction of Joel and Marjorie Warkentin. The invitation to work in the country grew out of conversations that Dr. Joe Grimes had with leaders of Suriname education and culture at an Inter-American Linguistic Congress.

4   In 1974, Biola University and Talbot Theological Seminary conferred on John Beekman an honorary Doctor of Literature degree for his distinguished service in Bible translation, and for his outstanding contribution as a translation consultant for hundreds of Bible translators worldwide.

5   See Hugh Steven, *The Man with the Noisy Heart, The John Beekman Story* (Chicago: Moody Press, 1979), 78 ff.

Paul Robinson and Henry Crowell, visiting the Piro village of Huau on the Urubamba River, eastern Peru, March 1949, enjoy the hand-woven Piro "cushma" robes and other gifts.

June 7, 1955: The Catalina airplane from Yarinacocha arrives at the Beni River village-sugar plantation on IVON, near Riberalta, NE Bolivian rain forests, bringing 26 linguists and support personnel (plus children) to initiate a new SIL branch in the Bolivian jungle. Seated on wing: George Insley, John Shanks, an unidentified person, Larry Montgomery. Waving: Cornelia Hibbard, Cameron Townsend, Mary Key, Leon Schanely, Betty Schanely, Delores and Bill Richmond.

Chapter Eleven

The Attacks

To borrow a famous phrase, the months of January to August 1953 would be "the best of times and the worst of times," for Cam and the SIL group in Peru. For Cam and Elaine, the best of times occurred on January 20, when Elaine gave birth at the SIL jungle center at 3:50 AM to their fourth child, a son whom they named William Crowell Townsend. Cam wrote:

> Our son's first name will remind us of our dear friend, William Nyman who has been a tower of strength to us personally and to the whole Bible translation movement. His second name stands for a greatly beloved brother in the Lord, Henry Coleman Crowell of Moody Bible Institute. He too, has served us in many wonderful ways.

The worst of times began in February when the first of a series of outrageous newspaper attacks from four bishops accused SIL of propagating Protestant dogma. The articles listed fifteen specific points, two of which were that SIL was attacking "holy Catholic dogma, and teaching a faith that is vague, abstract, and without principles or truths." Cam responded that these and the other points were erroneous and without foundation. As to the accusation that SIL attacked Catholic dogma, Cam wrote, "We aren't in Peru to attack or 'protest' against anybody or anything." To the accusation that SIL taught "vague or abstract truths," Cam wrote, "We teach the Apostles' Creed and avoid sectarianism."

At the same time there were complaints coming from Wycliffe supporters in the U.S. and Canada about SIL's flight policies in Peru. Letters came from churches demanding to know if the rumors were true that SIL pilots carried nuns and priests in their planes—along with these passengers' icons. Since MAF was not required to perform this service, a Baptist pastor from Fort Worth, Texas wanted to know why JAARS did it. Another group wanted to know why SIL would be linked in a cooperative literacy agreement with UNESCO (United Nations Educational Scientific and Cultural Organization), then considered to be a humanistic and atheistic organization. Cam answered the UNESCO inquiries in a series of personal letters. He also wrote one to the Wycliffe board of directors, who received a flurry of letters after *Translation* magazine carried an article on the UNESCO connection. Some on the board too, wanted to know why SIL was involved with UNESCO; they also asked Cam to comment on the question of flying priests and nuns in JAARS planes. His response to the pastors and to the board:

> After working for thirty-five years in Latin America I've never known of a priest or nun being converted through a "chip-on-the-shoulder" attitude toward them. I've known several who have been won through kindness. Humanly it is not easy to treat them with love when you know their organization is fighting against you and undermining and trying to stop your ministry. ...it also helps to know that every time you show them kindness it makes it all the more difficult for them to block us.

To the board, Cam wrote:

> It must be clear to the readers of *Translation* that we stand uncompromisingly for the fundamentals of the faith. We would never get ourselves in a position with anybody that would weaken our testimony. However, this doesn't mean we should not accept opportunities to reach indigenous peoples with the Word just because it's an agency of UNESCO that opens the door.

I am reminded of the example of Moses' mother when she accepted a commission from a member of the royal family of Egypt. It was from a family that bitterly opposed the people of God. Very likely she was criticized for being on friendly terms with Pharaoh's daughter and even for taking wages from her. Hebrews chapter eleven tells us that she did it by faith, knowing that it would turn out to God's honor and glory. In addition she was able to nurture and train the child she loved. Eighty years later the services she rendered to Pharaoh's daughter resulted in the liberation of Israel.

Ken Pike also weighed in on the debate, writing:

Our whole approach to closed fields is based on the fact that we can and must cooperate with governments and agencies by sharing our linguistic and translation materials regardless of their theologies, even if they are rabidly anti-Christian. It is precisely our desire to serve such groups that has opened the doors of ministry for us. I believe the abandonment of this principle would be catastrophic, and would be vastly more dangerous to our whole program than the loss of one or one hundred supporters. If it comes to a choice we should unhesitatingly choose to maintain the principle through which God has blessed us, even though there may be heavy censure.

Today there are many areas of the world closed to ordinary mission work. God's people are being forced to determine new ways to get a testimony of His love and saving grace to such people. In Bible times God raised up special ways to get His message of redemption and love to people behind closed doors. God raised up Daniel to work with a pagan, blasphemous king in Babylon. Daniel served the king by solving problems, and helped him rule his provinces. In all honesty Daniel did everything he could to serve that government. As a result, we have, I think, the first recorded instance of a testimony going out into every language and nation of the then-known world.

On March 20, 1953, Cam, whose theme was "by love serve one another," wrote the board of directors a lengthy explanation to answer the question of why JAARS was flying people other than SIL personnel. The following is part of that report:

> Since we began our flying service it has been advisable, and virtually unavoidable, to carry some people who are not members of our organization. Sometimes we have been asked to fly a mercy flight. Other times officials whom we desire to please have asked for our services. On other occasions we have flown people as a favor to evangelical missionaries or to "pour water on the gunpowder" of potential antagonists of other beliefs. This service has won us the goodwill of practically everyone in the jungle. But it has been done without legal authorization and with a certain amount of risk, if, in fact, we were to be involved in an accident.
>
> Recently I was advised that it was essential for us to fly all our aircraft at least twenty hours a month to keep them in proper flying condition. It is also necessary to fly them in order to keep our pilots in top form. In order to do this, it was necessary to extend our service to non-members. Therefore, to do this legally it became necessary to have some authority from the government. (We did not want to be seen as being in competition with the Peruvian Air Force.) I felt the best way to get this authorization was to carry out our JAARS service as an adjunct of the government airline. This would make the government responsible in the case of lawsuits. It would also make the government proud of all the flying we do rather than jealous and suspicious about what it is we do. This would also give our friends in officialdom ample grounds for continuing to grant us free gasoline on an ever-increasing scale. At the moment we have a tentative agreement with the Ministry of Aeronautics. I feel we are most fortunate in getting such an agreement, and believe further, this is the Lord's timing to counteract an attack against us that was published in the main Peruvian newspaper.

Clearly, this explanation satisfied Cam, but there were many people (non-members) who did not fully appreciate or understand this approach to SIL's mission. And the issue of carrying people of different faiths would continue to be raised against SIL for many years to come. While the UNESCO attack was something of a tempest in a teapot, more serious and disturbing attacks on SIL's credibility and ministry in Peru began on February 28, 1953. The first series of articles appeared in Lima's two leading newspapers accusing SIL of being an "organ for propaganda and dissemination of evangelical Protestantism." Part of that first long article that appeared in the Saturday, February 28th issue of the *El Comercio* newspaper said:

> We Catholic missionaries who are located throughout the Peruvian jungle are more or less in contact with the members of the Summer Institute of Linguistics. We have come to the conclusion that the Linguistic Institute is not merely a philanthropic and scientific institution, but it is mainly interested in converting and proselytizing. Their study of tribal languages and their medical work are employed as propaganda to enable them to infiltrate more easily into our national life and then to carry out an extensive and open campaign of evangelical Protestant proselytism.

The irony of these attacks was that those priests and nuns who actually had personal contact with Cam and SIL personnel in Peru had an altogether different view, as did many in the government. Peruvian friends of SIL were upset with the article's use of buzzwords, like "proselytizing, propaganda, infiltrate," and "extensive campaigning by evangelical Protestant sects," all of which conveyed untruths.

Curiously, just about a month before the February 28th article appeared in the Lima newspaper, Cam received a letter from Padre Pascual Alegre G., a local jungle priest, in which he wrote:

> As a Christian I congratulate you for the love you exercise on behalf of the Indians of these jungle regions. You and I do not belong to the same religion, but nevertheless we ought to be united by the common purpose of every Christian, which is to "love our brethren as Christ has loved us." Oh, how can this union in love become a reality, love toward the Lord who gave His life for all of us, and how can that hour be brought to pass when we shall all be truly brethren in love? As Saint John says, "God is love, and he who abides in love abides in God, and God in him." For my part, you can be sure that whatever I can do for others I will always do it without laying down conditions, for this is my obligation as an unworthy disciple of the one true Master, which is Jesus.

There couldn't have been a clearer statement of mission purpose and solidarity between two men of different theological and historic traditions than the statement given by Padre Alegre. One of Cam's favorite Scripture verses was the one Padre Alegre quoted from First John: chapter four, verse one, "Dear friends, let us love one another, for love comes from God." Cam did not want SIL to be accused of spreading propaganda. Cam and the members of SIL in Peru and in other parts of the world simply wanted above all else that ethnic peoples have a choice to come to know and share the truth found in Jesus Christ, and to become, as Padre Alegre described himself, "a disciple of the one true master, which is Jesus."

Unresolved issues remained, however. Cam still needed to answer the distressing allegations and to give an explanation to Dr. Pedro Benvenuto Murrieta, the Peruvian Minister of Education under whom SIL worked. Cal Hibbard, Cam's secretary and archivist for the Townsend papers, translated the following letter from Spanish. With the translated letter Cal wrote, "I send this remarkable letter to show the wisdom with which Cameron Townsend handled a sensitive and potentially dangerous situation that could have curtailed or stopped SIL's work in a country where church and state are united."

Distinguished doctor and beloved friend:

I write you regarding an important matter for which I need your help. In the nine years since SIL has been in Peru we've enjoyed good relations with Catholic missionaries, as the attached letter from Padre Alegre confirms. I admire and appreciate the help they have given to us. It has also been our privilege on occasions to serve them with our planes, carrying letters and transporting them to remote areas where there is no other means of transport, except by dangerous canoes and uncomfortable launches.

It has been my desire to expand this service, but during the past year, four of our planes have been down for maintenance and repair, mainly because of lack of funds to buy parts. I'm especially concerned for the repair of the Catalina *Moisés Sáenz* amphibian plane whose service I have made available to various priests.

We've recently organized a committee known as "Friends of the Summer Institute of Linguistics" in Lima. This committee has secured the help of various commercial houses and philanthropists.

But they've run into a problem with some who doubt the value of SIL's work. These doubts are based on disturbing articles that have recently been published by *Verdades Magazine* [and other publications]. The articles have done damage not only to us but also to the sacrificial Catholic missionaries in denying them air transportation. I beg you to talk with the editor of the magazine and explain the real character of our work. The dictionaries, grammars and reading primers we produce in each language will be available to the priests after the Ministry of Education publishes them.

Dr. Manuel Gamio, Director of the Inter-American Indian Institute [of Mexico], and recognized authority on Indian affairs, has testified to the value of the Indian languages for study, evangelization and for incorporation of the tribal people into the life of their nation. In a letter directed to Dr. Darcy McNickel dated 12 June 1952, he writes: "The investigations carried on by anthropologists and sociologists among these Indians frequently have deficiencies that would be avoided if these specialists could speak fluently the language of the Indians they are investigating. An example of this is the very important work that has been carried on for years in Mexico and Peru by hundreds of members of the Summer Institute of Linguistics, affiliated with the University of Oklahoma who, without being sectarian in religious matters, familiarize the Indians with the gospel by means of translations of the Bible into various aboriginal languages and dialects which they have previously learned and which they speak well, inasmuch as they are professional linguists. Additionally, they teach the Indians how to improve their living conditions as much as possible, taking into consideration the local geographic, cultural and economic factors uniting people into the fabric of the nation."

When I founded the Institute nineteen years ago, I stipulated that our work would be nonsectarian. I wanted to serve people in a Christian spirit, without distinction of creed or race. It could be that some Catholics would prefer that we not serve Protestants and that some Protestants prefer that we not serve Catholics, but I think such people are few in number. An institution like ours which works intimately with governments of six nations, has to serve everyone and I would myself not be pleased with any other *modus operandi* nor would I accept as a member any person who, through religious or racial prejudices, refused to serve persons not of his religious persuasion.

Also, I established a rule that no member of the Institute was to become involved in ecclesiastical matters. This, after all, is the work of clerics, whether Catholic or Protestant. By this I don't mean to imply that we are not believers or that we neglect the responsibility as believers to teach animistic Indians as much as we can about the God of love. On the contrary, we accept the responsibility, but our scientific and cultural work must not suffer due to ecclesiastic clashes. We are not in Peru to protest against anything, nor anyone, but to serve this grand nation that we have come to love as our adopted homeland. There has also been a challenge that SIL is not truly associated with the University of Oklahoma. The rector of the University of Oklahoma, Dr. G. L. Cross, on September 24, 1951 wrote to the director of our courses at that university, my nephew, Dr. Kenneth L. Pike, as follows:

"I want you to know that the University of Oklahoma values highly its association with the Summer Institute of Linguistics. Personally, I believe that the Institute is the finest program with which any institution of higher education could be associated. We shall do everything possible to continue the cooperation and fine relations that have existed in the past.

Cordially yours, G. L. Cross, President."

Let me also quote Dr. Charles Fries, the distinguished professor of the University of Michigan who has expressed on various occasions, his conviction that "our scientific labor constitutes the most significant advance in the science of descriptive linguistics of this decade."

Our plan is to study and give alphabets to the speakers of more than one thousand unwritten languages in different parts of the world.[1] At the same time we will help the governments of each region with their programs of incorporating those language groups into the national life. For such a difficult and extensive work, we need everyone's help. We are constantly grateful for the valuable help you have given to us on many occasions and I give you in advance our gratitude for whatever help you can be in solving the problem which I have referred to in this letter. I do want to assure you of my deepest respect and affection,

Guillermo C. Townsend, General Director

Before going with the first twenty young SIL members to the Philippines in April of 1953, Dr. Richard Pittman, a skilled and prudent mission statesman, wrote Dr. Cecilio Putong, Secretary of Education for the Philippines, explaining SIL's mission. It was, in effect, the same kind of letter Cam had given to the governments of Peru and Ecuador:

> Our organization, while dedicated to the service of the government with which it works, has no political affiliations and hence no political axe to grind. It is, furthermore, a private corporation and not an instrument or tool of any particular nation, administration or political party. Our membership consists of persons who desire to serve minority language groups in any educational, medical, agricultural, or social way possible. The desire of the Summer Institute of Linguistics is to produce scientific primers, grammars and dictionaries in the vernacular languages. In addition to translating scientific materials, we would also translate literature of outstanding educational and moral value, including the Christian Bible. The Institute is nonsectarian and non-denominational, hence not committed to the aggrandizement of any sectarian organization.

Without question, Cam and SIL were facing ecclesiastical authoritarianism. In a letter to Mr. R.G. LeTourneau, who had been invited by the Peruvian government to carry out a road-building project (Cam acted as his interpreter), Cam advised him not to have a public evangelistic service on his first visit to the country:

> The complaint of the bishops is that they are greatly concerned about the growth of evangelical work in the jungle. I am told the president does not like to give in to Rome, though the political powers of the church in this country where church and state are united is a factor that even the strongest ruler has to consider. Also the leading newspaper *El Comercio* is the most powerful force in the country outside of the Congress. There is also a law on the books prohibiting all Protestant propaganda. So holding a public service would not be advisable.

In spite of the newspaper attacks against SIL, the Sub-Secretary of Education, the Director of Rural and Indian Schools and nine other dig-

nitaries from Lima were in attendance at the closing ceremonies of the
first bilingual Indian teacher-training course, held at Yarinacocha on
Saturday, March 31, 1953. Elaine, in an April 1st letter to her parents,
gives us an intimate look at what took place that weekend, when eleven
bilingual teacher candidates representing seven language groups received their teaching certificates:

> Saturday was the closing day of our Indian teacher training school
> and ten officials from Lima came out for the occasion. Cam was to
> have arrived on Friday in the Catalina but just after they had flown
> a hundred miles out from Lima they had trouble with one of the
> magnetos and had to turn back. Cam returned to Lima by bus and
> took a special plane out to the SIL jungle base with the officials. Af-
> ter the ceremony at the Indian school, they were served a fine lunch
> and later were flown to tour a nearby village in the Norseman [air-
> plane].
>
> Our guests (we had seventeen in our house overnight) were to
> leave on Sunday morning on the plane. However, just as they were
> about to take off a terrific tropical storm broke out with all the high
> winds that go with it. I had already begun changing sheets when
> all my company returned to spend another day and night with us.
> It has been a lot of work, but it has also been a great privilege to
> have them in our home.

On Sunday, August 23, 1953, Elaine continued her correspondence to
her parents with the following disquieting news:

> We thought the attacks from the priests were going to die down.
> But on the front page of today's Sunday paper there is a big article
> with pictures of three archbishops and the cardinal attacking not
> only our work, but LeTourneau as well. The article appeared in all
> four of the Lima newspapers. They quoted from last year's article
> on LeTourneau that appeared in Time in which LeTourneau said,
> "God is my partner." And they have said they are very much op-
> posed to the road-building project. Most everyone you talk to says
> that even though they are strong Catholics they are on our side and
> feel ashamed of the way the archbishops are acting. However, these
> articles have tremendous influence ... since the majority of the peo-

ple believe what they read in the newspapers. There have been fifteen newspaper articles in the last two weeks attacking us and accusing us of all kinds of wrongdoing, and even going so far as to suggest we be reported to the police. Eight of the articles were on the front page.

The irony of all this is that after the president returns next week from a trip to Brazil, he plans to confer on Cam The Order of the Sun, Peru's highest civilian honor. The president told his cabinet not to pay attention to these attacks against our work and the LeTourneau project.

In an August letter to Dick Pittman and Mr. Nyman, Cal Hibbard confirmed that the situation in Peru was "very grave," and for Cam it constituted a more serious situation than he had ever faced in Mexico. He said the articles were having a serious impact on SIL's image. For this reason, and for the future of the work in Peru he said Cam had postponed his planned three-month trip to the States, and to the SIL branch conference in Ecuador, "until the Lord has completely won the victory." Cal also related that at the urging of many Peruvian friends, Cam published a rebuttal to the many recent accusations. Said Cal:

> At first Uncle Cam did not want to write the article, saying he believed the Lord would take care of the problem. But finally he agreed and spent all day until 10:30 at night writing the article. I typed a number of drafts, and when the final article was completed, I said, in my judgment this is the finest piece of writing he had ever done.[2]

Notes

1   Carolyn Miller, president of SIL, reporting to the 2002 SIL International Conference meeting in Waxhaw, North Carolina wrote that it is estimated that there are approximately 3,000 languages in the world needing research, development and Bible translation.

2   A complete text of that eight-page, single-spaced article, published in Lima's leading daily on August 18, 1953, is available from the Townsend Archives, Box 284 Waxhaw, NC 28173. See Appendix E.

Padre Pascual Alegre on vacation in Lima, visits with Cameron Townsend, talking of mutual concerns for helping the tribal people of the jungle.

Beginning in 1953, promising students gather at Yarinacocha for 3 months for a teacher training course under the joint sponsorship of Peru's Ministry of Education and SIL. Eventually these represented 15 to 20 tribal groups living in isolated corners of the Peruvian jungle.

Chapter Twelve

Why Are You Working with the Enemy?

Almost from the beginning of Eugene Nida's 17-year association with Wycliffe and SIL, there had been wary tension and long-standing differences between him and Cameron Townsend, in both philosophy and personality. In October 1936, Nida was assigned to work alone with the semi-nomadic Tarahumara people, who live in the rugged sierra and canyons of the state of Chihuahua in northern Mexico. The assignment proved to be an unhappy fit for Nida. After three months, broken in health, Nida, on his own initiative, left Mexico for his home in Garden Grove, California. Both Cam and Ken Pike were unhappy with Nida's decision to leave Mexico without first contacting them and the SIL administration in Mexico City. Cam had recognized Nida's great potential as a scholar and was anxious to seek an avenue whereby Nida could continue using his linguistic talent for SIL and Bible translation. Cam secured a part-time position for Nida with the American Bible Society (ABS).[1] Nida would indeed become one of the most influential scholarly consultants to impact the way Bible translators in the field handle the complexities of translating the Scriptures into previously unwritten indigenous languages. Nida is credited with pioneering what was once known as "dynamic equivalence," now known as "functional equivalence" translation. He also introduced young Ken Pike to some important linguistic insights. In 1947, writing under the direction of the American Bible Society, Nida authored *Bible Translating*, An Analysis of Principles and Procedures, with Special Reference to Aboriginal Languages. This remained a kind of Bible translation handbook reference text for all new SIL members until John Beekman and John Callow published their expanded work in 1974, called simply *Translating the Word of God*.

In addition to his involvement as a translation consultant for ABS, Nida was an integral part of each summer's teaching staff at SIL in Norman, Oklahoma. He was also a valuable member of the Wycliffe and SIL Board of Directors. However, over time, a lack of harmony between Cam and Nida resulted in a clash of wills between the two men. Eventually it led Nida to criticize, in public meetings and in one-on-one conversations with prospective Wycliffe and SIL members what he considered to be Cam's evasion of SIL's real mission purpose. Some accused Nida of intellectual arrogance, particularly when he spoke about Cam's lack of academic credentials. Nida, after all, was a Phi Beta Kappa scholar from UCLA with a Ph.D. in English. Cam was a third-year college dropout. (Few people knew that Cam was once offered a full Yale post-graduate scholarship to study linguistics under Dr. Edward Sapir but had declined in favor of allowing Nida and Pike to work on their studies.) The long-standing tension came to a head when Nida refused to recommend that the American Bible Society (ABS) publish Ken Pike's Mixteco New Testament, citing a lack of a sufficient number of readers. For several years after that incident, a series of lengthy letters were exchanged between Cam and Nida: Each championed his own approach to and criteria for translation priorities, including by whom, and when, a translated New Testament should be published. To be fair, there was intransigence on the part of both parties. Cam was genuinely convinced of the rightness of his position and could not imagine that Nida's position could possibly be in SIL's long-term best interest. Nida was equally convinced of his own position. His written responses were well reasoned and cogent. Aware that "two cannot walk together unless they be agreed," Cam wrote Nida in January of 1953 to suggest he establish his own linguistic institute in the New York area. When Nida refused to consider such an option, Cam wrote him the following:

> I really think [establishing your own institute] has tremendous merit entirely apart from the situation which has arisen between ourselves, due to your tenacious and constant opposition to so many of my policies. The relief I desire for this situation is only a secondary aspect of the suggestion I made that you found an institute of your own. I feel it is only right that a man of your great ability and worldwide experience and contacts should have an institute where he can promote his own ideas without constantly stepping on someone else's toes.

In a March 2, 1953 response to Cam's letter, Nida once again laid out the critical differences between ABS and SIL. Said Nida, "The Bible Society has two requirements when considering any New Testament for publication:

> 1) The acceptability of the text, i.e., the quality of the actual translation, and (2) a reasonable assurance of need and demand, and 'carry through' in the evangelistic program.

Cam very much agreed with the importance of a quality translation. However, he believed the Scriptures themselves are efficacious, and constitute the tool for the Spirit of God to use to bring people to a transforming understanding of themselves. Nida disagreed. "The ABS is forced to base its calculations on the existing need rather than any potential use." Cam reminded Nida that Wycliffe was founded on the principle that all unreached people groups should have the Scriptures as quickly as the Lord makes it possible. Said Cam:

> Other mission groups, in other parts of the world, are engaged in founding churches and then planning to bring the Scriptures to them later. The founders of Wycliffe believed that Bible translation should come first, at the earliest possible moment and be the foundation upon which the church would be established.

Nida did concede that SIL and Wycliffe were attempting to go about the task of translation and evangelism in a somewhat different manner than other groups, and therefore, said Nida, "the Society attempts to make due allowance for such differerences of program."

However, Nida in the ensuing months of 1953, continued to debate a variety of other policy issues and even recommended to Cam that some of Wycliffe's founding principles be abandoned. Cam, of course, rejected such a notion. Then on September 9, Cam received a letter from Nida that dealt what Cam described as a "severe blow." It was Nida's letter of resignation. He listed a number of SIL's operating procedures that were, in his opinion, incompatible and "against his own conscience and understanding" about how an organization should conduct its cross-cultural work. Chief among his complaints was the August 18, 1953 letter Cam had written to the editor of Lima's El Comercio newspaper in answer to repeated antagonistic criticism of SIL's work. Nida accused Cam of speaking in "veiled terms" about the true nature of SIL's mission. Nida further suggested that the result of serving Roman Catholics had alienated other groups, which had resulted in "widespread misunderstanding among colleagues from different Protestant mission groups." Said Nida:

> I believe the Wycliffe program is to be commended for its desire to serve [everyone] in an ever-increasing manner. Nevertheless, I am certain that in the final analysis the work of bringing the Gospel to men and women throughout the world will be accomplished more effectively if we do not alienate [our Protestant donors].
>
> You may be assured that I have only one purpose, namely, to help in any way possible in getting the Scriptures to people throughout the world. I shall be happy to continue to serve SIL and WBT as a group and as individuals. I very much appreciate the excellent work many are doing and I am *a sus órdenes* [Spanish for "I am at your service"]. However, I am certain that in view of the development within the Wycliffe program you are better advised to elect another member to the board of directors to fill the vacancy provided by this letter of resignation.

When SIL and Wycliffe had been officially organized in June 1942, William G. Nyman asked that all four men, Townsend, Nida, Pike and himself, all signers of the instrument of incorporation, get on their knees before God and pledge that no matter their differences, they would remain together for five years. Now six years beyond his commitment, Nida believed that since arguing his position was always ineffective, he was free to pursue his own agenda. Cam understood that to have a "house divided against itself," was not honoring to God or helpful to internal morale, so he gave his blessing to Nida's decision. But this tug-of-war over SIL's procedures, practices and philosophy did not end with Nida's resignation. Soon after the controversial article appeared in *El Comercio*, Cam wrote the following:

> A couple of days ago an English professor from the University of Michigan wrote to tell me that after reading the article with care several times he said it was a "magnificent" article. However not everyone who sent me letters agreed. One person who sent an unsigned letter said, "Your article is not only misleading, it conceals and distorts the truth." However, about 95% of the letters I have received have been favorable, many of them exceedingly so. About 5% have been unfavorable. A cabinet officer told me personally, "As a Peruvian, and as an educator and a government official, I thank you for all your organization is doing on behalf of the Indian tribes of the jungle." A Jewish merchant who heard about our fighting with kindness rather than with the brickbats of antagonism, asked me to call at his store. I have done so several times and this past Friday I told him how last September the Shapra chief Tariri[2] had let Christ come into his heart, and since then he hasn't wanted to kill anyone. As I left, the merchant said, "Do come often and tell me more, for this appeals to me."

In response to criticisms about his policies, Cam always wanted his letters to be calm, courteous and non-polemical. But in the case of a new member from the Ecuador branch who sent him a heated five-page challenge, threatening to resign[3] over Cam's August 18 article in *El Comercio*, Cam's response was not without its emotional component:

> You apparently are not at peace about continuing with SIL. I believe it is extremely important that you find God's mind [in these matters where you disagree]. For a new recruit to quit, and give as

> his reason that he couldn't conscientiously continue to work with
> us, will do serious harm to our organization. I am sure you would
> not want to do us, or anyone harm, unless you were convinced that
> God wanted you to. Before you joined us we took every precaution
> possible to inform you of our policies, both at Norman and in the
> special orientation meetings. Now it seems that all this effort was in
> vain and that you contemplate a step which would give a black eye
> to our Bible translation movement and hinder the evangelization of
> the Bible-less tribes for whom [at the moment] there seems no other
> hope than our movement. I am praying for you and am certain God
> will show you and us a solution.

While Cam believed his policies were absolutely biblical, some pastors
in the US and Canada were urging young people not to consider
Wycliffe as a service option. Some newer members found that their
churches categorically refused to support them. (The pastor of this author said, "Join any other mission but Wycliffe; they spend too much
time on their airplanes.") One pastor wrote asking a Mexico branch
member to change her mission board.

The following letter, which Cam wrote to a pastor who accused Cam
and SIL of "consorting with the enemy and compromising their testimony," is typical of the plethora of letters he personally answered:

> When you refer to damage that is being done by working closely
> with Catholics, the answer is that we do not work closely with
> them. We do however, whenever we have opportunity, treat them
> with courtesy and "pour coals of kindness" on their heads. As to
> your statement as to my being baffled by Catholic "attitudes," if
> you knew me, sir, you would know that I have a rather extensive
> understanding of their "attitudes." I've been in the thick of the fight
> for over thirty-six years in Latin America. I know whom I'm up
> against. But I have learned to use weapons that are both scriptural
> and effective. I know of no other way of winning people to Christ
> and being a true friend, except by showing respect, kindness, un-
> derstanding and love. The Apostle Paul endeavored to be all things
> to all men, that he might by all means save some. Paul was particu-
> larly considerate of the Jews, even though they persecuted him se-
> verely. On Mars Hill in Athens Paul followed a courteous approach

with the idol-worshipping Gentile philosophers and was willing to address them at their conference site.

Too often Christian missionaries forget this was Paul's attitude. Rather, they look upon people of opposite views as enemies who should be shunned. We are told by our Lord in Matthew 5:44-48 to "Love your enemies, bless them that curse you and DO GOOD to them that despitefully use you, and persecute you that you may be the children of your Father which is in heaven." It is my conviction that every missionary should endeavor to carry out those commands of his Master. Since we work behind "closed doors" it is essential for all our workers to treat our enemies, whether real or potential, with love. This means to give them a drink of lemonade on a hot day, give them a lift in your car or airplane and give them their customary titles while graciously standing up for your faith, should it be called into question. This is the Christian way, this is the way of Wycliffe Bible Translators and it is the way of victory over wrong.

In the midst of such negative attacks, people who offered their support and encouragement often heartened Cam. In January of 1954, Grady Parrot, president of Missionary Aviation Fellowship (MAF), sent Cam a letter in which he told about MAF transporting a critically ill priest from the Indian village in Mexico where SIL translator John Crawford worked. Said Grady: "I want to personally commend you for what I feel is a proper scriptural interpretation of 'walking as He walked.'"

January 1954 also brought a warm letter from Nida who commended Cam for attending and participating in the 30th anniversary of the founding of the Robinson Bible Institute in Guatemala.[4] Cam had written Nida that he had been able to give three messages in the Cakchiquel language and was grateful to the Lord that He had "revived" his knowledge of the language after so many years of not using it. Cam also mentioned that there were over 1,000 Cakchiquel delegates to the convention. Surely Robbie Robinson would have been proud. V.R. Edman, president of Wheaton College, wrote to tell Cam that he was praying for the critical situation in Peru. He said, "In these days we have learned to keep our heads and knees down and our hearts strong."

But while Cam was encouraged by such support, he was unhappy over a report he received in January 1954 about the decline in new recruits. To Otis Leal, candidate secretary for Wycliffe, Cam wrote:

> We are seriously crippled on our bases for lack of supporting personnel. It takes three people on the base to keep one translation team working in a tribal village. Currently there are nine tribal workers serving in the Lima office when they should be in their allocations working on their languages and translation but they are all too busy working on group projects. I don't see how to relieve the situation unless more non-linguistic workers volunteer. The same is true at the base in Yarinacocha. There we have tribal people [translators] working in the finance office, as secretaries, buyers, and maintenance workers. I wish the board would send down some of the support people who are scheduled to go to Jungle Camp immediately.

On January 16, 1954, Cam received word that Ken and Elaine Jacobs, and their daughter Joyce had, on their way to Jungle Camp training in Mexico, suffered a serious, life-threatening accident. The report said that their car skidded on a slippery bridge while they were driving at night and butted up against a barricade. When Ken got out of the car to assess the damage, he leapt over the barricade, thinking there was a road on the opposite side when in fact there was nothing but a thirty-foot drop to a sand bar in a river. Cam learned Ken had fallen on his head and shoulder and suffered a broken arm, a broken collarbone, a punctured lung and several broken ribs, and had almost drowned in his own blood.[5]

In May of 1954, Cam received a letter from an Indian believer in the region of southern Mexico where translators John and Elaine Beekman and Wilbur and Evelyn Aulie worked with the Chol people. His name was Nicolás Arcos and, like the Apostle Paul, he had been jailed for preaching the gospel. The letter had a decided Pauline flavor. Juan began his letter much like Paul began his letters, also written from prison:

> I am a servant of the Lord Jesus Christ. I spread God's Word in all the villages. At present I am in prison with my friend Pedro though we have done nothing wrong. When we were arrested many people

gathered around and I thought our lives were in danger, but God undertook for us. I have no fear of being in jail because I know there is a better place prepared for me with our Lord Jesus Christ in heaven.

We continually talk to the Lord in prayer. When we pray, all the police and soldiers stand and listen to us. When I spoke the Word of God to one of the policemen he was very glad to hear it.

I want to tell you about what happens when we learn God's Word. Here in this world we sometimes suffer in our bodies. But if we truly believe in His Word the Lord will help us. God's Word tells us we are to be faithful, but we can't be faithful in our own strength. The answer is to read His Word and obey His commands and follow after the thing that gives us eternal life. I am in jail as I write this but I do not cease reading God's Word. We who are persecuted He calls "blessed." This means we are happy even though we suffer trials. My heart is happy because, thanks be unto Jesus Christ, the children of God have increased in numbers [in spite of persecution] in all of the villages. Please pray for me and my companions here in jail. Pray for the rulers. Love the unsaved and faithfully preach the Word of our Lord Jesus Christ.

Your brother in Christ, Nicolás Arcos.[6]

In August of 1954, Cam attended the third Inter-American Indian Congress in La Paz, Bolivia. And, in typical Townsend networking fashion, he met a man from Mexico who happened to be a personal friend of the Bolivian president. Wrote Cam:

My friend secured an interview with the president and he and I were able to tell the president about the work we were doing in Mexico, Peru, Ecuador, and the Philippines as well as with ethnic peoples in the United States. The president was so impressed that he authorized an agreement between his government and SIL to carry out the same program in Bolivia as we were doing in these other countries. I warned the president that we had been under severe attack by the prelates in Peru, but he assured me that there would be no such difficulty in his country. The president was in complete accord with our writing into the contract our desire to translate portions of Scripture into the various Indian languages where our SIL people would work.

This wide-open door was coupled with a somewhat limited invitation to begin work among the indigenous tribes of Brazil. This invitation was received through Esther Matteson, who represented us at the Americanist Congress in Rio de Janeiro. It presents a tremendous challenge. We are going to need a lot more prayer support, translators and support personnel, not to mention all the other aspects and logistics of opening a new work. Our God is able!

On Christmas day, 1954, Cam wrote to tell Dale Kietzman that for him and Elaine this truly was a merry Christmas. He informed Dale that the Bolivian Ambassador had granted courtesy visas for SIL personnel to enter the country and that Harold and Mary Key would direct the Bolivian advance. There was also a kind of footnote at the close of that difficult year, 1954. Without a word of commentary, on November 24, Cam wrote an unidentified friend or family member the following:

> The Peruvian cardinal died suddenly on Friday. He will be buried on Tuesday. The president has decreed a day of national mourning. Next to the Franciscan bishop, I guess he was our most antagonistic opponent.

Love to all from here,
Yours, as ever, Cameron

Notes

1   For a fuller account of Nida's early career with Wycliffe and SIL, see Hugh Steven, *Doorway to the World, The Mexico Years, 1934-1947*, (Wheaton, Illinois: Harold Shaw Publishers, 1999).

2   See *Tariri, My Story, From Jungle Killer to Christian Missionary* as told to Ethel Emily Wallis (New York: Harper & Row Publishers, 1965).

3   The member in question did not in fact resign, but went on to serve faithfully for many years.

4   See *Wycliffe in the Making*, Hugh Steven (Wheaton, Illinois: Harold Shaw Publishers, 1995), 138.

5   Miraculously, Ken survived that accident and he and Elaine were assigned to work with the Chamula people in southern Mexico. In November of 2001, Ken and Elaine, with thousands of Chamula believers, attended a special dedication ceremony with over 7500 guests in attendance. They celebrated God's faithfulness. In spite of more than thirty years of persecution the Chamulas officially received the entire Bible translated by Ken and Elaine and a corps of Chamula co-translators. For more on this remarkable story, see Hugh Steven, *They Dared to be Different,* Huntington Beach, California, Wycliffe Bible Translators, revised edition, 1991.

6   To learn more about the Chol church see, Hugh Steven, *The Man with the Noisy Heart, the John Beekman Story* (Chicago: Moody Press, 1979).

The "Bridge of Pain" was a long-forgotten memory on the day Ken and Elaine Jacobs (above) addressed the Chamula believers on the occasion of the dedication of the Chamula New Testament. Below: two young Chamula men are part of history as they examine the Chamula New Testament for the first time.

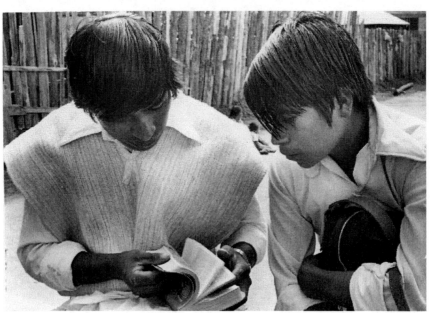

Chapter Thirteen

"Let's Stop Killing or God Will Be Angry with US!"

Nineteen fifty-five and 1956 were trend-setting years in the United States. The nationwide newly franchised McDonald's restaurants, along with the introduction of a courtly southern gentleman in a white suit and goatee holding a bucket of Colonel Sanders' Kentucky Fried Chicken forever changed the palates of the world. But the most important story of 1955 was a medical breakthrough by Jonas Salk, a young doctor who was proclaimed a hero for developing a vaccine for one of the world's most terrible childhood plagues, poliomyelitis, commonly known as infantile paralysis or polio.

There was another story in 1955 that millions of Americas received with the same sense of expectancy and political hope as the Salk vaccine. Rosa Parks, an overworked and weary black seamstress in Montgomery, Alabama was arrested for refusing to give up her seat on a bus to a white man. That incident sparked years of unrest and energized the American civil rights movement.

In Peru in January 1955, Cameron Townsend and other SIL members were called to special prayer asking God to quell the fierce inter-tribal unrest and murders among the Candoshi-Shapra people. Supporters of

SIL's work in Peru first learned about this unrest when, on January 18, 1955, Cal Hibbard wrote his pastor (and Elaine Townsend's), Lance B. Latham of the North-Side Gospel Center, of Chicago to pray for what Cal termed "a most serious situation":

> Uncle Cam has asked me to write you folks at the center for special prayer. You may know the Shapras, where Dorothy Svendsen and others are working, have been known for their fierce inter-tribal wars and killings. About eighteen months ago, Chief Tariri and a dozen other Shapras showed encouraging signs of being born-again and have continued to grow in the Lord. About a month ago Dorothy, during her first assignment to that tribe, went out to the area to replace Doris Cox, one of the regular translators who was in need of a vacation and also needed to do some concentrated language work here at the base. A few days ago we learned by radio that there have been three killings in the up-river section of the tribe. Normally, this would call for retaliation since there is deadly rivalry between the up-river and down-river groups. None of the Christians were involved in the killing. The relatives of the Christians who were killed are experiencing strong tribal pressure to retaliate. The chief, himself, a growing Christian, with a strong influence over the tribe, was away when the killings occurred. This has placed some Christians in the face of temptation to do violence since they are without the conciliatory support and counsel of the chief, so we want you to pray.

Two days later, on January 20, 1955, Doris Cox sent an urgent message to her supporting churches with the disquieting news that "the Shapras are at war!"

> While I am safe here at the jungle base I wonder each hour how things are in the tribe. Lorrie Anderson and Dottie Svendsen are in the midst of a turbulent situation. Shutaka and his five sons, intelligent and so likeable, have been the terror of our part of the jungle ever since we have known them. We warned them of eternal judgment to come if they continued in their wicked ways. One son, Pinchu, has received Christ, and last month the eldest son, Wautista, returned again and again to listen intently to the Gospel.

But the recent illness and death of one of Shutuka's wives (he had two) did not soften him toward the Gospel.

We now hear that someone, perhaps a brother-in-law in an up-river village, has killed Wautista and Tayanta, another son. All this has greatly saddened us. We can understand the pain and anguish that drives the old warrior, Shutaka, to plan terrible revenge. His first threat was to kill every man, woman and child in the village where the incident occurred. Many of the women and children of that village fled down-river to Lorrie and Dottie's settlement. The men scattered in different directions.

During the time you folks at home were praying and interceding to prevent any more bloodshed, the old chief Shutaka and one of his companions encountered a group of the fleeing men. There was a lot of shooting at close range, but *no one was even hit!*

Word came to Lorrie that Shutaka felt the hand of God intervening in sparing lives during the several encounters between the two sides! Shutaka was reported to have said something like, "Let's stop killing or God will be angry and punish us." The fighting has stopped temporarily, without a single loss of life. Shutaka is waiting to confer with Chief Tariri, who has been absent during the feud. That Shutaka would humble himself to acknowledge the greater leadership of Tariri, especially in this situation, is another miracle. There are still angry hearts and words to be quieted. "We wrestle not against flesh and blood..." Please continue to pray that Shutaka and Tariri, fairly new believers, will meet and there will be a peaceful end to this trouble

During the beginning days of 1955 there was no shortage of excitement and problems for which there would be a call for special prayer of both praise and intercession. On January 15, Cam wrote Marianna Slocum and partner Florence Gerdel to congratulate them for the "glorious completion of the Tzeltal New Testament" [in Mexico, after ten years of hard work].[1]
Cam said this milestone took him back twenty-five years to Guatemala and the joy he felt upon completing the Cakchiquel New Testament:

I can appreciate something of the great faith and effort and all the tears and pain and trials that have been yours as you have faithfully worked on this project. But how utterly worthwhile it is, and how gracious the Lord has been to give both of you the strength, wisdom, courage and helpers to complete the task. May He use it mightily to reach thousands of Tzeltals for His great glory.

On February 3, 1955 Cam wrote a general letter to the Wycliffe family to remind them to praise God for His blessings on the work:

> As of December 1954, the total WBT membership stands at 918, less 365 children making 553 adult SIL workers translating the Bible, getting ready to translate, or else helping the translators at the base as in the case of our JAARS pilots, mechanics and radio men and women. May all of us be faithful in remembering them in prayer.

Cam could also have reported that there were nine expectant mothers at the base. He stressed in his letter that prayer indeed changes things and included a number of details surrounding the Shapra crisis.

> Here at the base we are constantly monitoring the situation by radio. We had a plane standing by ready at a moment's notice to start the long rescue journey. The difficulty was that the plane could only reach a point six hours away by canoe from the women. Anything could happen during the minimum of twelve hours (six by plane, six by canoe) that would elapse before a rescue party could reach Lorrie and Dorothy. *The only sure recourse was prayer.* It seemed everyone at the base was constantly in prayer. Then the situation miraculously changed. One of the Shapra men was shot at, six times from close range, but we believe prayer warded off the bullets. If this Shapra man had been killed the incident would have prolonged the blood feud. Recalling what our women translators had been telling him and his people, the Shapra up-river chief said, "We had better stop killing one another or God will become angry with us." I was reminded of Psalm 28:6, "Blessed be the Lord, because he hath heard the voice of my supplication."

In 1955, people in the United States were being given practical advice on what to do in the event of a nuclear attack. For most SIL personnel, the irony of living in the Nuclear Age in 1955 was that they were working with people who were still in the Stone Age. In place of nuclear armaments, some of the most fearsome Stone Age people in Ecuador were using fire-hardened wooden spears to kill each other. The people were known simply as the Aucas.[2] One person who became interested in reaching the Aucas was thirty-four-year old SIL member Rachel Saint, whose brother Nate was a pilot with MAF stationed in Ecuador. In March of 1955 Rachel wrote the following letter to her praying friends and supporters:

> The object of Wycliffe Bible Translators has been to give the unreached tribes of the world translations of the Scriptures into their own languages. Today in Ecuador we are faced with the task of reaching a tribe which, humanly speaking, is unreachable. On the maps of the eastern jungle of Ecuador, bounded by the Napo and Curaray Rivers is a large section marked "Unknown Territory" with the further designation "Auca (Savage) Tribes." Besides being bounded by those rivers, that Indian forest is "bound" by the spear killings which through the years have reminded both Indians and whites not to cross into or travel in Auca territory.
>
> Twenty years ago a missionary traced the immense footprints of an Auca man on paper and sent it back to his home church asking prayer for these wild killers of the forest. Six years ago I visited my brother Nate, an MAF pilot of the Oriente in Ecuador. At that time he told me he never flew *over* Acua territory, he always flew *around* it. He knew if his plane developed a problem and he had to set it down, he would be in mortal danger from Auca spears. Yet in spite of all the frightening stories I had heard, the Lord in a strange way began to burden my heart for that little-known group of jungle people.
>
> Three and a half years ago, I visited Ecuador again and heard more about the killers in the forest. The Shell Oil Company had spent thousands of dollars establishing an oil-searching base too near Auca territory, and one day the Shell workers were attacked. The assailants passed their spears to the headman, who hurled them from quite a distance with an accuracy that fatally wounded six out of the seven Quichua Indians working on the project. The seventh dove into the river and lived to tell the sad tale. The feather

headdress that he brought back, dropped by some of the Indians in their flight, was exactly like those of the Shapra Indians.

Rachel's letter continued relating further incidents in her timeline of events, leading up to her concluding paragraph:

> Arrangements have been made for Catherine [Cathy] Peeke and me to go to the hacienda [plantation] of Don Carlos Sevilla [near Auca territory] where four Auca women refugees live and work. Don Carlos has invited Cathy and me to live on the hacienda in order for us to begin a study of the Auca language. How we praise God for this wee opening! Will you pray that He who is not willing that any Auca should perish will, in His own time, make a real entry into this tribe possible and enable us to do an Auca translation for Him?

On March 4, 1955 Rachel wrote yet another update on her life on the hacienda. It was "pleasant," she said, and the weather was better than she had hoped for. "And amazingly we haven't seen a mosquito!" In addition to describing their daily routine, Rachel eagerly shared news about one of the four young women who had fled from her Auca village after her father had been speared and killed by another Auca group:

> Her name is Dayuma and she is turning out to be an excellent language helper. She has learned some Quichua (which I haven't) but is a whiz at helping me learn the Auca language. If I ask her the word for moon and sun, she also gives me the word for stars! If I ask her the name for the Napo and Curaray Rivers she proceeds to name all the other rivers she knows. I feel like singing the doxology.
>
> Everybody here is quite interested in the language work, especially the family at the hacienda. I need not remind you to pray for me. In a very definite way I feel I must be depending on the Lord, not only for the immediate work but also for entrance into the tribe. Everybody here has plenty of respect for Auca spears, and with reason. Folks just don't travel where they are.

Simultaneously (and completely unknown to Rachel) as God was working in her heart and mind, he was preparing and burdening five young men from several faith missions to begin what they called "Operation Auca." It was September of 1955. Jim Elliot, one of the five men, had heard about the Aucas as early as 1950 and had sensed God burdening his heart for the elusive Auca people. Shortly after Jim and his partner Pete Fleming arrived in Ecuador in 1951, Pete wrote in his diary:

> I am longing to reach the Aucas if God gives me the honor of proclaiming His Name among them. I would gladly give my life for that tribe if only to see an assembly of those proud, clever, smart people gathering around a table to honor the Son,—gladly, gladly, gladly! What [greater honor] could be given [to one's] life?[3]

Within four months from the time "Operation Auca" began, Pete Fleming, Jim Elliot, Ed McCully, Roger Youderian and Nate Saint would become household names. On January 8, 1956, word reached the outside world that on a sand beach at the confluence of the Napo and Curaray Rivers deep in Ecuador's rain forest, the five young, talented missionary men were speared to death by an isolated "ethnic group, know as the Aucas." *LIFE* Magazine carried the haunting photos, taken by renowned photographer Cornell Capa, of the body of a young man floating face-down in a shallow river. There were also photos showing the fabric of their MAF Piper Family Cruiser (piloted by Nate Saint) torn, stripped, mutilated, and pierced through by wooden spears.

In the days following that fateful January 8th, there was a great deal of confusion and finger pointing among several Christian organizations that criticized the men for going into such dangerous territory. There was also criticism from the same evangelical groups for what they considered SIL's capitalizing on world publicity and making it appear that the Aucas were *their* work. The reality was that Rachel tried desperately to distance herself from news releases and reporters. In addition to the heartache of losing her brother Nate, she also felt a responsibility to support her sister-in-law Marj, Nate's widow—to help Marj make the adjustment to being a widow and single mother as she moved from the jungle back to Quito, where she had applied to Radio HCJB to act as hostess of their guest house.

On January 17, 1956, Cameron Townsend wrote Rachel:

We all have been deeply moved by the news of the homegoing of your brother Nate and the four other men who gave their lives in an effort to reach the Aucas, particularly when we learned that they had received a friendly welcome from one of the Auca groups. The news of them paying with their lives is all the more difficult to understand. Yet we have seen God work in mysterious, yet wonderful ways. This verse from John 13:7 came to mind: "Jesus answered and said unto him, what I do thou knowest not now, but thou shalt know hereafter."

We have been remembering you in prayer, not only because of your loss, but also because of the burden you have for the Aucas. My first prayer after hearing the news was that you would have the privilege of leading to the Lord the man who killed your brother. You will be thrilled to know that yesterday at the Fourth Presbyterian Church in Spokane, sixty-five young people dedicated their lives to the Lord for service as He leads. This came about as a result of the challenge presented by the death of Nate and his companions. This is probably the firstfruits of a great good that will come of this. "Except a corn of wheat fall into the ground and die, it abideth alone, but if it die, it bringeth forth much fruit."[4]

The charges by some that Wycliffe was "capitalizing" on the publicity of this tragic event were hurtful criticisms for Cam. Just a few months before (March 11, 1955) he had written to a Wycliffe lay-representative about "not being over-anxious, not running ahead of the Lord, and not to depend on vigorous slick deputation for funds."

Cam's letter to Rachel continued with some insight into his philosophy of mission:

I feel the history of missions, or should I say Christian work in general, presents two extremes. One is where man's effort is in the forefront and everything depends on his skill in raising money. The other, which I refer to as the "George Mueller method," is where man's effort drops out of sight so much that there is a tendency to leave it all up to the Lord. If I had to choose between the two, I would most definitely take the latter. Our emphasis in Wycliffe has been toward the latter. From the beginning we have been thrown into dependence on the Lord. Just think about what God has done through our weakness and utter dependence upon Him. As you know, William Nyman, our invaluable secretary-treasurer and board member, volunteered to help us after suffering a serious heart attack. He has never been physically strong. When the Lord challenged me to begin this work I was recovering from tuberculosis. Our work started in Mexico during the Depression. We were without funds or backing from any major church denomination, yet God supplied our needs. In just twenty years Wycliffe and SIL have grown from practically nothing to over 550 workers with five important training centers. This is the Lord's doing and we would not give up depending on Him, now that we have so many energetic and capable friends.

On the other hand, as we lean on our Jehovah-Jireh[5] to do what we are not able to do I feel we owe it to our fellow Christians to present the challenge of Bible translation in a way that is forceful, yet winsome and always in good taste.

Cam also believed it was important that friends and supporters of Wycliffe "get in on the blessing" of what God was doing through the Bible translation ministry. In his letter to a lay-representative who wanted to present a project to an adult Bible class, Cam wrote:

When you present your project I am sure you will be careful to be more interested in giving them a spiritual blessing than in getting them to write out a check for your project. I take great exception to preachers or others who make their congregations feel that dollars are all-important. I think we should be very careful to speak in such a way that our friends will realize that our confidence and expectation are in the Lord and not in their checkbooks. Our position should be that we are merely offering them a privilege of buying in on some rich dividends as per Philippians 4:17, from the J.B. Phillips translation: *"It isn't the value of the gift that I am keen on, it is the reward that will come to you because of these gifts that you have made."*

With this as his mindset, Cam wrote Rachel Saint on February 14, 1956 to tell her that he had been on a speaking tour to Seattle, Spokane, Reno and Turlock and was writing from Pasadena, California. He reported that the tour was strenuous and confessed that his energy level wasn't as high it once was. In fact, in an earlier letter to William Nyman, Cam shared that he was, on occasion, experiencing unexplained dizziness in addition to a loss of physical energy. For this reason, Cam said he was thankful for Peru director Harold Goodall who was assuming many of his administrative duties in Peru. Cam continued his letter to Rachel:

> One of the challenges I presented on these speaking occasions was that the death of these five heroic men in Ecuador should not have been in vain. From what I hear, much fruit has already resulted in volunteers for service and funds for MAF and probably other organizations as well. What concerns me is that we take steps to see that the "exceedingly much fruit" redound from it for the glory of God. He has set the stage through favorable publicity in newspapers, magazines, radio and TV coverage across the country for a great tidal wave of missionary endeavors on behalf of Bible-less tribes. It won't come about, however, unless all of us do our part. Someday I believe you will have an important link in bringing about this "exceedingly-much fruit."
>
> In the meantime, let's be much in prayer that when the time comes we will both be found ready to cooperate to the utmost in utilizing the interest that has been aroused, not just for the Aucas, nor just for the three organizations involved, but for the more than 2,000 Bible-less tribes and for every organization and movement that tends towards reaching the unreached for Christ.
>
> Also, Rachel, please do not engage in a race for getting to the Aucas first. Get Dayuma free[6] and concentrate on working with her in an environment that is conducive to concentrated language study. And under no cirmstances put yourself in a situation where your life might be in danger. I realize that you are under the authority of your director in Ecuador, but inasmuch as this request involves the good name of our entire organization and the reputation of the Summer Institute of Linguistics, I feel that in my capacity as general director, who according to the constitution, is responsible for the good name of the organizations, I make this definite request of you. I have no doubt that your local director will concur with me in it.

Cam ended his letter to Rachel by telling her that he had received a letter from the Russian Embassy in Washington inquiring about the possibility of "sending workers to that land. God is faithful. Praise His Name!"[7]

Notes

1   See *The Good Seed* by Marianna Slocum with Grace Watkins, published by Promise Publishing Company, Orange, California, 1998. See also *Never Touch A Tiger*, by Hugh Steven, (Nashville: Thomas Nelson Publishers, 1980.

2   The Quichua people called their nearest neighbors "Aucas," meaning "savages." For years the Auca lived up to that fearsome name. Today the Aucas are known as the Waorani, a word meaning "people."

3   Elisabeth Elliot, *Through Gates of Splendor*, (Wheaton, Illinois: Tyndale House Publishers, 1981), 26.

4   Since the world first learned of the killing of the five missionaries, scores of books, articles, plays, a movie, and other media events have been written and performed about that pivotal moment in time. It was a time when God galvanized the world's attention to the need of the isolated ethnic minorities without any gospel witness or translated Scripture. Perhaps the most important and memorable books to emerge out of that tragedy were *Through Gates of Splendor* and *Shadow of the Almighty: The Life and Times of Jim Elliot*, authored by Jim Elliot's widow, Elisabeth (Betty). In 1960, two years after Betty's second book, *Shadow of the Almighty*, Wycliffe author Ethel Emily Wallis wrote *The Dayuma Story, Life Under Auca Spears*, which became a bestseller. In 1981, Jim and Marti Hefley wrote *Unstilled Voices*, an important look back at the Auca massacre and the lives it touched.

5   Cam is using one of several names for God that describe his attributes and dealings with his chosen people. The name appears in Genesis 22 and the story of Abraham's greatest risk and step of faith, the offering up of his son Isaac. In this context, and in Cam's mind, Jehovah-Jireh is "the God who will provide."

6   When Muipha, a much-feared leader of the Aucas, killed Dayuma's father and brother, Dayuma fled her village and found refuge on the hacienda of don Carlos Sevill, vowing to return one day and kill Muipha. To carry out this threat she needed a gun. In order to buy the

weapon she went into an indentured servitude debt to don Carlos. This man was willing to release Dayuma for a payment of approximately $200 US dollars. Cam informed Rachel that such a sum of money had been raised for this whenever she needed it to pay for Dayuma's ransom—not to buy the gun!

7   In 1969, the President of Ecuador, Dr. José Velasco Ibarra, decorated Rachel Saint and Catherine Peeke with that country's highest award for service by a foreigner. The award was given in recognition of their outstanding linguistic and humanitarian work among the ethnic Waorani (Auca) people. This was the first time in Ecuador's history that such an honor had been given to women.

Chapter Fourteen

A Burden Shared Is a Burden Lightened

Gentlemanly conduct, civility, and good manners were hallmarks of Cameron Townsend's personality and leadership style. But in January, 1956, and for at least two years thereafter, Cam's habit of responding with diplomatic courtesy and civility in response to antagonistic, unkind accusations about his person, his mission methods, and his practices was severely tested.

Archival documents for the years 1956 to 1960 (the basis of these next three chapters) reveal an overwhelming support and appreciation for Cam and for the hundreds of dedicated and highly motivated Wycliffe and SIL workers. But just as a single rotten apple can spoil the whole barrel, so a single belligerent letter (among the hundreds of affirmative and supportive ones) tested Cam's psychological and spiritual equilibrium.

While Cam often took a philosophical attitude toward criticism from outside the organization, it was the challenges and criticisms from those within the group, from his own colleagues, that caused him the most pain and distress. In a May 14, 1956, letter to Ken Pike, Cam revealed a seldom seen or expressed character trait, "battle fatigue" and exasperation over why a member could not, or would not, follow his leadership without a challenge:

> It's almost midnight, but I can't sleep thinking about Ecuador. To-day I received another [letter from the Ecuador member].... I have been praying that God would use you to get him into a better frame of mind. I've had so much grief from the Ecuador Branch; I feel that some other board member, perhaps Harold Goodall,[1] should take over the responsibility of liaison between the board and the branch.

At issue was a debate between John Lindskoog, representing the Ecuador Branch as chairman of Ecuador's Executive Committee, and Cam over the location of a new jungle base of operations to serve the ethnic minorities living in Ecuador's Oriente region.[2] In 1955, Bob Schneider, Dr. Ralph Eichenberger and Glen Turner had gone overland from Shell Mera to carve out a new base site on the Llushin River—against Cam's better judgment. During the course of clearing the jungle for an airstrip, Bob Schneider sustained a multiple fractured leg when a large branch of a huge tree that was being felled struck the back of his leg as he ran to escape it. This required a dramatic and dangerous rescue evacuation by MAF pilot Nate Saint. The only cleared area on which to land near the site of Bob's accident was a short, unstable sandbar. Before taking off from Shell Mera, Nate deflated the plane's tires in order to give greater braking friction when he landed on the sandbar. The softer tires also prevented the plane from sinking into the soft sand. Thus, at lift-off from the sandbar, Nate needed the help of Glen and Ralph pushing hard on the tail as Nate revved the engine to overcome the resistance of the soft sand. The lift-off was successful, and eventually so was the heal-ing of Bob's leg. However, all the work the men had accomplished clear-ing and preparing the base site was washed away when the Llushin River changed its course during flood season.

This incident sparked vigorous lobbying by the Ecuador Branch and John Lindskoog to have the Ecuador SIL base located in a more accessi-ble area, closer to hospital care, more economical ground transporta-tion, and other amenities. The obvious choice was Shell Mera. But Cam said no.

When Cam vetoed this suggestion, John appealed to the board of di-rectors to arbitrate what John considered to be "an urgent situation that

needed help in overcoming a stalemate." On January 9 and again on
February 15, 1956, Cam responded to John's letter to the board of directors. Cam said he understood John's desire to settle in Shell Mera,[3] and
that on the surface his arguments had merit. However, wrote Cam:

> For SIL to locate our main base in a village of 350 people in rural
> Ecuador where there are already headquarters for five missionary
> organizations from the United States would most assuredly go
> against Wycliffe and SIL's historic policy. From the beginning, our
> policy has been not to build on another man's foundation. For us to
> locate in an area with the largest concentration of Protestant mis-
> sionaries in Ecuador would be like two families living under one
> roof. There would simply be too much friction and misunderstand-
> ing among the mission groups who do not understand our basic
> policies. In fact, there has already been criticism that JAARS was
> superimposing itself on MAF. SIL would simply be an unwelcome
> guest in Shell Mera. It is a well-known fact that two families can't
> live under the same roof without friction.
>
> Another important consideration in the development of our SIL
> programs has been the question of God's guidance. We have always
> tried to let God direct our paths. To some of my many well-mean-
> ing Christian friends such an attitude has seemed foolish. They
> have challenged me to be guided by my own reason. Their argu-
> ment was, "since God gave us brains we should use them."
>
> When I went to Ecuador last July I was perfectly willing, as you
> recall, to have our base of operations at Shell Mera if the Lord so
> led. I prayed about this as did the board, and I even put out a
> fleece[4] on various occasions during my stay in Ecuador. In each
> case I felt the Lord saying no to each of the locations that were men-
> tioned. I felt I would be going against what I understand to be
> God's leading if I were to have anything to do with locating our
> base in Shell Mera. It was, as you know, against my better judgment
> to have a base on the Llushin River. At times I do like to follow the
> path of least resistance so I gave in to the wishes of the SIL Ecuador
> workers. Then the flood came and forced us to house ourselves
> temporarily in Shell Mera. The result has been that for over a year
> we have been "treading on the toes," as it were, of the missionaries
> who are already established there. And in some cases our policies

have been an offense to them. This should have shown us it wasn't healthy for us to be in the same area as other mission groups. Since we have experienced serious grief when we depart from our Wycliffe and SIL policies, the board found it absolutely necessary to take definite action to prevent such things from occurring again.

Cam concluded his letter by pledging to do whatever he could to raise money for the new base:

> Within the next five years I believe Ecuador will have a wonderful base and you will thank the board for being wise and far-seeing in its action [to support my veto]. We will help you in every way we can to secure funds for a new Ecuador base, providing it's not built on the toes of other missionaries. Keep looking up. There are wonderful things ahead.[5]

Cam's veto was much more than an older man wanting his own way. Rather, Cam believed, it was a strategic necessity, in SIL's future interest, to avoid being in the same geographical cluster as other evangelical mission agencies. Cam's stiff resolve was always intended to preserve SIL's good name as a nonsectarian organization without ecclesiastical ties to any mission or church-related agency. He wanted to honestly report to the Ecuadorian, Peruvian and Bolivian authorities and all other government agencies where SIL worked that SIL was a non-sectarian organization willing to serve all without regard to race, creed or religion.

This decision to serve all, including Roman Catholic priests and nuns when asked, was to bring about a great misunderstanding on the part of a number of mission agencies, independent missionaries in Ecuador, and pastors, constituents and supporting churches in the U.S., Canada and Great Britain. On February 14, 1956, branch director Don Burns wrote to Mr. Nyman and the Wycliffe Board of Directors about their final action in favor of Cam's veto of Shell Mera. Included were some of the criticisms being leveled against SIL and Wycliffe:

> We here in Ecuador are disappointed with the board's final action that Shell is out. At the same time we are happy to get a ruling on this [contentious] matter and we shall move on to other problems before us in the confidence of God's guidance.

On another matter, I am sorry to report that many of the missionaries from other missions here are accusing us of being imposters, counterfeit and insincere because we are showing kindness to people of other faiths they consider to be non-evangelical. I am greatly puzzled over such accusations.

Don Burns, handsome, athletic, with an outgoing personality and a marvelous command of Spanish, was in March 1956, the director of the Ecuador Branch of SIL. As such, Don passed on to Cam a variety of letters from people who were bewildered over practices that branded SIL as being "guilty of subterfuge and outside the bounds of what a Christian mission agency should be." One mission director wrote saying:

I confess I am in disagreement with Wycliffe's fundamental principle, operating as a missionary organization in the homeland, and at the same time operating on the field as a secular linguistic organization. As long as you hold to such a principle you must accept the fact that you will be in trouble with other missionary organizations. Here in Ecuador the cat is out of the bag, you are not fooling anyone. In a recent enemy publication you are positively identified with Gospel missions in this country. Let me say again, that even though I am opposed to your operating principle, I would not personally allow this to be a source of friction between our respective organizations.

This man's argument was that SIL and Wycliffe were guilty of not keeping faith with the Christian public because SIL was not "punching away with the Gospel." Such an accusation was of course, entirely correct and entirely wrong. Cam's personal credo was never to let a day go by without having had some kind of personal witness. Yet Cam did not believe that "punching away at the gospel" meant he had to conduct open-air evangelistic meetings. This held particularly true in Latin American countries where it was against the law to engage in overt public "religious proselytizing."

At the same time, few could match Cam's consistent personal witness. He always carried a pocket New Testament, and looked for appropriate opportunities to speak to anyone, of any status, about his faith. Sometimes, after witnessing to a taxi driver, Cam would try to barter his

New Testament in exchange for the cab fare. In answer to the accusation
that SIL was guilty of "subterfuge," Cam wrote:

> What makes you think our being of service to others in order to
> make us welcome guests in our host country implies subterfuge?
> Thirty years ago in Guatemala, a Cakchiquel evangelist asked me
> for a set of barber's equipment. With tears in his eyes he said when
> he tried to explain the way of salvation to his fellow Cakchiquels in
> the rural areas, they wouldn't listen. He said, "If I could go and of-
> fer my services as a traveling barber, I would have a captive audi-
> ence, to explain the way of salvation, particularly while I am
> shaving them." I gave him the tools. In time he reported that those
> who before had chased him off their property, now listened to him
> with perfect attention. It wasn't long before there was a congrega-
> tion of believers in that difficult area.
>
> I suppose the devil may have accused this Christian of "subter-
> fuge" because he traveled as a barber, but was also concerned for
> the eternal souls of the people he shaved. The reality was that as he
> gained their confidence and friendship and manifested an interest
> in their practical need for haircuts, he earned the right to speak to
> them about eternal truths. I believe the Lord applauded the efforts
> of this Indian man for his ingenuity and humble spirit of service.
> His name was Francisco Díaz and I have tried to follow his humble,
> adaptable spirit in my own ministry.
>
> Here in Latin America, high government officials and dignitaries
> are almost always suspicious of preachers and those representing
> foreign missions. However, when we come with a servant attitude,
> such officials will listen to us. The first official we led to the Lord in
> Mexico listened to us because we had first served him through our
> linguistic research. This, coupled with Bible translation, is SIL's ba-
> sic service, but we find other ways to serve, like literacy and avia-
> tion and community development as well. SIL's fundamental
> principle is that we serve *with* them and in no way are we in com-
> petition with their government programs. We never hide the fact
> that we are evangelical in faith, nor that we're endeavoring to give
> the Word of God to the ethnic minority people who as yet do not
> have a written language, and therefore do not have access to the
> Scriptures. We publish these facts and refer to them with fervor at

our banquets and dinners that we frequently give to honor a government official or celebrate special occasions with invited dignitaries. In every case we hand out copies of the Word of God in Spanish, and give opportunity for testimonies from national believers, as well as from our own members. We also maintain this friendship by writing them friendly letters. We have a ministry among the ruling classes, most of whom would not go near a church or missionary preaching service. In our personal witness we never preach denominationalism, religious dogma or *churchianity* [sic] of any type. We just present Christ and Him crucified.

What was true of Cam's personal witness was also true of most SIL personnel. In the early part of 1956, Dick Pittman was striving to negotiate a contract for SIL to work with Vietnam's ethnic minorities. He wrote Cam frequent detailed letters about his progress, his adventures and the people he was meeting. From Saigon in March 1956, he wrote to tell Cam that a high-ranking government official who had been less than cooperative and even cynical toward the notion of SIL's program of Bible translation for ethnic peoples had barely escaped with his life in an airplane accident:

> Today I providentially met Mr.__ in the post office, and learned of his narrow escape from death. I visited him that afternoon to tell him of my plans to leave for Delat the next morning. I told him since I believed the Lord had spared his life, I wanted to share some verses of Scripture with him. I thought he would laugh them off in his usual slightly cynical manner. But today he was much more serious than before the accident. I said when everything was right between a man and God, he did not need to fear death. This resulted in a lengthy conversation about ultimate reality. I left with a prayer that God would work in his heart and bring him into a saving knowledge of Himself.

During the spring and summer of 1956 and much of 1957 and 1958, Cam spent hundreds of hours answering in great detail the criticisms from people who accused Wycliffe in one way or another of being "neither fish nor fowl." In answer to a man who wanted to know why Wycliffe workers on the field did not refer to themselves as Protestant missionaries, Cam answered that the word "Protestant" in Latin America would give an altogether wrong impression of SIL's ministry since in fact, SIL was not "protesting" against anyone. In fact, to do so would result in the possibility of being expelled from a country altogether. Furthermore, Cam wrote:

> Our members are not translators only, neither are they missionaries only. They are Christian men and women who are translators. They are young people who in response to a call to do the will of Christ have given themselves to a task that requires scientific skills. Should it be thought a strange thing that a scientific organization can, and in this instance, does have a membership composed entirely of evangelical Christians? Furthermore I believe the church and missionaries as well need to rethink their mission strategy and be willing to break away from the time-honored shackles of *churchianity* [sic] and become all things to all men for the Gospel's sake.

Aware of the heavy stresses and burdens Cam was bearing from these and other criticisms, Don Burns, on March 6, 1956, wrote Cam the following:

> Since these have been such difficult days, I feel led to share with other branches the unique criticisms we have been getting from other missionaries. I do so in the hope that *a burden shared is a burden lightened*. It seems that opposition to our work by other missionaries has reached its climax and at long last we have established direct contact with some of the sources that have accused us of practices, which as you know, have been so ridiculous that I am ashamed to write about it. While it is true that SIL does things differently from the standard "missionary handbook," I can't help but feel the true cause of this underground wave of resistance comes from the enemy of our souls. Satan's devices are to stifle the work of the Holy Spirit by sowing discontent and bitterness any way he can. Let's not be ignorant of the enemy's insidious devices.

Perhaps more than most, Cam was indeed aware that the battle he was waging was not against flesh and blood, but against "the rulers, against the authorities, against the powers of this dark world and against the spiritual forces of evil..."(Ephesians 6:12). To an assembled group of friends on August 26, 1976 after an Americanists Congress in Paris, France, Cam was unapologetic about who the real enemy was and had this to say:

> Our linguistic approach has never been equaled in the history of mission, anywhere at any time. God has led us into a wonderful system of taking the message to those who have never heard. And the enemy of our souls, Satan, is riled up over this. He knows his time is due to end, if not before, at least when the last tribe has been reached. And though we have over two thousand tribes to go, Satan looks at the six hundred and fifty tribes that have been reached, and says, "My, it's getting pretty dangerous." Therefore, he is trying to stop us with every possible means. But I say if we continue on with the methods God has given us and move in the same direction He has been leading us over the years we will not be stopped. My confidence is in God who will take care of us and see us through to the completion of our historic task of Bible translation for every ethnic tribe that doesn't yet have the Scriptures in their own language.

The criticisms against SIL and Wycliffe and their diverse style of ministry were criticisms against the unique methodology Cameron Townsend had developed in Guatemala and now employed to carry out his historic vision. Among some Christian leaders of his generation, this methodology was considered suspect and guilty of bringing a new radicalism to mission outreach.

What was clear in Cam's mind, but not to his critics, was the common ground shared by Bible translation and the science of descriptive linguistics needed to execute this task, and thus the need for an over-arching nonsectarian organization. On July 1, 1977, a year after the congress in France, at the Wycliffe International conference Cam gave the following address:

> My critics frequently ask me to explain why we call ourselves the Summer Institute of Linguistics instead of something like "Bible Translation Mission." I say I am sorry you don't understand, but we

are not your regular kind of mission. We have a job of science to do. Early in my ministry God led me to begin something entirely new and different. Since we're tackling a scientific task, I needed an organization that would willingly serve everyone. This meant the nature of SIL was to be non-sectarian. Admittedly we have paid a price for this. What many people have failed to understand or even appreciate is that SIL is primarily a scientific [linguistic] organization, whose linguists are Bible-believing Christians.

Furthermore, every SIL linguist who has been assigned to do a language analysis of an unwritten language willingly spends ten to fifteen years of hard study in an effort to figure out how a particular language works. This is important because he or she is going to translate the Bible. And you can't hand an ethnic person a Bible you have translated into their language and say, "Here is God's Word in your language," if it is full of grammatical errors. No, the translation must be accurate or else the individual will say, "Well, isn't it strange that God doesn't know how to use good grammar?"

And so our linguists study hard, they take courses, and get academic degrees and credentials in order to do the best possible job of translation. I am often asked, "How can linguistics be considered missionary work?" My answer is that the study of linguistics, which enables a translator to do a scholarly job of Bible translation, is the same as a physician working in a mission hospital. Both the linguist and the physician are doing Kingdom work while each is practicing their scientific professions.

Let me hasten to add that in addition to scientific research, the translator-linguist has the responsibility to teach people to read and write their own language. The translator can do this or bring in an SIL literacy expert. The other responsibility is to lead at least some within the language group into a saving knowledge of Christ.

I said these were the goals for a translator, but there is yet another. I am convinced that once a translator has accomplished the first goals, the final goal should be for the translator to move on to another assignment. For a translator to stay longer makes it appear that he or she is building an ecclesiastical body. The translator's work is done when there are a handful of believers with God's Word to feed on and the Holy Spirit is in their hearts to strengthen and lead them to build his Church in their midst.

Notes

1. Harold Goodall was the new director of SIL in Peru.
2. The area Ecuador calls the Provincia del Oriente is part of some two million square miles of thick jungle forest beyond the eastern cordilleras. This vast area of rivers, jungle, fog, insects, snakes and animals is shared by six South American nations, Brazil, Bolivia, Venezuela, Colombia, Peru and Ecuador. Of this vast area, Ecuador has the smallest portion.
3. Shell Mera is an end-of-the-road jungle frontier town. In 1940 the Shell Oil Company based their oil explorers there, hence the name Shell Mera. But since Ecuador has a small army base with an airstrip there it's officially known as *Base Militar Pastaza*.
4. The term "fleece" refers to the story in Judges chapter 6 when Gideon wanted a tangible sign from God that he was to make war against the hitherto invincible and all-powerful Midianites. For centuries Biblical scholars and theologians have argued the merits of such a practice as normative for Christians. Some scholars suggest the incident in Judges was a one-time event, that to ask God for a tangible, concrete sign exhibits a lack of trust in God. Others argue that God is God, and can, if he chooses, do for a believer what he did for Gideon and make his will known in a tangible way.
5. These were not idle words. According to Ken Watters, who was gradually assuming greater responsibility as treasurer replacing Mr. Nyman for Wycliffe, "Cam was deeply burdened for an Ecuador base and wondered how he could find $10,000 to help." In 1957, the Ecuador SIL branch found a beautiful location on an oxbow lake called Limoncocha. And Cam was as good as his word and gave monies received from his article, "Two Thousand Tongues to Go," that appeared in the August, 1958 issue of *Reader's Digest*. More about this in Chapter 17.

"Friendship of Orange County" Helio-Courier was presented to Ambassador Fernando Berkemeyer of Peru by Vice-President Nixon on September 6, 1956 at the campus of Santa Ana College, Orange County, California. Nixon, a resident of Orange County, presented the aircraft to Peru on behalf of the people of Orange County.

Chapter Fifteen

Marching Around Jericho

C am's theological understanding of Christianity was utterly practical. He believed that the gospel's admonition to be salt and light in the
world is a challenge for Christians to work for the well-being of the
larger society in which one resides. Cam further believed that this was
what God had in mind when He told Jeremiah in chapter 29:7, "Seek
the peace and prosperity of the city to which I have carried you into ex-
ile."

Most SIL workers in the late nineteen-fifties and early sixties felt privileged to work for the social, cultural and spiritual well-being of their
adoptive countries. They fell in love with the many aspects of the national cultures in which they worked, including their foods, music, art,
often stunning scenery, and of course their people. Few worked harder
than Cameron Townsend to foster cultural and political understanding
between the people of the various countries where there was an SIL
presence. Cam occasionally lobbied the U.S. State Department and other
U.S. government agencies and companies on behalf of a particular
country over an issue that was important to that country's economic
and national interests. Cam's most celebrated advocacy was his support
of Mexico's sovereign right to self-determination over its oil reserves. As

early as 1938, Cam became the official goodwill spokesman for Mexico's president Lázaro Cárdenas.[1]

In a May 30, 1956 letter to his sister Lula and brother in-law Eugene Griset, we glimpse Cam's thinking about what he called "standing on the threshold of yet another possibility for an epoch-making [program], through SIL's indirect ministry":

> We have pioneered in goodwill projects in Latin America and the Philippines that involve diplomatic ceremonies, good-neighbor banquets, picnics, conferences, etc. These efforts have reaped wonderful dividends in making friends for our program and our message, as well as opening doors of opportunity and keeping them open.
>
> I now feel we should extend (in a limited way) this ministry to the homeland. Last December we sponsored an Inter-American Friendship Rally in Chicago. This resulted in contributions for a new type of airplane for our work in Ecuador. It was christened the *City of Chicago*. The mayor of Chicago, along with the ambassador of Ecuador in Washington, gave speeches. Later, to honor the Ecuadorian Ambassador at a banquet sponsored by the Pan-American Council, Don Burns, the director of the Ecuador Branch, and I, told of our spiritual service to the ethnic peoples of Amazonia.
>
> When the *City of Chicago* aircraft reached Ecuador the Minister of Education at yet another ceremony received it in Quito. This remarkable airplane, called the Helio-Courier, will, under the blessing of God, continue to make friends for the Gospel and for our nation for the next twenty years. What a marvelous goodwill investment! We are now in the midst of strengthening our ties of friendship with other countries and suggesting that similar goodwill airplanes be given to Bolivia, the Philippines and Peru. We are promising that JAARS will cooperate with these projects by taking the responsibility of operating and maintaining the goodwill planes for the benefit of the ethnic peoples of the jungle. When the funds for the three planes come in, we plan to hold ceremonies at which the ambassador from the land to which the plane will be going will express the gratitude of his country.[2]
>
> The verse God gave me as I launched out on this new approach was: By faith, the walls of Jericho fell down after they were com-

passed about for seven days. I doubt if the marching around had any more to do with the crumbling of the walls than Naaman's dipping seven times in the Jordan River had to do with his cleansing of leprosy, but both were indispensable preludes to the great miracles that followed. I'm wondering what all may be involved in the "marching around" as regards the subject of American friendship toward the lands where our translators serve. We want to do whatever marching He requests even though it seems humanly to be as futile as dipping oneself in water to cure leprosy. The miracle will be of God as we obey.

Cam ended his letter with the admission that while he had success in promoting international goodwill in Latin America, he was not as confident about how to do this in the United States. Cam asked Eugene and Lula for their prayers and counsel and said that if he were mistaken about God's leading, he would be the first to drop the project. Cam admitted that the diplomatic affairs associated with fund-raising involved a great deal of effort, and said:

> Who wants to march, march, march around Jericho unless God orders it? Thus far when inadequate financial returns have had me longing to quit marching and to give up the project, God has given me no liberty to do so but has said, "Have not I commanded thee? Be strong and of good courage" (Joshua 1:9). With those words ringing in my ears, I dare not quit. Yours to reach an unevangelized world whether by direct or indirect methods, whatever God directs.

The historian E.H. Carr once said, "The facts of history are nothing, interpretation is everything." If Carr's premise is correct, then we can interpret Cam's letter to be an oblique request for his relatives to become partners in financing at least one of the proposed airplanes. In the letter, Cam included the amount of monies on hand for each of the planes. "Forty percent for the Bolivia friendship plane, thirty for the Philippines and eighteen percent for the Peruvian plane." This polite yet fully informative letter was an example of Wycliffe's policy stated in the SIL's November 26, 1955 board meeting, "As to needs, full information, as to funds, no solicitation."

Cam's letter is also notable for his expression of ambivalence about his program. Seldom did Cam's public presentation of his proposals express equivocation. But in this private letter to his family, he expresses his need for special prayer and "counsel." There is no record that Eugene or Lula offered their opinion or contributed money to the project. A month later, however, Cam wrote that "a friend" had contributed $5000 toward the goodwill plane project.

The question still remained whether to ask secular organizations and "unsaved" people for project funding for the goodwill planes. The policy was coming under scrutiny by many Wycliffe constituents, not the least of which was the board of directors. Longtime board member John A. Hubbard was particularly upset and wrote Cam that he believed raising funds for a new Helio airplane from secular sources was in violation of the November 26th board action. To answer the inquiry as to why he was involved in such a program, Cam, in a no-nonsense letter to the board dated June 7, 1956, said he was going to "rehearse" the facts concerning the "inaccurate statements made about the Inter-American Friendship project." There were two points of contention that concerned the board. One was the complaint made by a number of Tulsa, Oklahoma businessmen who said they were tired of "people from the Inter-American Friendship committee coming into their offices asking for money to fund an airplane for Bolivia."[3] The other was the issue of how Cam was interpreting the board's policy of "full information, but no solicitation." Cam's response to the board began with his explanation that he wasn't asking for money for just SIL or himself. Rather, the Helio-Courier planes would serve the country where there was an SIL presence. The airplanes would be entrusted to JAARS people who would pilot and maintain them. In this way the planes would be at the disposal of anyone in need of assistance where there was no commercial air service. In response to the criticisms of unwelcome visits to Tulsa businessmen, Cam said:

> Actually the Tulsa committee, Bill Nyman Jr. and myself have visited only nine firms. We wanted to give them an opportunity to cooperate in this good neighbor project. Of the nine, six contributed. Second visits were made on only four firms. We also visited two foundations. Neither of the foundations contributed. We also con-

tacted several pastors and a fine Christian physician, not for donations but for their help in any way they saw fit.

My answer to the criticism that we have approached "unsaved"
people for their help, is this: If a Christian operates a bus line he
doesn't hesitate to collect fares from unsaved people. Our planes
serve in areas where there are no commercial planes. Of necessity
our planes become common carriers for anyone who calls on us for
aviation service. I would consider it mean and unbecoming to our
testimony if we didn't help when asked. My position is that charity
[love] must always prevail.

The question now becomes, who is going to equip us adequately? We're not a commercial airline and when the day comes
for a commercial airline to take over, we will heave a sigh of relief.
In the meantime, we serve as a goodwill organization and it is
proper to ask men of goodwill to cooperate, especially if it's in their
own best interests, as in the case of U.S. firms operating in Latin
America. Furthermore, an Inter-American Friendship project cannot be limited to Christians. For over twenty years I've been inviting Latin American leaders regardless of personal creed to
cooperate with us in welfare projects that develop their hinterland
and improve the status of their ethnic peoples. Many of these influential people have come to look upon us as partners in progress.
They even become willing sooner or later to listen to our gospel
message because we have shown them true friendship. We haven't
rejected friendship to "publicans and sinners" any more than the
Lord did. No matter what part of the world we work in we can't
have a good-neighbor policy unless our aim is service to all, regardless of religion or creed. This has been Wycliffe policy from the beginning.

One of Cam's friends who expressed concern over the ethos of the goodwill project was Philip Howard, editor of the Philadelphia-based *The
Sunday School Times* and father[4] of Elisabeth Elliot. Howard had been a
good and empathetic friend to Ken Pike, Dick Pittman, and L.L. Legters,
and had followed the work of Wycliffe and SIL with support and
prayer. He told Cam that he was one who prayed regularly for him and
was convinced translation was a most important ministry. But on the
question of promoting the goodwill program, he wrote:

> Do you not run the risk of departing from your pilgrim character
> and our Christian life of faith and work when you seek help from
> people outside the faith who do not understand or approve of the
> need to get the gospel to the unreached tribes of earth? Is there not
> a danger of minimizing the real heart of the gospel message to
> please people and obtain diplomatic help?

Cam did admit that he and the committee were somewhat inexperienced in dealing with American businessmen in the Tulsa area, many of
whom he said did not have an interest in international affairs. But at the
heart of Cam's letter to the board was a challenge for people willingly to
serve in the spirit of Jeremiah. Unfortunately, this kind of "social spiri-
tuality" was unsettling to some who clung to a more traditional,
exclusionary religiosity that did not include social action outside their
own often tight-knit community. The Goodwill Friendship Committee
of Tulsa, designed to raise money for the Bolivia Helio-Courier airplane
was, as Cam admitted, an experiment. While this "experiment" was
running into a buzz-saw of criticism in Tulsa, the idea of a lay-run service organization dedicated to the practical, hands-on ministry of helping Wycliffe translators was the forerunner of what would become in
1967 Wycliffe's adjunct organization, Wycliffe Associates (WA).[5] Years
later, when Cam spoke to a WA gathering he said:

> We want lay people to be involved with Wycliffe because of the
> blessing it will be to their own lives as they are used to bless others
> through the translation of God's Word.

But that was eleven years after the Tulsa "experiment." At the time of
the "experiment," some of Cam's closest friends threatened to withdraw
their support from Wycliffe over his practice of asking the secular community for project funding. One of those friends was Amos Baker. Cam
had met Amos while walking in a park in Sulphur Springs, Arkansas,
around 1934. In Cam's own inimitable style, he won Amos as a friend,
and then introduced him to the Lord. Amos became one of Cam's dearest friends and strongest supporters. Amos often took on the personal
support of several new Wycliffe translators until they had time to build
up their own partnership base. Thus, when Cam learned the Bakers had

threatened to withdraw their support from Wycliffe, he wrote the board:

> When I learned from Mrs. Baker that she and her husband were considering withdrawing their support from Wycliffe because of what we were doing in Tulsa [Amos's hometown] I was stunned! Amos has faithfully worked with us ever since our Bible translation program got underway in 1934. I now regret we started this experiment in Amos' hometown. We certainly can't afford to lose such friends who are dear to me and to the work. I now want to withdraw from Tulsa as soon as possible. Perhaps the Lord intends to provide the money that is lacking for the Bolivian goodwill plane without my marching around Jericho any longer. I wonder if I got the wrong Jericho? Maybe the goodwill chairman, Mr. Wakefield, will have a suggestion when I have an interview with him. Perhaps when Amos returns from his business trip he will be able to throw some light on my pathway. On the other hand, we have gone too far to draw back completely. Only God can solve the problem. The one thing that is clear to me and some others is that the need remains for our organization to serve our country as well as strengthening international goodwill. God has greatly blessed our work on the field. Now we should find a way to extend this blessing here at home. This is a serious matter, please pray. Your puzzled servant.

Whatever was puzzling Cam, it most assuredly wasn't his commitment to be a friend to humanity. To deny such a friendship would, in Cam's mind be to deny that Christ was the Lord of his whole life. There was no division or compartmentalization between his secular and spiritual life. Cam's argument was that to be a Christian one should not have a "Christian role" that is different from his "sociological role."

Thus, Cam could answer Philip Howard's letter on June 12, 1956, by admitting he was aware of the misgivings many Christians have over appealing for financial help to a secular source for a "spiritual" ministry. Wrote Cam:

> We in SIL and WBT have been criticized, as your letter indicated, because we are kind and show no hostility toward priests and nuns. The reality is that I love to serve whomever the Lord brings

across my path. It's the Lord's command to love our enemies and do good to them that hate you. There have been many lately who have tried to stir up people against me. When this happens it allows me the opportunity to prove that we hold no malice, even toward those who oppose me and our organization and all the while maintaining our evangelical position.

There is an additional reason why we serve everyone, that can't be disregarded with impunity. When you are deep in the jungle, you're supposed to share your canoe, food, shelter and companionship, with those in need, even your worst enemies. That's frontier etiquette and no one can afford to break it, least of all a servant of Christ.

On Sunday June 10, 1956, Dawson Trotman, who had served on the board since 1942, wrote Cam a candid letter of extraordinary support for his inter-American friendship program. It would be his last letter to Cam. On June 10, Dawson Trotman drowned at the Word of Life Bible Camp in Schroon Lake, New York while rescuing a young girl who had fallen overboard. Dawson successfully rescued the girl, but just as he lifted her out of the water into arms that pulled her to safety, Dawson suddenly suffered a cardiac arrest, slipped beneath the water, and drowned. Here is the last part of his letter:

> My position is that it is right to ask unsaved people to help. There is much of God's money that has been used to serve the devil long enough. Let's get all we can to serve Him who created all the earth and its substance. If I had any criticism of you and this project it would be why haven't you contacted more of the business leaders and given them a chance to contribute? I know most of the board opposes me on this issue. However, let me say I wish I could talk to you face-to-face. It's hard to write what I now want to say without being misunderstood. I am afraid there are several fine leaders of our organization who are unhappy because they feel you occasionally make unilateral decisions. Yet, I hasten to say that almost without exception, these same leaders will admit that in hindsight your decisions were correct. You know that I have had trouble making up my own mind on some of the decisions you have made. At the same time I know you have a very strong sense of being led of God.

I freely admit that I look at things from a common-sense point of view. I also admit that in many of the decisions you have made I did not have the same faith and sense of God's leading that you had.

Your practice has been that you reach a decision because you believe God has prompted you to move in a certain direction. You express this opinion, but there are others, perhaps the majority, who are not in agreement. Yet in light of past experience the board or others agree with your decision, and action is taken. This happens because over time you have, almost without exception, been proven right in your decision to move in a certain direction.

On June 18, 1956, notwithstanding the resistance and disapproval from some in the Tulsa community, Cam invited Mr. John Simmons, chief of the U.S. State Department Protocol Office to attend the upcoming christening ceremony of the Helio-Courier for Bolivia. The ceremony took place at the Oklahoma City airport on the afternoon of June 27. Later, Cam sent out a general letter covering the event, in which he mentioned that Billy Graham was holding his mass evangelistic campaign in Tulsa. Cam wrote:

> What a privilege to get acquainted with Dr. Graham personally and to feel the warmth and fervor of his dedication to God and the humility and wisdom he manifests in his daily life.
>
> When Billy preached to a multitude in the stadium at Tulsa he announced the promotion to glory of our beloved friend and fellow Wycliffe board member, Dawson Trotman. When Billy told how "Daws" had died as he lived—busy saving others—we were all challenged to greater consecration to our God-given task. How we shall miss Dawson!
>
> We had another unforgettable day when the president of the University of Oklahoma, Dr. George Cross, presented a high-performance airplane (a Helio-Courier) to Bolivia's distinguished Ambassador Víctor Andrade, for our work among Bolivia's jungle peoples. Mrs. Cross poured a bit of Oklahoma crude oil on the plane's prow from an Indian bowl, naming the aircraft "Friendship of Oklahoma."

The whole program, beginning with a 19-gun salute for the ambassador, and ending with a quotation from the Word of God (Galatians 2:20)[6] at the banquet, evidenced the Lord's blessing. He even hung a cloud over the hot June sun to protect the large audience during the outdoor part of the program. Directly after the christening ceremony Cam left for Seattle to lay the groundwork for yet another friendship committee. After a special luncheon, hosted by the Mayor of Seattle, to kick off the *Friendship of Seattle* goodwill project, a businessman said to Cam, "Thank you for this emphasis on international goodwill. You aren't just helping those countries; you are helping the United States as well, because she too, must have friends."

On July 30, Cam cabled Bob Schneider in Lima about yet another ceremony to be held in Santa Ana, California on behalf of Peru. He then sent Bob a letter with the following details:

> The Chamber of Commerce of Santa Ana is sponsoring the ceremony at which the "Friendship of Orange County" goodwill airplane is to be presented to the envoy of the Peruvian government. Inasmuch as Vice-President Nixon was born in Orange County, and in view of the importance that President Eisenhower's administration is placing on building up our friendship with Latin America, the Chamber of Commerce believes the vice-president will accept the invitation to give a speech at the time the airplane is christened and presented to Peru.
>
> I realize, of course, that the plane itself does not merit such extraordinary attention but it can be the occasion for a strategic emphasis on the need of strengthening our good-neighbor associations on a personal level. I believe these ceremonies are highly worthwhile and will usher in a new era in Inter-American diplomacy when people of our respective countries and their private institutions get together to forge stronger ties of friendship as people rather than just government to government.

Notes

1   See Hugh Steven, *Doorway to the World, The Mexico Years, The Memoirs of W. Cameron Townsend 1934-1947* (Wheaton, Illinois: Harold Shaw Publishers, 1999), 105 ff.

2   See Appendix C for a complete list of all Goodwill airplanes and the countries that received them.

3   Bernie May, former director of Wycliffe USA, and longtime friend of Cam's, relates an incident when he and Cam asked one of the DuPonts, in Miami, Florida, for a contribution toward a plane for SIL's work in Colombia. Mr. DuPont rose from his chair, grasped both Bernie and Cam by the arms and ushered them (none too gently) out of his office toward the elevator saying, "I am not interested and don't have time for such a project, good day." Bernie said when they got out of the elevator and went outside, Cam straightened his shoulders, smoothed his jacket and said, "What a shame for that man to miss an opportunity for a great blessing." Bernie said the incident so unsettled him that he wanted to go home, but not Cam. Said Bernie, "Uncle Cam looked at his watch, looked around at the skyline and said, "Who can we visit now?"

4   *The Sunday School Times* was in its day the leading religious journal for evangelicals, and was as influential as later magazines like *Christianity Today*. Philip Howard was, as his father before him, and his son David Howard after him, a trustee of Wheaton College.

5   When the ministry of Wycliffe Associates first began, there were only three or four service opportunities for lay involvement. These included forming a local chapter to pray for the work of Wycliffe, taking field trips to Mexico and pledging money at a dinner banquet. As of this writing, the service opportunities have greatly expanded to include work and building construction parties in almost every country were there is an SIL presence. For further information on WA's extraordinary lay ministry, See Hugh Steven, *What a Difference a Team Makes* (Cloverdale, British Columbia, Canada: Credo Publishing Corporation, 1988). Also available from Wycliffe Associates.

6   "I have been crucified with Christ and I no longer live, but Christ lives in me. The life I live in the body, I live by faith in the Son of God, who loved me and gave himself for me"(NIV).

Tariri Nochomata, chief of the once-feared Shapra group of Peru's northeastern jungle, came to faith in Christ after translating The Life of Christ Gospel portions into his language, working with Lorrie Anderson.

Chapter Sixteen

Some of Us Will Answer
for You

On October 9, 1998, the White House Press Secretary released a memo telling of a meeting between President Fujimori of Peru and President Mahuad of Ecuador. The press release said the White House was helping to mediate a diplomatic settlement to a long standing and complex border dispute, which had existed since colonial times and had long created friction and unrest between the two countries.

Forty-two years before this press release, Cameron Townsend, aware of the unresolved conflicts, took it upon himself to try to ease some of the diplomatic tensions between Ecuador and Peru. On September 18, 1956 after a fourteen-month absence from Peru, Cam wrote to Ecuador's president, Dr. Camilo Ponce Enríquez, and offered his services and those of SIL in Ecuador to operate what he called a "Peace Boat," which, said Cam, would:

> Bring about the establishment of a small transport service on the Napo River that would allow Ecuadorian farmers to have free access to the Amazon for their produce [and thus be an important commercial outlet for the farmers].

Cam had been in high spirits over the first two successful Inter-American Goodwill Friendship airplane ceremonies. Still fresh in his memory was Vice-President Nixon's speech given at the ceremony in Santa Ana, California at which the wife of the Peruvian consul general of Los Angeles christened the new Helio-Courier *Friendship of Orange County* destined for Peru with a mixture of water from the Amazon and orange juice from Orange County.

Encouraged by these successful enterprises to be bold for the Lord, Cam wrote his longtime friend Henry Crowell, of Moody Bible Institute, about his river transport dream.[1]

Henry Crowell had often encouraged Cam in his projects with financial support and warm letters of endorsement. But the "Kilo Kid," as he was fond of calling himself, was also an outspoken critic when he felt Cam was treading on the toes of evangelical sensibilities. Like Philip Howard, Crowell had become perplexed over recent reports that Cam and SIL were "aiding and abetting" priests and nuns in their work in Peru. Thus, completely ignoring Cam's Peace Boat project, Crowell wrote that he, along with the Moody board, was unhappy over what he termed "building a bridge over the stream at our expense so the enemy, whoever that might be, can more easily attack us." Crowell said he agreed with Cam that it was right to do good to an enemy in need, to give him a meal, dry him out, give him new clothes if need be and then send him on his way. (Crowell referenced a priest who had been rescued from drowning by SIL members.) And, said Crowell in his October 16, 1956 letter to Cam:

> As long as I am in a growling mood, let me say further that I am becoming increasingly worried about your program of obtaining airplanes for Wycliffe's use by having them donated by civic groups around the nation. Is there any danger, Uncle Cam, that this "friendship program" and other diplomatic adventures and cooperation with governments will weaken the spiritual emphasis of your organization? Well, I have growled enough for today. Let me hear your side of the story, which, I am sure, will be a good one. Praying for you as always.

On October 19, Cam responded to Crowell in a letter in which he once again outlined his convictions and policies of defeating an "enemy" by serving him.[2] Cam concluded his four-page letter with:

> I feel so dependent upon you and your colleagues that it's awfully hard to have to disagree with you. Only strong convictions based on His leading make it possible. As long as you and your colleagues trusted my colleagues and me in our new approaches to the vast Bible-less areas of the world, we really made progress. Surely you won't abandon us in our daring innovations that have been so successful when the weak methods of the past left over 2,000 tribes without the Word of God. Let's continue and accelerate our efforts to reach all peoples with God's Word in their own mother tongue in this generation. I know you are also interested in making a greater impact for the gospel. I therefore ask that you please continue to stand behind us even when you can't understand our strategy. Just remember the old methods brought limited results and culminated too often in closed doors. God is using us to open doors. Let's not regress and go back into old methods. In the meantime, we need you and your colleagues badly. Together we can reach, under God and by His methods, every tribe in this generation.

For Cam the most effective mission strategy (and one that for him was irrefutable) came from the Apostle Paul's words in Galatians 5:6b and 14-15:

> The only thing that counts is faith expressing itself through love. The entire law is summed up in a single command: love your neighbor as yourself. If you keep biting and devouring each other, watch out or you will be destroying each other.

In the context of world mission, to "love one's neighbor" for Cam meant to find out how to serve in practical ways and to identify with what was good within a given culture. This was as natural and easy for Cam as it was for him to breathe. Yet Cam knew this non-confrontational strategy did not always sit well with a certain segment of his U.S. constituents.

In the face of increasing criticism, Cam made every effort to reassure his supporters that his goodwill strategy was one of the ways the gospel could be preached quietly and effectively and was, in fact, responsible for keeping the doors open for the gospel even in the face of government and ecclesiastical opposition! In a report to Henry Crowell on the events of the Orange County Inter-American goodwill ceremony, Cam's intention was clearly to convince Crowell that his Goodwill Ceremonies were paying handsome diplomatic dividends for SIL:

> The Lord has again given us a great victory through the Inter-American Goodwill Ceremony in Orange County. The publicity for this ceremony came on the heels of an attack by the prelates who were trying to turn the new president of Peru against us. It didn't work. This situation reminded me of 1951 when the cardinal in Peru was attacking our work. In the midst of the attacks the president of Peru took part in the big goodwill ceremony of the *Moisés Sáenz* airplane. After the press reported this event at the Lima airport, the opposition immediately stopped.
>
> Amazingly the same thing has happened again. This time our position seemed more difficult, not only because the new president is a strong supporter of the Vatican but also because the tendency in the Peruvian Congress is to be critical of what the former government did.
>
> The new president had questioned the Director of Education with whom we work about our contract and asked him to make modifications. But then came the goodwill ceremony with Vice-President Nixon's translated speech given in impeccable Spanish by the U.S. charge d'affairs, Mr. Clare H. Timberlake, to Peru's president, Manuel Prado. The newspapers gave favorable reports, along with photos of the many dignitaries, including senators and congressmen as well as Dr. Jorge Basadre, the Minister of Education, who gave the closing address in which he expressed high praise for our institute and in the name of President Prado thanked the people of Orange County for the plane. After President Prado received a written copy of Vice President Nixon's speech, the modifications he had asked for were dropped. The timing of these goodwill events could not have been more perfect, for which we thank our Lord.

In the United States, the primary buzzwords of 1957-58 were "new" and "futuristic." Concept automobiles designed "for the year 2000" were appearing in auto shows and magazines. The Wankel rotary engine was the first new internal combustion engine since the nineteenth century. In 1957, however, only the wealthy could afford the new gull-winged Mercedes, but thousands of first-time car owners were buying the new Volkswagen Beetle. On January 31, 1958, Explorer I became the first U.S. earth satellite to go into orbit.

And in January 1957 Cam wrote that Dr. James Dean and his wife Gladys would be taking a team of twenty young SIL workers to begin language studies in the highlands of what was then called the Territory of Papua and New Guinea. Dale and Harriet Kietzman were also on their way to Brazil to head up SIL's new work among the three hundred or so ethnic people groups of that vast country. In his 1956 Christmas letter, Cam said that hundreds of new translators and support workers would be needed to adequately meet the challenges just in these two new countries. Cam concluded his letter by saying:

> As I look ahead to this coming year it promises to be a year of extraordinary advance in many directions. [A survey was underway to locate a site for SIL's first Arctic Training Camp.][3] At the same time I realize the task before us is too big and the needs so great they could overwhelm us. But then I am reminded "since God did not spare his own Son but gave him up for us all, will he not with him graciously give us everything else?" (Williams). Yes, alongside that GREAT GIFT we commemorate at Christmas time, everything else you or I need in his service to make known that GREAT GIFT to those who don't yet know it, is insignificant.

Also in 1957 the question of how to make the needs and challenges of Bible translation known to a wider audience of young people was one that was always on Cam's mind. And when Cam had an important idea, he was constantly looking for ways to bring his ideas into reality. As a way to bring greater attention to the needs of all unwritten tribal languages of the world, Cam sent a confidential letter to TV personality Ralph Edwards, host of the popular show, "This Is Your Life," proposing that Edwards feature Rachel Saint and her Auca language assistant Dayuma in a future program. (This proposal was unknown to Rachel.)

While Cam was dealing with preparations for the Edwards TV program with Rachel, news came from Dick Pittman that his dear friend and strong supporter of SIL, Ramón Magsaysay, president of the Philippines, had been killed in a plane crash on March 17, 1957. This was followed by the news that Cam's dear friend, John Brown of the John Brown Schools had died. To his son, John Brown Jr., president of John Brown University in Siloam Springs, Arkansas, Cam wrote in tribute to his father's memory and to the important partnership they had had during the early days of Wycliffe and SIL. The letter is a significant illustration of how important friendships were to Cam:

> When I was in Sulphur Springs last spring and learned that your father was to speak at the university, I told my wife that even though it was inconvenient for me to attend, I was going to put everything aside to go and hear him. When we received word that he is now with the Lord he served so long and so well, it made me glad I took the time to hear him speak. Few men have influenced me, as did your father. His guidance wasn't limited to people in the U.S. God used your father in a chain of events that opened up Mexico for our translators. Later it was he who influenced us to establish our children's home and conference center in the Ozarks [Sulphur Springs]. You also know that many of our Wycliffe workers received at least part of their training under his leadership. We praise God for all that He did through your father.

Someone once wrote that a friend is one who "strengthens you with prayers, blesses you with love, and encourages you with hope." During the years 1958 and 1959 Cam and SIL continued to experience a period of severe criticisms from many within the U.S. evangelical community over SIL's policy of "Service to All". Yet interestingly, in the midst of this criticism, many evangelical leaders acknowledged the important contribution the SIL schools were making in training future missionaries. Rev. R.T. Ketcham wrote an open letter entitled "The Wycliffe Bible Translators and the Roman Catholic Church" which was highly critical of many of Cam's mission policies. However Ketcham prefaced his remarks by saying,

"There is probably no finer school in existence, which is better qualified to train missionaries regardless of field of service. This article should not deter missionaries and Christian workers who desire a thorough linguistic training from attending the Wycliffe School at the University of Oklahoma. However, I have some serious concerns over such statements by Dr. Townsend as the following:

I, your servant do not belong to any denomination.[4] However, I respect them all, and try to be a good neighbor to all. The Summer Institute of Linguistics (SIL) founded by me and directed by me, does not protest against anything and does not attack anyone. On the contrary, we endeavor to promote a spirit of love and brotherhood. We try to serve all. We don't call ourselves Protestants, but simply believers in Christ.

Rev. Ketcham's open letter was filled with quotes from several Catholic priests and others Ketcham considered to be "enemies of the gospel" and Ketcham thus wondered how it was that Townsend could refute the charge that SIL workers were not "wolves in sheep's clothing." At a time when Cam greatly needed prayers, encouragement and support, he received it in a letter from a good and true friend, Billy Graham. On December 9, 1958, Billy Graham wrote the following:

The Lord has gloriously blessed Wycliffe. In my opinion, He has honored your objectives and methods beyond any missionary society of modern times. Some of the criticisms you have received may be sincere [but coming] from confused people who have only part of the facts. Some may come from envious and jealous hearts. Some of it may come from people who have taken a false Scriptural position on *separation*. I hope you will not be discouraged or disturbed by these rumors [and criticisms].

During the past few years I also have come under severe criticism from some of these same groups. At first I was disturbed and discouraged and it sent me to my knees and to the Scriptures. Out of this came a clear conviction that the Holy Spirit had been leading us in the right direction all along. I refused to answer these critics, basing my position on the fact that when Christ was reviled, He reviled not again. I also remember the words of I Peter 2:15, "for so is

the will of God, that with well doing ye may put to silence the ignorance of foolish men." I am convinced that those who take this ex-
treme position are now in the process of eliminating each other and
eventually causing much harm to the work of the Lord.

I deeply regret that you must be subjected to these rumors, criticisms and outright lies. However, this has been the price that every
true servant of God has had to pay. Please, my beloved friend, do
not allow these criticisms to disturb you. The overwhelming majority of evangelicals are back of you one hundred percent. Some of us
will answer for you in a positive way. In fact I have decided to
preach almost an entire sermon on the "Hour of Decision" on the
effectiveness of Wycliffe's work.

I believe your methods, tactics and strategy are from the Lord.
Do not flinch in the midst of criticisms no matter where they may
come from. Be assured of my wholehearted support and constant
prayers on your behalf. With warmest personal greetings and lots
of love.

In the February, 1960, issue of *Eternity* magazine, Donald Grey
Barnhouse, founder and editor-in-chief of the magazine published an
article entitled "A Survey of Missions in Spanish America." The article
grew out of his recent tour of Latin America. Under the section "The
Case for Wycliffe," Barnhouse had this to say:

Before going to South America I had learned there was deep-seated
animosity against this work on the part of some of the workers in
other faith missions. I would not bring this up here if I had not been
approached by a mission executive who wrote me long letters
against Wycliffe, who said he was determined to stand against that
organization.

Barnhouse then related the many complaints against Wycliffe and SIL
that have been mentioned, but toward the end of the long article,
Barnhouse wrote:

Let it be said immediately that I think so much of the work that
Wycliffe is doing that I am going to devote a major article to a description of their base at Yarinacocha, Peru and the actual mechan-

ics of getting an Indian language reduced to writing. I find the accusation of spiritual compromise to come from ignorance, jealousy and misdirected zeal. This is one of the most fascinating missionary stories of the world today.

On June 13, 1960, William (Bill) Bright, director of Campus Crusade for Christ wrote:

> It is our desire to cooperate with Wycliffe Bible Translators in helping recruit men [and women] to help take the Gospel to the remaining ethnic peoples who do not have God's Word in their own language. The work you and your colleagues are doing is one of the most significant ministries for Christ in the history of the Christian Church. Be assured of our most cordial, enthusiastic and continued interest. With warm personal regards.

Notes

1   In spite of many months of investigation and planning, including even the selection of a boat, the Peace Boat program never came to fruition. One reason had to do with the intransigence of both Ecuador and Peru, who were not interested in seeing commerce develop along the disputed borders.

2   Cam's letter to Henry Crowell dated October 19, 1956, Document #11977, is available from the Townsend Archives, Box 248, Waxhaw, NC 28173. The letter is too lengthy to include in full in this chapter.

3   A group of sixteen recruits attended the Arctic Training Camp on the Nenana River in Alaska and then moved to village locations in May and June of 1959.

4   Cam was supported by, and had his membership with, the nondenominational Church of the Open Door, then in Los Angeles, California.

In June 1957 Ralph Edwards of the once-acclaimed television program "This is Your Life", wove the stories of converted Chief Tariri of Peru and converted Auca woman, Dayuma, of Ecuador, into a thrilling program presented in June 1957. Left to right: Ralph Edwards, Tariri, Tariri's wife Irina and baby, Rachael Saint, Dayuma.

After fleeing her tribal home years before, Dayuma, seated at Rachel Saint's right, taught Rachel the Auca language and eventually returned to her people with Rachel to tell them of the love of God.

Chapter Seventeen

"Did That Reach Your Heart?"

N ot all of Cameron Townsend's ideas were successful. Despite much effort to launch his Peace Boat project, it was scuttled. There was just too much acrimony between Ecuador and Peru over their contested borders. A second attempt, led by Jack Henderson, to negotiate a contract with Venezuela for translation work also failed. Jack's report to Cam came immediately to the point: "This is not a good time to try to negotiate a contract. The government is not making any new agreements with anyone at present."

When the U.S. proposed tariff increases on lead and zinc from Peru and Mexico, Cam sent a lengthy telegram to Sam Rayburn, speaker of the House of Representatives in Washington, D.C. asking that the U.S. reconsider their proposal. Such increases, Cam argued, would have a disastrous impact on the economies of Peru and Mexico. More Americans North and South would suffer than would benefit from the increase. Wrote Cam:

> Keeping tariffs low will benefit the U.S. in the long run. Certainly consultation with our partners is in order before [implementing this increase.] Having good neighbors and friends in Latin America

is invaluable in the defense of democracy. Let the United States be
true to this partnership, let us act as brothers.

Not one to leave any stone unturned, Cam next wrote to John Foster
Dulles, U.S. Secretary of State, and to President Eisenhower. Cam's letters described the destabilizing effect the tariffs would have on the "Jef-
fersonian devotion to democracy in the Western Hemisphere." Yet for
all his goodwill efforts on behalf of Peru and Mexico, the only response
Cam received was a polite letter from the Acting Secretary for
Inter-American Affairs explaining why it was necessary to raise the tariffs. In South America, the president of Ecuador, Dr. Camilo Ponce, recognized Cam's humanitarian efforts on behalf of Pan Americanism,
decorating him with the *Orden de Mérito* (Order of Merit).

While Cam wasn't able to lower tariffs or resolve border disputes in
South America, he did advance the cause of Bible translation when
some thirty-five million television viewers watched the popular program "This is Your Life" on the evening of June 5, 1957. TV host Ralph
Edwards featured Rachel Saint, Dayuma, and Chief Tariri of the
Candoshi-Shapra Indians of north central Peru. During his research for
Rachel's story, Ralph Edwards learned about the remarkable conversion
of Tariri. So intrigued was he with the striking and dignified chief who
had once taken the heads of his enemies, Edwards requested Tariri's
presence on the show.

However, when Cam proposed the idea to Lorrie Anderson and Doris Cox, translators among that people group, they raised serious questions about Tariri traveling so far from his home, into such a strange
and alien North America culture. Cam understood their concerns and
even voiced his own reservations about such a trip, but then he remembered how impressed the Peruvian ambassador, cabinet officers and
embassy staff had been with Tariri when he was presented at a special
reception in Lima. Said Cam:

> In clear, unequivocal language Tariri told how he used to kill peo-
> ple and take their heads. But since the women of the Institute had
> come to his village he had learned about God's love and accepted
> Jesus Christ as his Savior; he was now a different man. He said he
> no longer wanted to be the greatest chief, because Christ is now the
> greatest. He said we should all learn about Jesus so we could all

live in peace with one another and there would be no more killings. The entire embassy staff had turned out to hear him and you could tell they were all deeply impressed. Then, on his own, Tariri removed his ear ornaments of polished beetle wings and gave them as a gift to the ambassador. It was a tremendous occasion.

Cam added:

When I understood the impact Tariri had made on the ambassador I realized we could use Tariri in an unprecedented manner before the large audience in the U.S. who would watch the television program "This Is Your Life." While Rachel would give her testimony about the positive results of Bible translation, I thought something would be missing if Tariri did not go on [TV] as an example of the power of the translated Word in the vernacular language. This I felt would be one of the strongest testimonies for Christ that audience had ever heard or seen. I also thought Tariri's presence would encourage believers, and perhaps silence those who prefer to leave [ethnic peoples] without a message of hope.

By all accounts, the program was a rousing success. William Nyman wrote Cam to tell him he had had a conversation with representatives and sponsors of the program in which they said, "It was the best show we have ever put on. The TV studio audience broke into spontaneous applause; that had never happened before." Ken Pike wrote to say:

Once more you've shown yourself a man of much more courage and imagination than I have. I frankly held my breath about the "This Is Your Life" program. When I learned about this I informed a handful of officials at the university. I later learned that the wife of the vice-president said she "never watched that program" (she didn't like it) but on the assigned night she did in fact watch it and said she was greatly pleased with what she saw, as was her husband.

On June 18, Dr. Pete Kyle McCarter, acting president of the University of Oklahoma, wrote to say "As I watched the program progress, I had feelings of deep gratification that the Linguistic Institute [SIL] is a part of the University of Oklahoma." Bill Wyatt, Wycliffe's regional public relations representative in Chicago, wrote to tell Cam, "A week after the program aired, twelve hundred people gathered on a Sunday night in Moody Church to hear Rachel and Tariri's testimony." And so letters of congratulations flowed in from all across the country.

But then, Bill Nyman, Jr. contacted Cam about a phone call he had received from the ambassador of Peru. Bill said the ambassador had received a lengthy cable of complaint from Peru's president regarding Chief Tariri's appearance on national television. The government did recognize that Tariri was a free citizen and could do what he wished. At the same time the Peruvian government expressed their concern that the American public might acquire the false notion that Peru was entirely made up of headhunters. Bill said the Peruvian government would greatly appreciate it if Tariri were not to appear on any more U.S. television programs, including a proposed interview with Billy Graham[1] and Vice-President Nixon. In the interest of diplomatic harmony Bill said he hoped Wycliffe would comply totally with Peru's request, which they did. When Tariri returned to Peru he reported to Cam and others about what he had said to people in the United States. The following is part of Tariri's report that was published in the Peruvian press:

> Friends, I went to see your country [the United States]. I talked to everyone as my brothers. I said, "Let your ears listen to me." I used to think only of killing and cutting off many heads but I quit that custom. Now I live well. Let us all live well. Let us love Jesus only. Let's follow His example. Why should we live wrong and get drunk and kill and have only hatred and do evil things? Jesus suffered for our sins and died to pay our debt. Why shouldn't we serve God?

When Cam received word about the Peruvian ambassador's request that Tariri to not make any more U.S. TV appearances, he accepted the decision philosophically and said when God closed one door He would open another. That new door opened sooner than Cam expected.

On August 6, 1957, Clarence W. Hall, senior editor of *Reader's Digest*, wrote Cam asking permission to do a feature story on the work of Wycliffe Bible Translators. That letter set in motion the machinery for the far-reaching and well-received *Reader's Digest* article, "Two Thousand Tongues to Go," published in August of 1958.

In the U.S. the years 1957-59 became a period of unprecedented publicity for Wycliffe. Books, articles and new films. Along with the public endorsement by Billy Graham, all were used by the Holy Spirit to draw several hundred bright and dedicated university and Bible college-trained young people, as well as others from business and industry, into the Wycliffe and SIL family.

In September, Billy Graham advertised the *Reader's Digest* article on two of his Hour of Decision radio programs. And on "young people's night" at a San Francisco rally, Billy Graham urged his audience to consider Wycliffe as a way to serve God through Bible translation.

In December of 1959, the book *Two Thousand Tongues to Go*, written by Ethel Wallis and Mary Bennett about the early history of Wycliffe and SIL became a popular seller. A year earlier, Moody Press had published Eunice Pike's book *Words Wanted..* (Eunice was also at work on a sequel, *Not Alone*, which would be published in 1964.)

In addition, SIL was able to advance into new countries—God was blessing the translation ministry. Many ethnic peoples were, for the first time, coming to faith in Christ, and some, like Dayuma, were being baptized.

On April 15, 1957 Dr. V. Raymond Edman,[2] president of Wheaton College, baptized Dayuma at the Wheaton Evangelical Free Church. In attendance at Dayuma's baptism was Dick Pittman, who sent the following letter to Cam:

> Mr. Robert G. LeTourneau flew Rachel, Dayuma, her infant son Sammy and me up from Fort Smith, Arkansas for the occasion. Sammy was also dedicated at the same time. The parents of Jim Elliot, the mother of Ed McCully, Tom Howard (brother of Elisabeth Elliot) and Reuben Larson of HCJB were present. Tom stood with Sammy for his dedication. The pastor of the Free Church, Wilbur Nelson (Marge Saint's pastor), and the Wheaton College Chaplain, Evan Nash also took part. Although Dayuma had never seen a baptism by immersion before, she participated with wonderful poise, joy and cooperation. Most of the Wheaton Wycliffe community [in the area] was present. Rachel, Dayuma and Sammy then flew to Philadelphia on Thursday.

After Dayuma's baptism, Elisabeth Elliot reflected on the impact the gospel had had among the community of Aucas responsible for the killing of the five missionaries in 1956. She wrote:

> How did this come to be? Only the God who made the iron to swim, who caused the sun to stand still, in whose hand is the breath of every living thing—only *this* God, who is *our* God could have done it.[3]

In April of 1957, Ben Elson, the director of SIL in Mexico, took a month-long trip to southern Mexico with his wife Adelle to see what God was doing among approximately 50,000 Tzeltal believers, where Marianna Slocum and Florence Gerdel worked. In the space of nineteen years, Marianna had translated two New Testaments, one for the Highland Tzeltals (thirteen years) and the other for the Lowland Tzeltals (six years). During this relatively short period of time, a people notorious for their open killing, hostility to outsiders, frequent drunkenness, and rampant disease and poverty had been transformed. They had become a community full of pride, with schools and productive cornfields, with over three hundred churches and chapels, and eighty clinics. (Florence, who was a registered nurse, trained more than thirty paramedical workers, some of whom acted as itinerant medical workers to remote clinics.) Ben Elson reported that the highlight of his trip was attending a Tzeltal Sunday church service:

> We went from the clinic where we were staying to the church building across the valley. As we walked we could see Tzeltals coming along the trails from all directions. Some had left before sun-up to arrive on time. Once inside the church, we were invited to sit on the raised platform. I was amazed to see the benches completely full. People were sitting or standing in the middle aisle. Those who could not find room inside stood outside looking in through the open shutters of the windows. I estimate that it was a congregation of over one thousand people.
>
> The lay preacher for that morning (preaching responsibilities are shared among fourteen elders) read Matthew 13 from the Tzeltal New Testament. The sermon was expository, and when he finished he asked the congregation, "Did that reach your heart?" The crowd

replied that it did, except for one young man who said, "No, it did-
n't reach." The preacher then went over the same point again.

The service began at 10:30 and ended at 12:40. If people began to
get sleepy they stood up to stay awake. After the sermon there was
prayer, during which the congregation knelt.

On December 9, 1957, Mexico's leading news magazine *Tiempo* (Mexico's counterpart to *Time* magazine) featured a photo of Marianna
Slocum on the front cover and carried the story of the amazing social
and spiritual developments taking place among the Tzeltal people in the
highlands of Mexico's southern state of Chiapas. When Ken Pike saw
the magazine, he wrote Cam:

> Once again I shake my head in amazement at the way the Lord has
> guided you completely outside of the range of my own imagina-
> tion. We pray that God will use it for His own glory.[4]

On his trip to Chiapas, Ben Elson was also able to observe the practical
help John Beekman (translator to the Chol people) was providing as a
consultant. John worked with a number of translators who were unsure
about how to make their translations more accurate, less literal and
more idiomatic, reflecting the way a person would actually speak his or
her own language. In a letter to Cam, Ben proposed that Beekman be released from his duties as director of the SIL branch in Guatemala to
spearhead and develop a series of workshops where translators could
be given advanced training in Bible translation techniques and consultant procedures.[5] Ben observed that even seasoned translators in Mexico
were sometimes frustrated about how to handle complicated translation
problems. Said Ben:

> It is clear that our translations into Indian languages will have to
> compete with Spanish and the tremendous prestige that Spanish
> has in most of the Indian communities in Mexico and other Latin
> American countries. This means in order for a translation to be ac-
> cepted and widely used, it must speak the language of the people,
> to the heart of the people.

That memo was perhaps one of the most important of Ben Elson's long and distinguished leadership career as director in Mexico, and later as Executive Vice-President of Wycliffe. Ben's insight set in motion the machinery for the training of translation consultants and the development of translation workshops. These have benefited hundreds of translators worldwide, giving them new tools to produce quality translations. After attending one or more of the Beekman workshops, some translators completely scrapped whatever translations they had done and began from scratch to implement the new techniques. Once freed from his administrative duties in Guatemala, Beekman, who had been part of the team translating the Chol New Testament several years before, devoted his time to developing the translation workshops. One of the many by-products of this new translation department was a series of practical exegetical helps for each book of the New Testament. Among the books resulting from this project was the widely helpful *Translating the Word of God,* by John Beekman and John Callow.

While many newly literate people were enthusiastic about the clarity of the idiomatic translations, Cam and others occasionally received letters like the following, from people outside of SIL and Wycliffe:

> We have worked on the [---] language for over twenty years. And while we appreciate the desire of missionaries to produce a translation easily understood, we are convinced that the colloquial language is not chaste or dignified enough to present the Word of God. We are thankful for the work your group is doing to translate the Word of God into ethnic languages. However, we earnestly hope that Wycliffe will cease to emphasize the use of paraphrase and colloquialism in their translations.

One man who had recently received the Scriptures in his own language was Juan López Mucha. On the occasion of receiving the Tzeltal New Testament for the first time he said:

> Our hearts are happy because today we have received in our own hands the Word of God in our language in order that we may understand it. The Word of God is powerful. It makes the hearts of the people turn in the other direction. It is like a fist and like a fire—very powerful. It makes our hearts upright before the Lord.

The heart of every believer is upright because of it. God is the one who uses the Word to reach our hearts. It is He who makes it remain in our hearts. By the means of the Book of God we know we have eternal life. I want His Word to remain there. I want it to work in my heart and put an end to all evil there. I now have His Word in my hands. I also have it in my heart.

Among the many SIL translators who understood the importance of an idiomatic translation to meaningfully convey the truth of Scripture were Cathie Peeke and Rachel Saint. In February of 1959, Rachel and Dayuma returned to Ecuador after several months of concentrated study in the U.S. and took up residence by the Tiwaeno River, where a group of fifty-six Aucas, mostly from Dayuma's extended family, were living. In an amazing work of the Holy Spirit and through Dayuma's faithful witness, all fifty-six Aucas had affirmed their faith in Jesus Christ. Kimo, one of the Auca men who had been involved in the spearing of the five American missionaries, now a believer, had, with another relative, Dyumi, gathered the Aucas Sunday after Sunday to hear "God's carving" [God's Word]. Kimo told Rachel they had counted the days while she was away from them and said, "On God's day we spoke God's carving." When Rachel expressed amazement at how soon some of Dayuma's family members had believed, Dawa, Kimo's wife, said, "I told you we Aucas would not take a long time to believe. Hearing [God's carving] we believed."[6] After Kimo came to faith in Christ, he said, "Not understanding, we killed your men. We believed them to be cannibals and we were full of fear. It was a mistake. Now we will hear about God."

Yet along with many heartwarming reports and the evident blessing of God on the ministry of SIL and Wycliffe, Cam continued to be harassed by Christians who considered Cam's push for overt publicity an offense to the gospel and to Scripture. One mission worker in Ecuador took exception to the "This is Your Life" program and wrote the following:

Your flair for publicity bothers me. It would seem to me that it has been a dreadfully long time since you have read the words from Matthew, chapter 6:1-4[7] My feeling is that any work of the Lord needs NO publicity before the world.

Later, Cam wrote to Bob Schneider, who had received a copy of the note and said:

> I hope and pray that our critics among the missionaries in Ecuador will begin to show a little more respect for the convictions of others than they have shown toward me. Mexico's great Indian statesman, Benito Juárez said, "Respect for the rights of others is peace."

The blessings Cam was experiencing at this point were often mixed with the pain of sickness and death among some in the Wycliffe family.

In July of 1958 Bob Schneider wrote Cam that one-fourth of the field staff in Ecuador were ill from various disorders. Some seriously ill with hepatitis were evacuated and sent to their homes in the U.S. to rest. Elaine Townsend and others had battled malaria. From Mexico, George Cowan wrote that people in the branch had been hit with "a wave of sickness." Several children had contracted polio. Some of the attacks were described as light, but the disease had left one young girl para-lyzed on one side of her face, another child was confined to a wheel-chair, as was an adult.

From the Philippines came word that SIL member Freeman Hatch had a confirmed case of polio. Years later, Freeman along with his wife, Corine, moved to California, where they worked for many years, he in the finance office and Corine in hospitality at the U.S. Wycliffe head-quarters in Santa Ana. In 1974, when these headquarters moved to Hun-tington Beach, California, Corine and Freeman became host and hostess at the new headquarters. And in June 1999, when Wycliffe's U.S. head-quarters relocated to Orlando, Florida, Corine moved once again to be-come part of the welcoming staff at the new facilities, this time without Freeman, who had died in 1998.

Corine was able to give encouragement to many who had suffered a reversal of health or the loss of a loved one by agreeing with Romans 8:28.[8] Elisabeth Elliot who had experienced the loss of her husband to Auca spears, said:

> We know that what happens [to us] is no accident. God performs all things according to the counsel of His own will. "Thou art wor-thy...for thou wast slain, and hast redeemed us to God by thy

blood out of every kindred and every tongue and people and nation." (Revelation 5:9 KJV).

Notes

1   In 1957 Billy Graham became an active member of the Board of Directors for Wycliffe.
2   Dr. Edman, himself a former missionary to Ecuador, spoke both Spanish and Quichua.
3   Elisabeth Elliot, *Through Gates of Splendor* (Wheaton, Illinois, Living Books, Tyndale House Publishers, 1981), 265 ff.
4   On July 17, 2003 Jim Heneveld of the Chiapas mission of the Reformed Church of America, in consultation with Florence Gerdel of SIL wrote the following:

> Through the translation of the Tzeltal New Testament, initially made by SIL [translator Marianna Slocum] and the work of the Holy Spirit plus the work of the National Presbyterian Church of Mexico and missionaries of the Reformed Church of America (who are soon to finish the Tzeltal Old Testament) there are today between 400 to 500 Tzeltal congregations. These congregations are served by about 60 ordained pastors. It is estimated that there are approxmenty 60,000 believers. Lay preachers and elders, many of whom have had Bible School training, are serving many of the congregations. Additionally there are an estimated 50 paramedics, including a number of trained Tzeltal dentists.

5   See Hugh Steven, *Man with the Noisy Heart, The John Beekman Story* (Chicago: Moody Press, 1979).
6   "Be careful not to do your acts of righteousness before men to be seen by them. If you do you will have no reward from your Father in heaven."
7   For more about this remarkable story, see *The Dayuma Story, Life Under Auca Spears* by Ethel Emily Wallis (New York: Harper & Brothers, 1960) and James and Marti Hefley, *Unstilled Voices, A Look*

Back at the Auca Massacre and the Lives it Touched and Changed (New York: Christian Herald Books, 1981). This book deals with the polio virus that invaded the Tiwaeno group, the Aucas' crises of faith and the outpouring of support and practical help from U.S. physicians and nurses.

8   "And we know that in all things God works for the good of those who love him, who have been called according to his purposes."

Chapter Eighteen

Our Purpose is Always to Help, Never to Hinder.

On December 1, 1959, the president of Wycliffe, George Cowan, had the responsibility to notify the missions of the Interdenominational Foreign Missions Fellowship of North America (IFMA) that as of February 1, 1960 Wycliffe would no longer be a member of that organization. Part of George's letter read:

> Whereas, it has become increasingly apparent that some of our God-given [mission] methods are the cause of misunderstanding with some of the board [members] of the IFMA, we of the board of the Wycliffe Bible Translators, Inc., hereby tender the resignation of our organization from the IFMA to become effective February 1, 1960. This action is taken after considerable heart-searching and prayer.
>
> We want to assure you that we hope to be able to serve you both at home and abroad as in the past and to experience the same cordial fellowship in the Lord's work, even though it has seemed best to withdraw from membership in the IFMA. With warm Christian greetings.

The words "considerable heart-searching and prayer" were the appropriate words for George to use; they reflected the deepest feelings of Cam, the Wycliffe board and many SIL members in taking an action that saddened them. But after more than four years of heavy correspondence, numerous face-to-face discussions, and even a visit by the president of IFMA to Peru to investigate SIL's mission methods, the Wycliffe board decided it was in the best interest of Christian harmony to withdraw its membership.

The IFMA had challenged Wycliffe's right to be a member as early as 1956 when there was a change of IFMA leadership. In October of that year Dr. Philip (Phil) Grossman, Wycliffe's Northeast Regional Home Director[1] along with several other SIL members, served as official delegates to the IFMA's annual meeting held at Grace Chapel in Philadelphia. One of Phil's responsibilities was to be part of a panel discussing the topic, "Aviation and Missions." In his report to Cam, Phil said:

> The first question put to me was, "What should pilots do about carrying priests in their planes?" I answered by giving some of the Scriptural and practical reasons, which I had used before from your mimeographed material. I then added, "The weapons of our warfare are not carnal" (such as boycotting individual priests who may be in need of our practical help). The Bible leaves no choice but to do good in practical ways to all without regard to race or religion.

In 1958 Harold Key, SIL's field director for Bolivia took part in yet another IFMA conference meeting, this time in La Paz, Bolivia. In his address to the conference, Key, like Phil Grossman, underscored SIL and Wycliffe's intention and desire to work together in a spirit of love and collaboration with all mission agencies. Key said, in part:

> Please consider that we will make every effort to advance the unity of the spirit and solidarity of purpose for the glory of our Lord and the spread of His Word. Since I have a military background, allow me to use a military metaphor to illustrate my point. In the army soldiers are supposed to shoot only at the enemy and not at each other. In battle the infantry does not fire at the engineers or the supply troops. Instead they are thankful to have these other classes of troops around. There are only three kinds of soldiers who fire at

their fellow troops: those that are ignorant of the location and identification of the others, those that fire as a result of their own care-
lessness and ignorance and those who are traitors to their own
cause. I feel, therefore, that we should take every possible step to
remove any of the above qualities from our spiritual battlefield.

None of us here wishes to hamper the Lord's service done by
others. Failure to understand the motives of another mission
should cause us at least to refrain from criticizing them, since this
not only nullifies our own value on the mission field, but it may
mislead some faithful supporters at home who depend on us as individuals to give an accurate report of our work.

We in Wycliffe are fully persuaded that each mission has its own
particular assignment and purpose given by God. We each have
different objectives, just as different types of troops have various
objectives assigned to them. This too behooves us not to speak de-
rogatorily of other missions or to belittle their efforts, either before
nationals among whom they work or the prayer warriors at home.
For those missions who feel called to work in Spanish, we feel no
competition or spirit of resentment. For those who feel called to
work with Indian languages, we feel only a spirit of companionship
and a desire for mutual aid and support on problems held in common. Our purpose is always to help, never to hinder.

A year later, in January of 1959, Jack Percy, IFMA's president, flew to
SIL's jungle base at Yarinachocha, Peru. His mission was to investigate
the "innumerable criticisms current in the U.S. and Canada as to
whether the Wycliffe program qualifies them as a member of a missionary fellowship." The charges against Wycliffe and SIL included "aiding
and abetting false teachers and [being] guilty of unscriptural mission
policies." As Jack Percy prepared to leave after his four-day visit, he admitted to Cam and Elaine that it is "easier to criticize from a distance of
8,000 miles than it is when one is actually present on the field." However, in a report to the Wycliffe board in April, 1959, Cam said:

Brother Percy has not written to me or anyone else as far as I know,
since his visit in January. However, he did tell a friend of ours
sometime after he had returned to the States that he thought the
best solution to the problem would be for Wycliffe to withdraw its

membership from the IFMA. Furthermore, I don't like the name "Interdenominational." We are <u>un</u>denominational rather than <u>inter</u>denominational.

More than twenty years ago Mr. Legters told one of our severest critics, "Brother, you are at perfect liberty to do your job the way you think best. Go ahead and demonstrate that your methods are best. Until you do, however, we are going to continue on with the methods we believe God has given us." If we canvassed the majority of the IFMA member organizations I am confident they would support us. In the meantime let's not be guilty of causing a controversy or an embarrassment to the IFMA. Since we realize we can't convince our critics of our mission policies and since our position is always to help and never to hinder, let's withdraw peacefully without ill will and let's do it without delay. We can help whatever mission group asks for our help just as well from outside the IFMA as from the inside, and we will be happy to do so.

Behind Cam's request to the board for Wycliffe to withdraw voluntarily from the IFMA was his knowledge that the IFMA members might vote to exclude Wycliffe. Cam knew that such an action would not be in the best interest of Wycliffe's public image on the homefront. But not everyone on the Wycliffe board was in agreement with Cam's request for withdrawal. Ken Watters said, "Cutting ourselves off from our evangelical brethren would send the wrong message to our constituency." Board member Ben Elson wrote Cam to say he wasn't in favor of withdrawal. To withdraw, argued Ben, would confirm to the IFMA member organizations that the charge against Wycliffe that its members would not associate with other evangelicals on the field was true. Wrote Ben:

> Not all evangelicals agree on all doctrinal points and I cannot see why it isn't possible for us to agree to disagree and still have fellowship within the IFMA organization. If they wish to expel us, then it would be them withdrawing from fellowship with us. I think we should give consideration to the fact that many within our organization are from churches that are affiliated with the IFMA and our withdrawal would cause us to make more [defensive] explanations.

In spite of Ben Elson's cogent argument in favor of retaining membership within the IFMA, the Wycliffe board on November 18, 1959 took the following action:

Moved that, with deep regret, Wycliffe Bible Translators, Inc. withdraw its membership with the IFMA in view of the statements made by the IFMA leadership to the board at Racine, Wisconsin on October 2, 1959 that the IFMA leaders could not endorse the policies and practices of the Wycliffe Bible Translators as explained in our letter of September 16, 1959. This action is taken after prayerful and extended consideration of the discussions had with the IFMA leadership over a period of the past 14 months.

As Ben Elson predicted, there were indeed a number of churches and institutions in the U.S. and Canada that sent letters to Cam like the following: "How can we as an institute officially endorse that of which the IFMA must conscientiously have no part?"

Another letter came from the pastor of a church in Maryland inquiring as to Cam's stand on "modernism and the new evangelical movement." The letter asked the question:

> Would you support in any way an evangelistic campaign, such as those conducted by the Billy Graham Evangelistic Association, that include modernistic churches and have liberals on the committees and leading in prayer? Do you earnestly contend for the faith, which was once delivered unto the saints?

As Ben Elson also predicted, Cam and others spent many hours writing letters to their constituents explaining why Wycliffe had withdrawn from the IFMA. George Cowan was asked to answer other critics:

> The IFMA leadership was not unanimous in its decision to ask for Wycliffe's withdrawal. I spoke with several IFMA mission leaders privately and they expressed their unhappiness at the outcome.

On May 11, 1960, in another letter, George Cowan wrote the following:

> From our mission statement you will see that that our policy with regard to "enemies" has been arrived at and carried out in a sincere desire to obey our Lord and the Scriptures. We do not claim perfec-

tion or infallibility for ourselves in our understanding of God's Word or in our policies. But we do believe God has led us through the years and has singularly blessed our efforts to love our enemies and to further the Gospel among the ...people who have never before heard of Christ or had His Word in their own tongue. It has been a matter of deepest concern to us that some have misunderstood our motives, maligned our leaders, misrepresented our actions, and sought even to turn others of our Christian brethren against us. I am sure you [Brother Maxwell] would not want us to change our policies against our conscience, and our understanding of the Scriptures, and the historic evidence that God has led us in our ministry.

In a letter from the Cicero Bible Church in Chicago, dated May 23, 1960, pastor William Currie wrote:

I am sorry to see the stand Wycliffe Bible Translators has taken in recent days to leave the IFMA. Personally, Brother Townsend, I rather question some of your mission's practices. However, I am not called upon to answer for you, or to judge your position. I do recognize, however, that because of the recent actions taken you have placed many of us on the spot when it comes to continued support of Wycliffe Bible Translators. Many of us feel strongly against certain issues and practices you embrace, which we regard to be incompatible with the Gospel. However, just as you have certain convictions, I do too. I dare not move against my convictions any more than I would expect you to move against yours.

What many of Cam's detractors did not understand or appreciate was that after dealing with hundreds of foreign officials, diplomats, and dozens of Latin American presidents, after forty years of service in Latin America, Cam knew that to antagonize or in any way threaten a host government's valued institutions, could result in a closed door for future ministry. Cam's *modus operandi* was a quiet and indirect, but engaged diplomacy. This was a strategy Cam had learned as a young Bible salesman in Guatemala when he, along with a fellow missionary from a different mission witnessed a plantation overseer beating and mistreating an Indian worker. When Cam's missionary companion challenged the overseer, the overseer beat the Indian all the harder and ordered the missionary off the plantation. Cam, on the other hand, stood by with head bowed and prayed silently for the Indian man. Afterward Cam went to the Indian and gave what comfort and psychological support he could. Because Cam hadn't challenged or antagonized the overseer, Cam was always allowed to speak and minister to the large group of Indian workers on the plantation.[2]

Cam chose the route of quiet or indirect diplomacy rather than overt denunciation or deliberate ostracism of persons of different faith or creed. Though some American and Canadian pastors and others took exception to Cam's desire to "light a candle rather than curse the darkness," this in no way deterred him from following his vision and policies. Cam understood that to "recompense evil for evil" (Romans 12:17) besides being contrary to the will of God, is an ineffective diplomatic instrument. Cam's prayer for his adversaries was that God would bring about a change of heart from the inside out.

It should be noted that Cam's non-polemical attitude should not be mistaken for silent passivity. Cam was far from silent about social injustices and inequities.

In a paper entitled "Wycliffe's Essential Sidelines," Cam set out his thinking on social action activities that, at first glance, did not seem directly related to Bible translation. In Mexico City on March 21, 1960 Cam addressed a group of first-term members and said:

> You simply cannot close your eyes to a bleeding wound or a starving child when you are in a position to help. One of our translators took time out from his translation work to help the people he worked with to use the hydraulic power of the river to grind their wheat, saw their lumber and light their homes. The project robbed him of time working on the language, but when the local priest ordered the Indian people to expel the translator from the village, they refused, citing the practical service he had been to them.
>
> In 1935 I spent considerable time and money raising a garden in the public square in the Mexican village of Tetelcingo. We ate and enjoyed some of the vegetables, but financially it was a flop. However, through that garden the president of Mexico, having heard of "a strange gringo" living and planting a garden in a hot, dusty Mexican village, came to see me. The results of that visit were

priceless. I called it "the sermon of the garden."[3] Later I wrote a biography of that president [Cárdenas]. It took a great deal of my
time, and a lot of effort by a number of people who helped me. Fi-
nancially it was a failure, but God used that book to procure vital
assistance from another president, Magsaysay, for our program in
the Philippines.

Cam could also have mentioned that many years before he had written
an anthropologically significant novel called *Tolo, The Volcano's Son*, set
in Guatemala in the late twenties and early thirties. It was an attempt to
acquaint the American public with the culture of the ethnic peoples in
Central America.

Even as Cam challenged the new members to be open to serving their
communities in practical ways, he was fully aware of the real and potential persecution from the religious authorities in Latin America. The
attitude of many in the traditional ecclesiastical system was that Scripture translation into indigenous languages was unnecessary. "The only
thing the unlearned require," said one religious authority "is to know
the catechism and a few prayers." Cam, of course, had an opposing
view. He believed in Martin Luther's dictum, "The salvation of the soul
depends on each individual's ability to read God's Word for himself or
herself." Cam also believed that biblical literacy would strengthen the
bonds of a national society. At the same time, he believed that being
kind in practical ways to his religious opponents would build friendships, lessen friction and in fact undermine the opponents' strategy to
discredit SIL's ministry. In Cam's words, "kindness pours water on their
gunpowder."

In his paper "Wycliffe's Essential Sidelines," presented to the new recruits in Mexico City on March 21, Cam concluded his remarks with a
strong affirmation of the important "ministry of hospitality" and the vital contributions of support workers on the field and in the homeland.
When Cam spoke of *support personnel* he was referring to home-as-
signed workers in regional and corporate offices, as well as those on the
field, like medical personnel, teachers, pilots, accountants, buyers, writ-
ers, printers, graphic designers, editors, mechanics, and assistants. Each
of these are team members contributing to the overall goal of Bible
translation.[4] Said Cam:

Wycliffe and SIL have a great need for support personnel. Other organizations might call them technical, medical or agricultural missionaries. But Wycliffe isn't quite as generous in using such terminology. But since I am one of the support personnel I don't object to the term. In fact I praise God for every member of my support personnel team! I have yet to see a field where there were enough support people to take care of the odds and ends that support people have to do to keep the field [translator] and home offices running smoothly.

Support personnel have the high responsibility of laying the tracks for the translation train. I have grieved to see translators taken from their allocations to do the work that a support person might do because there wasn't a support worker to fill in the gap.

I doubt if we would be in Peru today if it weren't for the people who visited us on the field. Enemies lied about us, but the people who came to visit us saw through the lies and on their own were convinced of the value of our work. Many returned to their hometowns and cities to defend and support us. The more people came to see us, the more we realized the truth of Hebrews 13:2, that there were indeed "angels" among them. Let us never be too busy to show visitors and tourists warm hospitality with real joy. Our so-called "sidelines" ministry has contributed enormously to the great advance of our work over these past twenty-five years.

Finally, let's thank God for our critics. Besides giving us free publicity, this experience has been a valuable means of grace. Through the letters and personal visits from friends and supporters, we have realized more fully our utter dependence on our wonderful Lord. Remember, even though our methods and practices are as old as Joseph and Daniel, our critics' look upon them with suspicion. Nevertheless our responsibility before God is to love each other, critics included, as brothers and sisters in the Lord. Our task is always to help, never to hinder.

Notes

1   Phil Grossman later became Associate Secretary of Wycliffe Bible Translators.

2   See Hugh Steven, *A Thousand Trails, Personal Journal of William Cameron Townsend, 1917-1919 Founder of Wycliffe Bible Translators* (White Rock, BC: Credo Publishing Corporation).

3   See Hugh Steven, *Doorway to the World, The Mexico Years, The Memoirs of W. Cameron Townsend 1934-1947* (Wheaton, Illinois: Harold Shaw, Publisher 1999), 51 ff.

4   One support team not mentioned in Cam's list were the now vital computer programmers and technicians. In 1960 no one in Wycliffe had a computer. At this writing, it would be safe to say no one in Wycliffe or SIL is *without* a computer.

Chapter Nineteen

What Mean These Stones?

Cameron Townsend loved to celebrate special occasions. Birthdays, anniversaries, national holidays and promotions were an excuse to have a party (always with cherry pie), and picnics and special dinners to entertain friends and diplomats were regular occurrences in the Townsend household. And when Cam visited an SIL field branch, a special banquet, lunch or dinner for dignitaries always seemed to be part of the agenda, in addition to many private get-togethers with SIL members.

In commemoration of the first Camp Wycliffe, held in 1934, and as a way to honor SIL and Wycliffe's early history, Cam and the board planned a nationwide celebration of twenty-five years of God's faithfulness beginning in Sulphur Springs, Arkansas. Held in September of 1959, after Wycliffe's biennial conference and with Billy Graham (Wycliffe's newest board member) in attendance, the opening of the celebration included a prayer of dedication at the unveiling of a stone memorial. The text on a bronze plaque embedded in the monument began with a phrase from Joshua 4:21: "What Mean These Stones?" with the following words:

These stones from the foundation of the farmhouse where the first Summer Institute of Linguistics (Camp Wycliffe) was held June to

September 1934 stand here as a memorial to God's faithfulness. From that small beginning with nail kegs from Tom Haywood's hardware store for chairs, board bunks for beds and only two young men as students have come the five Summer Institutes of Linguistics now held on three continents training hundreds of pioneers each year in how to learn unwritten languages and give them the Bible. From that beginning came also Wycliffe Bible Translators, a sister organization that has sent translators to 200 Bibleless tribes already and plans to produce or help other missionary organizations to produce God's Word in every language on the face of the earth. As this rock memorial is raised in September 1959 we gratefully say: "Hitherto hath God helped us." He will enable us to finish the task He gave us.

When reporting this event to family and friends, Cam noted that Billy Graham took the opportunity to hold a mini-rally in a local Sulphur Springs park where, said Cam, "Over 5,000 rural folk came to hear Billy preach. More than one hundred came forward to accept Christ as Savior." Cam's letters were also full of optimism for Wycliffe's future. To inaugurate the twenty-five-year anniversary, Cam sent letters to the membership and constituents that said in part:[1]

We now know the task we face is much larger than it appeared to be twenty-five years ago. How are we going to meet the challenge before us? By faith alone. It was by faith that L.L. Legters and I crossed the border into Mexico [on November 11, 1933] and it was by faith that we began our first summer linguistic school in 1934 in an abandoned farmhouse in the Ozark hills of Arkansas.[2] We began in a modest way to train consecrated, pioneer-hearted young people how to tackle the job of reducing unwritten languages to writing in order to translate the Scriptures into those languages. The audacity of the vision of reaching all the unwritten language groups of earth with the Word of God seemed matched only by the insignificance of the farmhouse quarters, the small enrollment [two students, Ed Sywulka and Richmond McKinney][3] and the unlikely staff. But God has honored faith. And today as the Summer Institute of Linguistics and Wycliffe Bible Translators, Inc. prepare to celebrate the silver jubilee of the organizations' beginnings, thousands of pioneer missionaries who have profited from the linguistic courses are working in many parts of the world with some fifty different denominations and faith-mission groups.

In this twenty-fifth year of remembrance our hope and expectation continue to be in God alone. Of course, we must be true to the proven methods God gave us. But along with them, and far beyond them, we are utterly dependent upon His miracle-working power, His love and His Holy Spirit. As we sing "Faith Mighty Faith" in this anniversary year, we must realize that in the next twenty-five years the Word of God must be taken to ten times as many ethnic groups as we have reached during the past twenty-five. We realize, too, that there are still many, many barriers to overcome. However, we have tasted of God's faithfulness and power and are not frightened by the obstacles that face us. We dare to sing again with the utmost confidence of the mighty faith that laughs at impossibilities and shouts, *"It shall be done!"*[4]

Officially, the twenty-fifth anniversary began on September 15, 1959 with the dedication of the historical stone monument in Sulphur Springs. It was to conclude on September 15, 1960. In the meantime, throughout the entire year a series of special public meetings were held in different parts of the U.S. and Canada. Cam proposed a series of roundtable discussions to be held across the U.S. for pastors and Christian leaders. The discussions would both challenge a new generation of young people and clarify the biblical mandate and responsibility of the church to be involved in mission, specifically in Bible translation.

At the University of Oklahoma, there were to be special lectures, with Ken Pike presenting his famous monolingual demonstration of learning a language by gestures. Ken scheduled several of these demonstrations throughout the country, including one at an InterVarsity meeting at Columbia University in New York. Said Cam of these events:

I want this anniversary celebration to serve as a means of quickening the whole church to complete her task. But with the celebration must come a new understanding of how world mission is accomplished. It's not enough for the mission enterprise to be more *prolific*; it must also be more *effective*.

Cam was calling for "experienced pioneer leaders" to participate in what he called "the year of challenge." The challenge was to freshen up Wycliffe's policies and fit them into the context of the changing social and political realities that missionaries would face in the next twenty-five years. Wrote Cam:

> It's my desire that competent workers be brought home from the different fields who are skilled in a variety of mission specialties such as Bible translation, literacy, medicine, aviation, radio, the establishment of indigenous churches, etc., who will demonstrate how each of these activities contributes to reaching Bibleless peoples in isolated areas of the world.

In addition to reaffirming the biblical and theological character of world mision, Cam called the church to pray for the unfinished task of Bible translation. On the bottom of Wycliffe's official twenty-five-year stationery were the signatures of thirteen widely-known Christian leaders who had covenanted with Cam and the Wycliffe family to pray for "those engaged in pioneer Bible translation." The signatures included those of Billy Graham, Dr. Charles Fuller (founder of the Old Fashioned Revival Hour), Dr. Oswald J. Smith (pastor of People's Church, Toronto), Dr. Harold Ockenga (pastor of Park Street Church, Boston), and Dr. V. Raymond Edman (president of Wheaton College).

One of Cam's ongoing prayers was that the Bible translation task would be completed "in this generation." Cam had never lost the burning vision born years before when his imagination had been challenged during his days as a student at Occidental College where he came under the influence of the Student Volunteer Movement. The rallying cry of the SVM, under the leadership of John R. Mott was "Evangelization of the World in This Generation." This was the phrase Cam used to conclude his letters during the year of challenge. Cam knew, of course, that reaching such a goal would require a large number of new workers. As he had done for the previous twenty-five years, Cam prayed for God to give the increase, and asked God to add six thousand more young people to the Wycliffe team by 1975.

The reality of prayer, and the way God chooses to answer the longing of our hearts is that he answers according to his own will and purpose. Cam's prayer had been, and would continue to be audacious and full of expectant faith. After all, Cam had seen SIL and Wycliffe grow from two students in 1934 to over eleven hundred workers in ten countries by 1961. Cam would live to see the group grow to over twenty-five hundred workers in twenty-three countries by 1982. He would also live to see a translation team enter the five-hundredth people group by that same year.

However, he would not live long enough to see the prayer of reaching every tribe in his generation answered. On Friday April 23, 1982, at six PM, William Cameron Townsend entered into the presence of the Lord he had loved and served for over half a century.

Wycliffe's statistics note that in 1999 the membership stood at a little over five thousand. By 2003, Wycliffe's membership was over six thousand.

But we are getting ahead of Cam's story. In 1960, Cam was just sixty-four years old and God still had many more important things for him to accomplish before he would be called home at age eighty-five. As one would expect during an anniversary celebration, there were opportunities to tell light-hearted stories about the "good old days." One such anecdote appeared in a letter by Cam to Clarence Hall, senior editor of *Reader's Digest.* Cam wrote Hall to try to interest him in writing a feature article on Ken Pike. In the letter, Cam extolled Ken's many outstanding contributions to the world of linguistics and academia and the important part he played in the development of SIL. Cam said in part:

> Dr. Kenneth Pike doesn't look very rugged. He was turned down by the China Inland Mission in 1934. However, he can stand more hard work than most anyone I know. Nevertheless, when he came to our little linguistic course in the Ozark hills in 1935, I had to see to it that he got an afternoon nap or else he would fall asleep in class.

Ken Pike was known for his sharp, acerbic wit, but he always demonstrated deeply felt love and concern for his colleagues. As area director for the Asia-South Pacific region, Dick Pittman's administrative load was heavy and often stressful. This resulted in frequent low-grade headaches. Aware of Dick's problem, Ken wrote him a letter which offers a glimpse of Ken's concern for his friend's physical and spiritual well-being:

I know you have enormous responsibilities for the Pacific area. I well remember Mr. Townsend under similar pressures. In 1935 in Tetelcingo he was having almost constant headaches. To counter these he had me read Bloomfield [a 564-page treatise titled *Language*] aloud to him to soothe his nerves while he drank cups of coffee to keep awake. (He liked me to read to him also, because, by his own admission, he was a slow reader.) The pressures of responsibility exact their price, sometimes pretty high, and sometimes with physical consequences.

I well know how easy it is to cast one's burden on the Lord and yet be unable to relax in such a way as to allow the old physical body to be normal. The Apostle Paul didn't do so well in this area. Again and again he referred to constant pain and anguish and the daily concern he had for the churches. It seems to me that Paul's life and responsibility parallel these that you and Uncle Cameron have had to bear.

All of this does not say however, that medical men cannot help us in such times. I myself cannot concur in the judgment that physical or nervous tension under falling bombs is not a sign that a person lacks spiritual trust. My prayer for you is that you can find a *competent*, understanding physician to whom you can talk and to whom the Lord will give wisdom to help you.

At the special anniversary year banquets and various meetings, younger members would occasionally ask Cam about his early experiences in Guatemala and how L.L. Legters came to be part of SIL. Others wanted to know when and how Bible translation became his passion. At the conclusion of these banquets, which also honored his forty-two years of mission service, Cam related the following abbreviated history of his call into cross-cultural ministry. He began by relating how he and his companion, Robbie Robertson, left San Francisco by steamer in September 1917. Said Cam:

It took us two weeks to arrive at Puerto José in Guatemala. The voyage was slow since the steamer stopped at all the ports along the way. A week after our arrival we attended a Bible conference in Antigua and were introduced as colporteurs. At the time I had never led anyone to Christ. I wanted to, and had read books on how to do personal evangelism. I had tried to lead the Pershing Square derelicts in Los Angeles to Christ, but I just couldn't do it. Now here I was beginning to be a colporteur in Guatemala and I had never led a single person to Christ. One summer I had tried to sell magazines. I may have gotten a few subscriptions from people who took pity on me, but I was never a good salesman.

At the Antigua conference the missionaries would all go out every afternoon and speak to people about the Lord. Reluctantly (I didn't want anyone to see my discomfort) I got some tracts and walked around town until I saw a man on the sidewalk. With trembling knees I went up to him, but then turned away. I tried a second time, but I just couldn't talk to him. I turned aside and walked down the street. I then saw a young man about my own age. At the time I didn't realize that the Spanish word for "Lord" is the same as "mister", nor did I know every tenth person is named "Jesús." I spoke to the young man and said, "Conoce usted el Señor Jesús? [Do you know the Lord Jesus?] The young man said, "You know, I am a stranger here too, I don't know him." That was too much for me! I went back to the little chapel where Robbie and I had been assigned a room above the stable. I got down on my knees and said, "Well, God, if ever there was a failure, it is me, right now. I have come 2,750 miles to tell people about the Lord Jesus Christ and can't do it."[5]

Cam continued with stories about his early days in Guatemala and how he began working among the Cakchiquel people and eventually translated the Cakchiquel New Testament. To the surprise of many in the room, Cam said he first requested to work among the Spanish-speaking population rather than with Indian peoples. Said Cam:

At first I struggled hard as a colporteur [Bible salesman] because I had such a low opinion of my selling ability. But then the Lord began to bless my efforts. Once in Honduras I sold forty-six New Testaments and sixteen gospels all in one day and my confidence began to improve.

Mr. Bishop under whom we worked had given Robbie and me a choice of two locations. He said, "To the west are the Indians. To the east are the non-Indian Spanish-speaking people." Robbie was interested in the Indians. I wasn't and so I went east. With me on these walking trips through Guatemala, El Salvador and Honduras was Francisco (Frisco) Díaz, a Cakchiquel [who spoke quite a bit of Spanish] man from whom I learned a great deal. As we traveled and worked together Frisco would tell me stories about his people. He said, "There are over 200,000 in my tribe, and they are held in virtual slavery under the domination of witchcraft and superstition. Why don't you come and work among my people?" This kind of conversation went on for nine months or longer, until one day I said, "All right, Francisco, I will go."[6]

In order to work among Cakchiquels I had to submit my resignation to my mission. When my co-workers learned about my decision they said I was doing a foolish thing and said the idea of translating the New Testament for the Cakchiquel people had no value.

In spite of the opposition I was determined to work among the Cakchiquels. To my delight the mission board in the States backed my decision to do a translation, but my co-workers were so upset that it almost split up the mission. If it hadn't been for the grace of God and our wonderful Lord I would never have completed the translation.

Speaking of God's grace, Cam told briefly how SIL was born and spoke of the vital part L.L. Legters played in getting the school started:

I first heard Mr. Legters in 1920 when he came to Guatemala and spoke at our first Bible conference. I was greatly impressed with his powerful message and energetic presentation. In 1926 Legters, as field secretary for the Pioneer Mission Agency whose job it was "to find men and money for missions," took an extended survey trip to the upper Xingu River region of Brazil.[7] When Legters returned from that trip and told stories about the ...Indians he had seen and showed me the pictures he had taken, my heart burned within me to reach out to these people. At the time I wasn't thinking of reaching all of the different tribes, I was thinking of only one. In the meantime my health broke and I came home to Southern California to recuperate from tuberculosis. In 1933 Legters came to visit me in California and we talked about the tribes in Brazil and how we might reach them with the gospel. However, this was during the Depression and no one had any money. As we talked Mr. Legters suggested that since the tribes in Brazil were isolated and expensive to reach I should choose a closer country like Mexico. I said, "Good. I will cooperate with you, if you will cooperate with me in starting a linguistic training school for missionaries. And to get them started we should begin with a short summer course in linguistics." And he said "All right." And that was that, no formal signing of papers or drawing up of a contract, just a gentleman's agreement to help in this new venture.

When I told Mr. Legters we had to begin with a short summer course in linguistics, I tried to prepare myself by reading all the books I could find on linguistics. The old books however, weren't very helpful, but at least I learned a little and was able to pass on to the students what I had learned. This was the beginning of what is now the Summer Institute of Linguistics (SIL), which we began in June of 1934 with two students in the Ozark hills.

Since that first summer of linguistic training in 1934, the growing SIL team has worked in more than 1,100 languages in sixty countries. Nearly six hundred language groups now have the completed New Testament. Wycliffe, and its partners have an enormous task ahead of them. At least 6,800 languages are spoken throughout the earth, and only 2,303 of these have even a portion of God's Word.

In 1967, the significance of the worldwide Bible translation task prompted the U.S. Senate and House of Representatives to designate September 30 as "Bible Translation Day," and to invite communities in America to observe the day with appropriate ceremonies. The words of John Wycliffe, the man who first translated the whole Bible from Latin into English (c.1328-1384) spoken six hundred years ago continue to be a powerful motive for the ever-growing number of Wycliffe translators: "Christ and his apostles taught in the tongue that was most known to the people. Why shouldn't men [and women] do so now?"

Notes

1   See Hugh Steven, *Wycliffe in the Making, The Memoirs of W. Cameron Townsend, 1920-1933* (Wheaton, Illinois: Harold Shaw, 1995), 253 ff.

2   In some of the Wycliffe editorials and official articles celebrating the twenty-fifth anniversary were references to a rent-free parcel of land called Breezy Point on Happy Valley Farm. In April of 1958 Cam wrote the Wycliffe Extension Department responsible for Wycliffe's PR with the following clarification about Happy Valley Farm: "Happy Valley was not the name of the little farm where we began our courses. It was the home of Loren and Laura Jones who offered us the use of their barn for a classroom if we couldn't find any place else. We only went to Happy Valley Farm to go swimming. Laura Jones also made the most delicious oatmeal cookies."

3   The following year, 1935, there were five students at "Camp Wycliffe." These were Brainerd Legters, Bill Sedat, Richmond McKinney, Max Lathrop and Ken Pike. In 1959, Cam sent out invitations for each of them to attend and participate in the special historical marker "rededication" ceremony in Sulphur Springs.

4   In the year 2003, SIL's website stated that it offers training for applied linguistics at a variety of institutions around the world. These included three SILs in the U.S., and one each in Canada, the UK, Germany, Latin America, Australia and New Zealand, and Japan. Course topics include phonetics, phonology, grammar, language learning, linguistic field methods, cultural anthropology, socio-linguistics, translation, and language planning.

5   For a complete history of Cameron Townsend's early life in Guatemala as a colporteur, see Hugh Steven, *A Thousand Trails, Personal Journal of William Cameron Townsend, 1917-1919* (White Rock, British Columbia, Credo Publishing Corporation).

6   This report differs slightly from Cam's earlier diary account, as recorded in *A Thousand Trails*, 200. There, Cam acknowledged the many conversations he had with Frisco and told of a specific moment when they were camped on a mountain ridge. Cam wrote, "When I

observed the Indians in El Salvador and Honduras and saw how they suffered less oppression and had more freedom than the Indians in Guatemala, my heart burned within me for Guatemala's suffering people. And when I saw how quickly Frisco learned and how eager he was to follow the Lord and do His will, and how many latent possibilities there are in him and his people, I am stirred even further to recognize the [spiritual] need among the Cakchiquel people. I have come to realize that it is imperative that people be reached with the gospel in this generation with the message of salvation. God has given me youthful vigor, faith and a challenge. Therefore, I have decided to devote my life to the evangelization of the Indian peoples." Cam then added that after he had said, "All right, I will go," Frisco, of course is gladdened to realize that his companion has come to this decision. "This made the rest of the trip so much lighter as we talked over plans for the future of our work."

In a January 20, 1919 letter to his parents Cam wrote, " As soon as possible, I want to have parts of the Scripture and the catechism translated into Cakchiquel (at present they have no written language except Spanish, which the majority understand but poorly). It is going to be very difficult to thoroughly evangelize the people without utilizing their own language."

7   For the story of Legters' trip to Brazil, see, Hugh Steven, *Wycliffe in the Making, The Memoirs of W. Cameron Townsend, 1920-1933*, (Wheaton, Illinois: Harold Shaw Publishers, 1995), 181 ff.

Dr. Kenneth L. Pike, former SIL director, was known for his sense of theater when lecturing potential Bible translators on the complexities of analyzing an unwritten language.

Chapter Twenty

Passing the Buck

The celebration of the twenty-fifth anniversary year of the founding of SIL ended appropriately. Cameron Townsend was honored in Mexico City on Tuesday, January 24, 1961, at a special banquet where he was presented with a *festschrift*. This 700-page commemorative volume of linguistic studies was edited by a committee of Mexican and American scholars, and represented sixty-one authors from North and South America, the Philippines,[1] France and Vietnam. In a letter to her parents Elaine Townsend wrote:

> From beginning to end the banquet was a time of great rejoicing as we remembered the faithfulness of our Lord and the wonderful co-operation of our Mexican friends as well as friends from other lands. There were ten countries represented, over two hundred distinguished guests and at least five ambassadors with their wives. There were also a dozen or more different Indian tribes represented. While making his speech, Dr. Jaime Torres Bodet, the [Mexican] Minister of Education, was so moved that his voice broke and many of us had difficulty holding back the tears. Cam ended his speech by quoting John 3:16[2] and telling the distinguished guests that if it hadn't been for our wonderful Lord and His faithfulness,

we could never have accomplished as much as we had during these past twenty-five years.

Telegrams and letters of congratulations added an extra dimension to the anniversary celebration. In view of some negative publicity after Wycliffe's withdrawal from the IFMA, the letter Cam received from Clyde Taylor, IFMA'S Executive Secretary, was of particular encouragement:

> We have appreciated the scholarship and the excellent work done by Wycliffe and the Summer Institute of Linguistics to reduce so many [unwritten] languages to writing and making the Scriptures available to those who have never had such in their own language.

Professor Dell Hymes of Harvard University said: "It is my belief that the work of the Summer Institute is perhaps the single most important contribution to the needs of linguistic science today."

And Billy Graham wrote: "Wycliffe Bible Translators are engaged in one of the most spectacular and important ministries in the world today. Never have so few contributed so much."

Wycliffe's twenty-fifth anniversary year was notable for more than just honorary banquets. After twenty-five years of spartan living conditions in overcrowed apartments in a converted hotel in downtown Mexico City, the Mexico branch of SIL was granted the use of five acres of prime land in Tlalpan on the outskirts of Mexico City. There they would build their new and enlarged headquarters.

To pastor Charles Blair of Calvary Temple in Denver, Colorado, Cam wrote:

> The [Mexican] Ministry of Education has given us a grant of land [five acres] for our new buildings. This will not only save us a great deal of money, the granting of land to our organization will also put the government's stamp of approval on our ministry.[3]

From his correspondence, pubic speaking, chapel talks and private conversations, one would have to conclude that Cam could be characterized as the absolute idealist. Cam, a man of remarkable vision, always saw his programs and ideas, and even the people he met, not as they were at a particular moment but as what they might become. So Cam's letter of January 13, 1960 to Dr. Oscar Vásquez Benavides, the Peruvian ambassador to Mexico is unusual for its note of concern about the future. It is unknown whether Cam was beginning to sense the stirrings of the deep social upheavals about to erupt in the sixties and seventies. Phrases like like "flower children," "hippies," "psychedelic drugs," "Civil Rights," and "student protests over Vietnam" were to become part of the historic fabric and lexicon of the sixties. It was a decade that would greatly alter American social and political structure. Without knowing what was yet to come, Cam's remarks to his friend Oscar seem to be the voice of a realist and a prophet:

> At dinner on New Year's Day with some of our mutual friends, General and Mrs. Cárdenas, Dr. and Mrs. Gamio, Dr. and Mrs. Juan Comas, wonderful friends all, asked me what I thought of the world situation, and if I thought we were heading for peace. I said peace might prevail for twenty years or so, but that sooner or later someone for some motive will most certainly set off a bomb that will ignite a terrible conflagration. In spite of this certain possibility, I said that all is not lost. The Bible teaches that some day the Lord Jesus Christ, the Prince of Peace, will return to earth and put an end to all injustices. In fact, I said, this is the urgency of our Bible translation task, namely, to hasten the return of Jesus Christ by making the Scriptures available to all those who have not heard of Christ's substitutionary death and resurrection for them.

Just as the sixties pulsated with youthful energy and marked new beginnings in America's cultural, political and social life, so were there new stirrings within Wycliffe and SIL. For almost half a century, Cam's folksy casual manner had been part of his leadership style. Those who joined the group in the thirties, forties and early fifties had had personal contact with him. They knew him to be a leader who was humble, approachable, caring and godly.

The early membership knew Cam wanted to inspire and foster within their lives and personalities a right relationship with God and a willing, authentic spirit of service through SIL's ministry. Furthermore, Cam believed that he and the group leadership ought to be mentors of every person God brought into the group. Not all directors had the capacity or inclination to follow Cam's nurturing lead. But most knew in times of stress or uncertainty there was an "uncle" who would listen, who loved and valued them, who sometimes acted on their behalf even before they sought his counsel, and who showed by example what selfless servanthood looked like. The essence of Cameron Townsend was that he treated people with care, dignity and respect and made everyone feel like an equal. He never talked down to people or made them feel inferior. He listened carefully and did not interrupt or speak until others were finished speaking. Nor did he underestimate the place of friendship in human affairs. It was these qualities and his servant-leadership style that resulted in the members' great affection for him. These were also some of the reasons for Wycliffe's and SIL's unique growth and the *esprit de corps* that many experienced in the early days of the organization.

But by the sixties, a growing number of new members, including some field directors from countries like Papua New Guinea, Vietnam, and other South Pacific and Asian countries, as well as the expanding British and European Wycliffe leadership, had never personally met the general director. In many ways, Cam had become a legend in his own time. His moral authority and the group's commitment to five core values—pioneering, translation procedures, the linguistic approach, service, and trust in God, were still in place.

At the same time, a growing number of mission strategists outside the group, and some within the group, began to challenge some time-honored SIL and Wycliffe policies (while still respecting the group's core values). Some of these challenges resulted in productive rethinking about how to apply Wycliffe principles in a complex and changing world. Some of this rethinking resulted in refocusing on different parts of the world. Latin America, of course, had been Cam's major interest. But the decades of the sixties and seventies would see Wycliffe and SIL responding to new challenges from Africa, Asia, the South Pacific, and Europe.

The demand for Bible translation was enormous. To meet these new challenges, many of the members were calling for greater connection with, and support from, the national churches. They also sought for nationals to be more actively involved in the translation process. Arthur Glasser, Home Director of Overseas Missionary Fellowship (OMF) wrote an editorial [May 1961] in which he stated,

It is both physically impossible and demonstrably unscriptural that missionaries from the West be responsible to evangelize all the people of this generation throughout all the world. The evangelization of the world is the task of the whole church throughout the world. No church attains fullness and maturity without participation to some degree in the missionary purpose of God.

At the same time, many leaders in SIL and Wycliffe were grappling with the effects and implications of the fundamental shift within modern Western culture toward a postmodern worldview.

In many third-world countries there was rising nationalism and reaction against American internationalism, which made the securing of visas more difficult for SIL workers. Many governments were unwilling to allow expatriate mission workers into their countries unless they were highly credentialed. In some countries a master's degree was often a necessary condition for granting a visa. Furthermore, many governments wanted their own people trained in linguistics and Bible translation procedures. They also wanted SIL to be in a position of accountability, and for translators to work under the authority of a recognized government agency. Cam, of course, had long advocated accountability to host governments. He had also urged each field director to form a sponsoring committee of national leaders, educators, and scholars to speak on SIL's behalf and to offer advice and guidance through what were sometimes political minefields.

In response to many of these major cultural shifts and the need to develop "flexible" approaches to new forms of Christian community, the 1973 International Conference of Wycliffe International and SIL cleared the way for the formation of National Bible Translation Organizations (NBTOs), which would share responsibility for first-time translations. The stimulus for founding an NBTO would come from SIL and Wycliffe but the NBTO would work under existing national church councils. These councils would promote and oversee translation and literacy work. Many SIL translators would shift from the traditional single-team approach to occupy roles as facilitators and trainers of nationals who, under the care and sponsorship of the church, would do translation with the help of SIL translation consultants.[4]

Cam, however, sometimes wondered if the Western church had abdicated its responsibility to be the the major provider of translated Scriptures for the world's ethnic minorities, and a failure to do this was, in his words, "passing the buck." In a published prayer that reads like a soliloquy, we see Cam's state of mind as he struggled to incorporate this new paradigm into his thinking:

> Lord, is the day of expatriates doing pioneer Bible translation work past? Are we, the Christians of the United States and the West, to declare our independence of the command, "Go ye into all the world and preach the gospel to every creature?" Are we to give as an excuse the anti-foreign attitude of countries that refuse to grant visas to missionaries? Are we to look to Him who told us to "Go!" and say, Lord, although it's true that there are many languages without the Bible in such-and-such country, the government won't let foreign missionaries in. Since we can't go, we have decided to give linguistic training to nationals and expect them to translate the Scriptures into those many, many languages. Please, Lord, don't think we have decided to "pass the buck." "Let the nationals do it," really makes sense. The reality is that if they can get adequate training, they can do a better job than we can. Of course, we have always worked with the [nationals]. We wouldn't have gotten to first base without their help. Now, however, we'll leave them to work alone while we seek financial help for them and provide a certain amount of training and consultant help. But please, Lord, we aren't "passing the buck."

Cam's prayer went on for several more paragraphs as he recalled how he had worked within the system during the early days of rising nationalism in Mexico. He spoke about how, through strong identification with the country's interests and ethnic peoples, he and the early SIL workers were accepted. He also confessed that he felt many newer SIL members had not identified themselves with the national culture and were, in fact, guilty of paternalism. If such was true, he asked God's forgiveness. Cam ended his prayer with:

> Lord, when I said we need to identify with the [national peoples], I also meant we should identify with the country's minister of education and other government agencies and officials that are responsible for our work. If we don't make frequent visits to these agencies

and treat them as true friends, they have every right to be suspicious of us. In the meantime, Lord, we will, by your grace, identify ourselves with the nationals wherever we go. Then you can continue to use dedicated people of every nationality.[5] In this way, we will not be guilty of "passing the buck."

Cam wrote to his constituents, in July of 1960, that the twenty-fifth anniversary year had far exceeded his expectations and that in spite of continuing criticisms from some who considered him to have "departed from accepted missionary policy," enrollment in the SIL schools was at an all-time high. Cam said he expected to welcome two hundred new recruits in 1961. He added, "We are well on the way to reaching our goal of six thousand members in the next twenty years." Cam also reported that JAARS had twenty-six planes servicing SIL personnel in Peru, Bolivia, Ecuador, the Philippines and Alaska. Brazil and Papua New Guinea would have JAARS service in 1961. There was also a new JAARS training and screening center being built on 256 acres of land (donated by Henderson and Anne Belk) in Waxhaw, North Carolina. And on July 30, 1961, the newly-built Wycliffe U.S. Headquarters were dedicated in Huntington Beach, California.[6]

Another major achievement at the conclusion of 1960 was the dedication of the Totonac New Testament, done by the translation team of Herman and Bessie Aschmann. Herman's co-translator was a young Totonac man named Manuel Arenas.[7]

There was a bittersweet sidebar to one of Cam's 1960 letters, telling of his longtime friend and colleague, Mr. William G. Nyman, who, due to failing health, resigned as Secretary-Treasurer on July 1. On that same day, Kenneth Watters succeeded the man who had guided the organization through the financial and structural shoals of growth. Mr. Nyman was indeed one of the unsung heroes of Wycliffe's early development. Six months later on January 10, 1961, William G. Nyman's heart failed, and he entered the presence of the Lord whom he had loved and served faithfully all his adult life. When Cam learned of his dear friend's death, he remarked that, besides being a faithful personal friend, Mr. Nyman had been a friend to all of the Wycliffe family. Cam said that the Bible translation movement had surpassed all expectations, in large part because of Mr. Nyman's wise counsel and acute financial skills. In a written tribute, Cam said:

In 1942, when I challenged Mr. Nyman to organize our business headquarters and become our secretary-treasurer, a post he occupied without salary for eighteen years, he wrote out his own mission statement. "First, last and always, I am prayerfully anxious that the Bible translation movement continue its God-given task of giving the Bible to every man in his own language. And to this end I am ready and willing to do all I can to further this effort until the job is done...."

In a strange way Mr. Nyman's ill health prepared him for the task God had planned for him. After his first heart attack, the doctors urged him to give up his lumber business in Chicago. When he did, he was then free to give his undivided attention to carrying Wycliffe's main administrative load in the homeland [aided at first by his two daughters Mary Ann Mooney and Eleanor Witt, who ran the little Wycliffe office over the Nyman garage].[8] Mr. Nyman began with forty-six pioneer missionaries in 1942. That number increased to over 1,000 at the time of his death.[9]

Mr. Nyman was a genius at handling the finances of our rapidly expanding organization. The rules of the group required that all donations go directly to the member on the field unless otherwise designated. The members then returned five percent to the home office and five percent to the field offices to take care of overhead and publicity, etc. Our rules also said we could not incur debt, thus there was very little provision for advertising and deputation expenses. With his hands thus tied, Mr. Nyman used his knees in prayer and business experience to keep us solvent. In amazing ways, money came in so that new workers could be sent to the field, and year after year our overhead for running Wycliffe's home office was seven percent of its total annual budget. One human feature about our steady income had to do with Mr. Nyman's gift for writing letters to donors. Every member appreciated this service and in turn the letters inspired the donors to give again even though there was never a hint of begging for money in his letters. Furthermore, every letter was different and personalized. He never used a form letter.

For most men of mature experience there is often a reluctance to change to new ways of doing things. Not so with Mr. Nyman. In most cases he was more than willing to adjust to new methods.

There was one issue, however, on which he conformed only out of loyalty to me. The issue was over the establishment of our own jungle aviation and radio service, JAARS. After two agonizing years in the Amazon jungle, I was convinced we needed our own air service. When it came to a vote by the board, he, together with most of our leaders, was at first strongly opposed to taking on this heavy responsibility. However, in the face of strong opposition from most of our leaders, Mr. Nyman cast the deciding vote in favor of establishing JAARS. Today JAARS is serving our translators in six countries. Two million passenger miles are flown a year, mostly where there are no other safe and efficient means of transportation. As the years passed and we saw the way God was using JAARS in so many different ways of ministering to our own people and others, it gave Mr. Nyman great joy to know that he had had a pivotal part in bringing JAARS into existence.

Notes

1   In recognition of SIL's fifty years of humanitarian and spiritual service to the Philippines and its ethnic peoples, the Philippine government, in 2003, issued a special edition of twelve commemorative postage stamps.

2   Cam made it a practice at all official banquets to give God credit for any success Wycliffe or SIL had. He was also faithful in reading or quoting a relevant passage from the Bible. It was Cam's intention and prayer that these references to Scripture would in some small way trigger a spiritual awakening in the hearts and minds of his guests. Cam's critics sometimes accused him of using such ceremonies to grandstand and "bring glory" to SIL. In a 1965 memo on Field Policy, Cam wrote: "God knows our hearts. The last thing we want is to bring glory to ourselves. What we do want is for the host government to help expedite our work. We also want the government to feel that we are in partnership with them, that they have a part in all we are doing. We don't want the government to accuse us of being in competition with their aims for the country. Ceremonies and banquets give us the opportunity (often with press coverage when a cabinet officer or president attends), to explain our program with tangible evidence that we are living up to our contractual agreement. Such ceremonies not

only build friendships, they help keep the doors open in countries that are hostile to expatriate mission work."

 Dick Pittman once said, "The best way to accomplish Bible translation is to be on the right side of the authorities [in the countries] where it needs to be done."

3   Dick Pittman would later write Cam to tell him he was doing the right thing by getting the government to grant SIL property for a limited time. He reminded Cam of a conversation he once had with a former missionary to China who warned him not to own property on the mission field, the reason being that ownership of property by foreigners continues to be interpreted in many countries as a lingering form of imperialism. Dick said further, "One feature that commends us to our host countries is that SIL is obviously not trying to carve out a real estate empire in the countries where we serve."

4   George Cowan, president emeritus of Wycliffe offered the following clarification of "the new paradigm" in how Bible translation was to be done in the 21st century. "The translator in a pioneer situation where there are no believers is usually an expatriate (non-mother-tongue speaker) who has learned the target language and is working with a speaker of that language as a co-translator. Where churches already exist the translator is preferably a mother-tongue speaker of the target language, assisted by an [SIL] consultant trained in linguistics and biblical exegesis."

5   By 1990, there were six NBTOs in Africa, four in Asia and two in South America.

6   These headquarters were relocated to Orlando, Florida in July 1999.

7   See Hugh Steven *Manuel* (Old Tappan, New Jersey: Fleming H. Revell Company Publishers, 1970), and Hugh Steven, *Manuel, the Continuing Story* (Langley, B.C: Credo Publishers Corporation, 1987).

8   Bill Nyman Jr. and his wife Marjory were involved as SIL translators in Mexico, and were later assigned to a variety of public relations ministries.

9   As of January 2003, there were 6422 members from thirty-four Wycliffe organizations working in sixty countries. Some of these were retired members, many of whom were still actively involved in a part-time Wycliffe ministry.

Chapter Twenty-One

If We Don't Start in the Face of Impossibilities, When Do We Start?

To the ancient Hebrews, the number seven symbolized completeness. Proverbs 9:1 speaks of the seven pillars of wisdom. In second Kings 5:14 Naaman was told by the prophet Elisha to dip in the River Jordan seven times as an act of faith to cure his leprosy. On the seventh day of marching around the city of Jericho seven times, seven priests of Israel blew their rams-horn trumpets and the walls of Jericho collapsed (Joshua 6). And God rested on the seventh day of His creation and "made that day holy" (Genesis 2:3).

On February 24, 1962, Cameron Townsend sent a handwritten letter to the Wycliffe Board, informing them that after seven diplomatic trips to Colombia, the Lord had, in his marvelous way, answered a long-standing prayer:

> A contract has been signed by the Minister of Government, the Director of Indian Affairs, the Director of the Colombian Indian Institute and myself (representing SIL) to begin work in the more than

130 ethnic minority languages of Colombia. We will work in a territory that was turned over to the Vatican by a concordat (an agreement with the Pope). Amazingly we are the first non-Catholics ever
to have been permitted to work in that area. SIL's contract, therefore, includes a clause stating that we will *respect* the concordat between the Vatican and Colombia. I foresee no problem about
respecting the concordat since I believe our attitude of love and
practical service will pave the way for a greater use of the Scriptures in the vernacular.

However, the papal nuncio (the pope's representative) was more
than a little disturbed about our contract, mostly because the government hadn't consulted him before the contract was signed.
When I visited him, he was at first stern and unfriendly. But when I
assured him that his workers among the Indians and our SIL workers would be of mutual assistance his attitude changed and he became friendly. When I left, he did something rarely done by a papal
nuncio—he accompanied me clear to the sidewalk and waved
goodbye. Of course, I was delighted and greatly relieved by his attitude, as was the Director of Indian Affairs. Later, when I visited the
U.S. Embassy, the man next in command to the American ambassador told me the nuncio has a reputation of being terribly stern. He
said we should consider ourselves very fortunate. And, of course,
we are "fortunate," and we give all praise to the Lord. *The Lord has
indeed done great things whereof we are glad.* At the same time, we
know the challenges in Colombia will be bigger and more complex
than the ones we faced when we started in Mexico. I am confident
however, that God will see us through until all the tribes in Colombia have received his Word.

Yours to finish the task,
Uncle Cam

Cam and Elaine began yet again to pioneer. This time in the field of Colombia. They set a target date to leave Peru in July of 1963. One must
conclude that Cam's strategic vision was central to this diplomatic
breakthrough. As early as 1953 Cam, Ken Pike, Bob Schneider and others had been praying and taking small steps toward establishing an SIL
presence in Colombia. In 1957 Cam and Elaine went to Bogotá (one of
seven trips by Cam) to work out a tentative agreement with officials in

the Anthropological Institute. The Minister of Education, however, rejected the agreement. And thus began a series of talks with functionaries of various departments of the Colombian government. In 1959, at the
Fourth Inter-American Congress held in Guatemala City, the head of the
Department of Indian Affairs, Dr. Gregorio Hernández de Alba, who
was familiar with Ken Pike's many published works, expressed openly
his desire for SIL to work in his country. Acting on this positive response, Cam asked Rosa Corpancho, a longtime Peruvian friend and
political insider, to open a dialogue between SIL and the Colombian
government. However, the official who met with Rosa said that because
of the concordat, a contract between Colombia and SIL would be impossible.

Throughout his distinguished career as a mission statesman,
Cameron Townsend had been confronted with many strategic "impossibilities." But over time, as God proved faithful, the word "impossible"
left his vocabulary. For over two decades, Cam's prayers and vision had
focused on Colombia, and "impossible" did not fit into his vision. Besides, as Ken Pike once said, "If we don't start in the face of impossibilities, when do we start?" The question remained, however—when *should*
they start in Colombia?

The answer to that question came in October of 1961. Cam, still at
Yarinacocha, Peru, received a midnight phone call from Harold Goodall
in Charlotte, North Carolina. Harold told Cam the Colombian ambassador was attending a trade fair in Charlotte and would be spending that
weekend with Cam's longtime friends, Henderson and Anne Belk. Cam
spent a fitful night wondering if the Lord had planned this unusual development to pave the way for SIL's entrance into Colombia. Said Cam
in a later report:

> The next morning after Harold's call I talked the matter over with
> Marianna Slocum and Florence Gerdel, both of whom had been
> praying for over a year about taking a new assignment in Colom-
> bia. As we prayed about these new developments I was impressed
> that I should fly immediately to Charlotte and speak with the am-
> bassador. The following day, Friday, the 13th, I flew to Charlotte,
> arriving just after dark.
>
> When I phoned the Belks' home, Anne told me she had received
> an earlier call from the ambassador's secretary in Washington, D.C.

saying that the plane on which the ambassador and his wife had reservations had been delayed and the ambassador had decided not to go to Charlotte. Anne then explained to the secretary how disappointed everyone would be if he didn't come and urged the ambassador to book another flight. So ably did Anne present her case that the secretary promised to speak to the ambassador.

Anne immediately called the JAARS headquarters in Waxhaw and asked people to pray that the ambassador would make the right decision. Just prior to my call, the ambassador's secretary phoned again saying the ambassador, Sanz de Santa María, and his wife would be arriving a little before midnight.

At 7:30 PM on October 15, while flying from Charlotte to Washington, D.C., Cam wrote Marianna Slocum to tell her that he was at that very moment sitting across the aisle from the Colombian ambassador and his wife. Cam explained that in a conversation on Saturday evening at a banquet given in the guests' honor, the ambassador had said that, in spite of the concordat, he hoped the Cardinal would not oppose an agreement between the Colombian government and SIL. Cam added:

> The ambassador put me in touch with a former Minister of Education, Dr. Betancourt, who just happened to be in Washington attending a special congress. Interestingly, the ambassador told me that though he was a conservative and Dr. Betancourt was a liberal, he esteemed Dr. Betancourt highly.

Cam later reported that he asked Bob Schneider to accompany him to his meeting with Dr. Betancourt, who, said Cam "was favorably impressed with our program and promised to help in any way he could. Later I thought how wonderful that through this unexpected trip the Lord had given us friends in both political parties. God does indeed work in mysterious ways his wonders to perform."

On October 20, Cam again wrote to Marianna and Florence, this time from Bogotá. He wrote that in a single day he had run between a number of government offices, including those of the Director of Indian Affairs, the Ministry of Education and the office of the President. On a second day he visited the office of the Cardinal and the office of the Secretary of the Interior. Said Cam:

The Secretary of the Interior, Dr. Hernández de Alba, was friendly but still looked upon the concordat as an insurmountable obstacle for our spiritual ministry. After he talked for a while, I showed him two letters from Franciscan nuns who had been helped recently by our JAARS airplanes. I told him also of my visit with the Cardinal. Over lunch he said he would make a slight correction in our proposal. He added a paragraph stating that we would be willing to serve the Roman Catholic missionaries in technical matters. This he said will enable the government to defend itself against possible clerical criticism of us.

That evening at 6:25 the president gave Dr. Hernández de Alba and me a careful hearing and then told Dr. Hernández de Alba to prepare a contract and asked how soon we could begin our work. I assured the president we could begin in six months. At that point the president offered us an old army post with a landing strip on the Putumayo River for our base of operations in that part of the jungle. God is faithful!!!![1]

On November 7, 1961, Cam wrote a general letter to the group, in which he recapped many of the items he had written to Marianna, then added the following:

It seems that we are to begin work in Colombia in six months, but how can we do it? We are involved in a variety of new building projects that include the international JAARS headquarters in Waxhaw, the new headquarters building in Mexico City, the translation workshop in Ixmiquilpan, Mexico, as well as new headquarters in Guatemala City. These are just a few of the special projects we all need to be praying about. I am assured by Philippians 2:13, "For it is God which worketh in you both to will and to do..." He will enable us.

Some of you who receive this letter may feel led to help in Colombia. Please write me if you do. However, don't apply unless you are willing to go the extra mile in serving folks of other faiths, particularly monks and nuns. The tribes of Colombia will be reached only by loving service and patient faith in the Word of God. Above all, pray.

Four months later Cam again wrote Marianna Slocum to give her the unsettling news that in spite of the president's blessing and an official contract with Colombia's Department of Indian Affairs, the local padre and regional bishop had petitioned the government of Colombia to cancel SIL's contract. Said Cam:

> This is certainly a call to prayer. In one way it's good that they have done this before we got started. When the government defends its position regarding SIL it will make our position stronger when we actually begin work [in Colombia]. Since the Vatican Council is calling for greater harmony and peace among all brethren (Protestants included) the government should have an easier time defending its action. This will also give us a chance to show love to the padre and the bishop who have signed the petition to keep us out (Romans 8:28).

As Cam predicted, a high-ranking government official insisted the contract be upheld, countering the bishop's objection to SIL's presence in Colombia. This paved the way for the first group of SIL workers to arrive in July 1962.

On July 25, 1963, on the eve of the Townsend family's journey from Peru to Colombia, the Minister of Foreign Affairs, Vice-admiral Luis Edgardo Llosa, honored Cam and Elaine for seventeen years of distinguished service on behalf of Peru's Indian peoples. Both were awarded the insignia of the Peruvian Order of Merit, in the grade of "Comendador." A week before this event took place at the elegant Torre Tagle Palace in Lima, Cam went to the Peruvian city of Ayacucho to accept the honor of being made an Honorary Professor of the University of Huamanga. Cam said that he had great liberty in speaking on linguistics and that he "flavored it with the gospel."

After a fond farewell from many distinguished Peruvian friends and members of SIL in the Peru Branch, Cam, Elaine and their family went by ship to Colombia to continue making vital contacts in Bogotá and the jungle, establishing the work of SIL. In a letter to Jerry Elder and others in Peru written from Bogotá on August 25, 1963, Cam thanked the Peru Branch for the gracious send-off. Cam later wrote he had many opportunities aboard the ship to witness for the Lord. He said he had met five Jesuit seminary students on their way to study in Spain. Said Cam:

The students were very interested in all I had to say. One day they spent three hours with me asking all kinds of wonderful questions. It was I who finally broke away.

The day after Cam wrote that letter, he and his family left Colombia to spend six months of family time in Charlotte. The Henderson Belks offered them the use of their summer home. In January of 1964, the Townsends flew to Bogotá to continue the work there. In the meantime, Cam was involved in a staggering list of new projects. During the years 1962-64, Cam traveled between Mexico, Washington, D.C., New York, North Carolina, Peru, and, of course, Colombia. There were speaking engagements and businessmen's luncheons to attend in the hopes of raising interest and money for the JAARS Center in Waxhaw. There was a new Helio Courier airplane christening ceremony and an endless succession of visits to supporters and to functionaries of foreign governments. In August of 1962, Cam took part in the inauguration of SIL's new Manuel Gamio[2] Linguistic Center at Ixmiquilpan, Mexico. In attendance was a large group of Mexican government officials and academic leaders. On October 1, Cam returned to Mexico City to welcome India's Minister of Foreign Affairs. Sixteen days later he was hosted at a special dinner for twenty-five Peruvian officials at SIL's group house in Lima, Peru.

And high on Cam's agenda of important projects was the New York World's Fair and the construction of a special building to be called the Pavilion of 2,000 Tongues. The fair was to run from April to September of 1964, and during the same months in 1965. Not since the debate over the establishment of JAARS had a project raised so much concern from the Wycliffe board. It would be a costly endeavor, and it resulted in a great deal of tension between Wycliffe's finance officers and those responsible for administering the project. The pavilion would include the great mural "From Savage to Saint" by Douglas Riseborough. The one-hundred-foot mural was a larger-than-life portrayal in graphic detail of the "before" and "after" lives of the headhunting Shapra people of Peru and of the conversion to Christ of Chief Tariri. Cam had hoped to recoup the cost of the mural, the construction of the pavilion, and Wycliffe staff expenses by charging a one-dollar admission fee. Unfortunately Cam overestimated the World's Fair attendees' eagerness to pay to see a mural and listen to a narration.

While the staff represented Wycliffe's ministry with dignity and pro-
fessionalism, the crowds at first bypassed the handsome pavilion when
they discovered there was an entrance fee. It didn't take long before the
fee was dropped and large groups of people began to view the mural.
Nate Waltz, an SIL tour guide, wrote Cam to tell him he calculated the
flow of visitors to the Pavilion of 2000 Tongues to be an average of one
hundred people every fifteen minutes.

One of those who helped develop the pavilion was former Time-Life
photographer Cornell Capa. He had been a friend of Cam's and of SIL's
since the fateful day of January 8, 1956, when Auca spears killed five
missionaries. Cornell had been one of the photographers who joined the
search party and subsequently chronicled the painful hours of the five
wives waiting for news of their husbands.

In 1963, Cornell's work appeared in the book, *Who Brought the Word?*
This was the first in a series of Wycliffe "coffee table books" to have
Cornell's imprimatur on them. The second book, *Language and Faith,*
published in 1972 was a joint photographic venture between Cornell
and various Wycliffe and SIL photographers. Cornell was also the still
photographer and producer of the Wycliffe film, *Now God Speaks
Tzeltal.*[3]

In order to give himself greater freedom to develop high-level public
relations projects and new advances, Cam asked the board to name a
deputy or deputies to relieve him of the many SIL and Wycliffe internal
administrative duties. In 1964, the board appointed Dr. Benjamin (Ben)
Elson as the first Deputy General Director for North America. George
Cowan, president of Wycliffe, was appointed Deputy General Director
for Europe and Africa, and Dick Pittman assumed the same position for
Asia and the South Pacific. Ken Pike declined the title of Deputy General Director for Academic Affairs since, as president of SIL, he already
had responsibility for academic affairs. These were the first steps toward a major reorganization and restructuring of Wycliffe Bible Translators.[4] Cam had lobbied hard for over four years to get the board to
create these positions. These appointments and restructuring changes
would, as Cam hoped, permanently change his responsibilities as general director.

By 1964, the home offices and the SIL branches were functioning as
Cam had envisioned, with their own duly elected directors and executive committees in each field branch. For many years, Cam's watchword

had been "direction of the field on the field," or "SIL on the field, and Wycliffe at home."

In the mid-sixties, the board began to examine the whole organizational structure of Wycliffe and also to deal seriously with the inevitable time when Cam would no longer have the energy to function as general director. As a first major step, the board requested help from Spencer Bower, a business management consultant who, after examining Wycliffe's organizational structure recommended that a position of executive vice-president be established. The board accepted the Bower report and in May, 1966 Ben Elson became the first executive vice-president for Wycliffe (a post he held through 1975.)

In 1971, in a further administrative change, the board accepted the recommendation by a special steering committee that there not only be an executive VP, but also vice-presidents for finance, development, operations, academics (and a year later) personnel. In his December, 1995 paper on a "Brief History of the Development of the Organization," Ben wrote:

> The system of vice-presidents was put into effect in the early seventies. When I first assumed responsibility as home office director, the main function of that office was to receive and receipt funds for the members and forward such funds to the field. Other responsibilities included the promotion of Bible translation work through literature [film] and deputation. [It was assumed] the branches could handle their own affairs. But many of the smaller, distant branches wanted more help than they were getting from headquarters. This concern resulted in an expanded international administration, WBTI, whose role was to be coordinating, responding, and supporting rather than directing. Work was still to be done primarily through the branches.

The implications of these new policy and reorganizational changes would have a direct impact on Cam. On Tuesday, May 25, 1967, he met with the Wycliffe board to discuss agenda item #4. Under debate was the issue of whether the office of general director had become an anachronism—whether there was a need for his successor to be chosen.

Notes

1   The government later gave SIL 250 acres of land on a lake just off the Ariare River, near the little town of Lleras.

2   This new linguistic workshop center was named in honor of Cam's longtime friend, the distinguished Mexican anthropologist, Dr. Manuel Gamio.

3   The third book, *Pass the Word* published in 1984, was produced exclusively by Wycliffe and SIL personnel, as was the fourth book in this series, *The Alphabet Makers* published in 1990. The fifth book, *Any Given Day in the Life of the Bible*, was published in 1992.

4   The need for such reorganization became apparent as the group grew larger. When people began to join from countries other than the U.S., they became members of SIL and Wycliffe USA. But in order to receipt funds properly in other countries, legal organizations were needed. Therefore people became members of their own legally organized Wycliffe organization and of Wycliffe, Inc. (USA).

At first, the board called these organizations "divisions." This meant each home country would have a separate Wycliffe office and that Wycliffe, Inc. USA would become an equal partner. When this idea was finally accepted the (USA) board wanted the then-already incorporated Wycliffe to be its legal organization, and a new Wycliffe International was formed, to which all members joined.

In 1991, the reorganization continued with an internal name change, i.e., from divisions to Wycliffe Organizations (WOs)— a grouping of legally organized distinct entities, each with its own board.

Chapter Twenty-Two

After this, the Harvest

Cam was not pleased. On Monday, May 22, 1967, he gave a progress report to the board that was well received. However, the issue of the position of general director was still on the table and had not been resolved. Part of his May 22nd report covered the status of Wycliffe's World's Fair exhibit in New York. He then made it clear he was unhappy over the Bower management consultant report. He believed the report leaned too heavily toward a centralized government. Cam had vigorously opposed the idea of board members who lived in the States issuing orders and giving direction to people on the field without first-hand information. "Field-directed" was a principle he had championed ever since his first days in Guatemala, when his mission board required him to ride four days on horseback to ask a senior missionary for permission to spend fifty dollars.

Cam was also unhappy because the board had neglected to consult him on any of the issues covered in the Bower report. But mostly, Cam argued for the board to continue the office of general director.

The following day, Tuesday May 23, Cam again addressed the board's agenda item #4. Said Cam:

When the Bower study was made I wasn't consulted on any of the matters. It seems strange to me that when the issues of reorganization within the family are contemplated that the "daddy" of the family is not consulted. Let me say that I consider the post of general director to be most important. You all know I have been against the build-up of bureaucracy. At the same time, I know our executives and other officers are absolutely essential for the smooth running of the organization. Where would we be without a treasurer? Each of our executive officers carries an extremely heavy load. They should not be expected to have the additional burdens of vision strategy, policy, advancement to new fields, plus the heavy loads of personnel diplomacy and public relations.

Just consider the millions of pages of free publicity the group has gained as a result of the vision of the general director. We would not have had the worldwide coverage of the Tariri story, the World's Fair or the building [in Tlalpan, Mexico City] we are now in, or the movie, *Now God Speaks Tzeltal*. Nor would we have received the many other government concessions that required patience, vision and perseverance. I beg you to go very slowly with your decision to do away with the post of general director. Please experiment for at least two years before coming to a decision. In the meantime, I beg you to consider Dick Pittman as my successor. He is a godly, dedicated man who thoroughly understands our Wycliffe policies.

After Cam excused himself from the meeting to attend to other matters, Dick Pittman said he really did not seek or want the job of general director, should the board consider continuing that post; then he, too, excused himself from the meeting. In the discussion that followed, Ken Pike said that many of the statements just made were "dangerous half-truths":

When the general director said he did such and such, that was true, but it is only half-true. The other part is that it was *the founder* that did what he did. Uncle Cam is both our general director and the *founder*, a position that will forever be unique. That is the full truth.

Bus Dawson agreed with Ken and said:

We are dealing with two kinds of authority. There is legislative authority that belongs to the executive director. And there is respect or moral authority which belongs to Uncle Cam and which he will retain whether or not he holds the office of general director. [I don't think anyone else can hold that office.]

The board took Cam's advice to move slowly on this matter and waited until 1971 to make their final decision to change Cam's title. In Cam's letter dated June 5, 1971, written from Waxhaw, where he and Elaine then lived and where he would live out the remainder of his life, he wrote Earl Miller about his retirement plans:

I missed the board meeting when they held the elections. But I don't think my voice would have helped very much. The board also turned down Dick Pittman in spite of my strong recommendation for his continuance on the board. The board wants younger men, like David Cummings of Australia. This past May, the Lord led me to retire from the post of general director [I am now known simply as the founder], and thus I no longer hold an executive post in SIL or Wycliffe. Among my reasons for retiring at this time are that I need to concentrate on learning Russian and getting a Bible translation program started in the Caucasus. This I know seems impossible, "but God..."[1]

In May of 1971, at the opening session of the SIL corporation conference, Cam gave his last report as general director in the form of a final charge to the membership and to the board. He began by giving great praise to the Lord for the way the group had grown, but said that the goal SIL had set for itself in 1934 of reaching five hundred people groups in a generation had not yet been achieved. Cam acknowledged that, in 1971, they knew a great deal more about the needs for worldwide Bible translation than he knew in 1934. "Instead of five hundred people groups needing a translation, we now know that there are over 2,000," he said.

Cam was also thankful for new organizations and sectors of the church that had in recent years come alongside Wycliffe to form partnerships in the translation task: groups like the Lutheran Bible Translation Society, Evangel Bible Translators, Wycliffe Associates, World

Home Bible League and others. Cam, of course, did not fail to mention the people staffing Wycliffe's home and regional offices. Cam also saluted the many thousands who had supported and prayed for the work of Wycliffe over the years.

He reminded the board of Wycliffe's long-standing policy of not incurring debt when considering new building projects. He praised a number of people who he felt were doing outstanding linguistic work in difficult places. And he singled out Marianna Slocum, Esther Matteson, Herman Aschmann, and others who had moved on to do a second and even a third translation project. Cam said, "My hat's off to these and others who keep on pioneering." Cam cautioned the board not to be blinded by the "forest of bureaucratic detail," which he said would impede progress. On the question of who would succeed him, Cam again asked the board to continue the office of general director and appoint Dick Pittman to that position.[2] Then Cam said:

> God has been good to us. He has led us into our unusual policies [and core values]. Let's be true to them. People who do not accept our polices or are offended by them should not join us. Those within the group who can't accept such policies should resign and thereby avoid jeopardizing our position, as regards working in "closed countries." God will raise up substitutes for them. Let's forge ahead till every tribe has heard God's Word in their own language.
>
> To do this involves close adherence to our five basic points:
> 1. The linguistic approach.
> 2. The Bible first, last and always.
> 3. Non-sectarianism (within the Christian framework).
> 4. Service to *all* without regard to race, color or religion.
> 5. A faith that takes God at His Word and forges ahead wherever there are Bibleless tribes regardless of barriers.
>
> In closing, I wish to express the gratitude Elaine and I feel toward you all for the special way you have [in so many different ways] shown your love toward us.
>
> God has been marvelously good to me in giving me Elaine and giving us your fellowship. God bless you. Great things lie ahead. I look forward with expectation to the time when every tribe will have heard in its own tongue the life-giving Word. And then, if not

before, we shall behold, and lo a great multitude which no man can number, of all...tongues...shall cry with a loud voice, salvation to our God (Revelation 7:9).

Yours in Ephesians 3:20, 21,
Uncle Cam Townsend

The 1971 conference and the Board of Directors received Cam's report and his decision to step down as general director with deep gratitude. It then passed the following resolution:

In view of the great debt the organization owes to Dr. William Cameron Townsend for the vision for Bible translation work he imparted to us, for the love he has shown in leading us over the years, and for the wise and courageous policies he has taught us, and because of our deep love and esteem for him, it is moved that we ask Dr. Townsend to allow us to refer to him as our "founder and general director emeritus."

Over the years, Cam received hundreds of letters from members who expressed their love and appreciation for his love, leadership and extraordinary vision. One letter, from Linder and Mae Tanksley, early Wycliffe and SIL members who served in the Mexico Branch, encapsulates most exactly the essence of Cameron Townsend the man, the mission statesman, the visionary, the friend, and the faithful follower of Jesus Christ. The letter was actually written in 1957 when the group honored Cam for forty years of mission service (1917-1957). The sentiments the Tanksleys expressed in 1957 are timeless and speak for all who knew and loved William Cameron Townsend:

Faith Mighty Faith
Without the faith and vision that laughs at impossibilities there would never have been a Wycliffe [or an SIL or JAARS]. But we know the Lord was leading and training you forty years ago when you made your first trip south of the border.

And because you made that first trip, and many others since, the rest of us have been able to make our "first trips" and follow in your footsteps.

Wherever we go we know that "Uncle Cam" has been there first, if not in person, at least in spirit and in prayer. We thank you, Uncle Cam, for the example you have set for us and may the Lord grant you many more years of service for Him.

When Cameron Townsend died of acute leukemia on April 23, 1982, a great company of people came to the JAARS center where his body was laid to rest in Waxhaw, North Carolina to pay him their last tribute. His tombstone reads:

Dear Ones: by love serve one another. Finish the task. Translate the Scriptures into every language. Uncle Cam

The evening after the funeral (or his "coronation," as Elaine prefers to call it), family, friends and colleagues met together to give their personal remembrances of Uncle Cam. It was especially moving to hear the four Townsend children recount their memories of Cam as a loving, caring father. I was there and said, among several things, that Uncle Cam had taught me by example a theology of friendship. I recalled a conversation I had with him in February of 1982, which I discovered later was something he had shared in March of 1971 with a gathering of SIL directors and Wycliffe leaders:

I wish all our people would be very careful when dealing with friends or others who at times criticize us. When we are criticized, it is vital that we deal with them in love. We must never forget how important it is to show kindness, forgiveness and honor to those who oppose us. Rather than repay evil for evil, invite such people to your table for a meal. And perhaps you can even send them a birthday cake.

Let me say further that you must take time to be with people, take time to visit them. We will always have more work than we have time to do. But this must not excuse us from being with people you are trying to win for Christ or with professional colleagues outside the group. When such people come into your life, don't preach at them; learn to become their friend, learn to listen to them and learn to take an interest in the things they are interested in. And when the time comes when you have an opportunity that is natural and unforced to share your testimony, they will listen to you because you won't be preaching. You will just be talking together as friends. I urge you not to forget this.

This book now ends, as all books must, but the story does not end. The story of William Cameron Townsend, of Wycliffe Bible Translators, of the Summer Institute of Linguistics and of JAARS will continue because Cam and the three principal organizations he founded are all greater than the sum of their parts. Elisabeth Elliot reminds us all of this reality when she writes:

> Death is not the end of the story. Jesus showed us this on the cross. It was evidenced there in "the grain of wheat" that death is not the end. As in all cycles of nature the grain must die, then the harvest results.

> *After this I looked and there before me was a great multitude that no one could count, from every nation, tribe, people and language, standing before the throne and in front of the Lamb.* Revelation 7: 9a.

Notes

1   From October 1968 to March 1969, Cam and Elaine made the first of eleven trips to what was then the USSR. Between his first and third trip, Cam wrote a highly acclaimed book on the merits of bilingual education in the USSR, called, *They Found a Common Language.* During their third trip, April 17 to June 28, 1972, Cam and Elaine spent time with many linguists and educators distributing his new book. They were also invited to 107 private homes for meals. As was his custom, Cam always read his favorite Scripture verses from 1 John 4:7-15.

2   Dick Pittman was used of God to help open eight countries for SIL work. They were the Philippines, Nepal, India, Papua New Guinea, Indonesia, Australia, Cambodia and Vietnam.

On September 21, 1959 Billy Graham [left], new Wycliffe board member, spoke to the group as he and Uncle Cam dedicated a plaque commemorating 25 years since the first Camp Wycliffe courses were held at Breeze Point, Sulphur Springs, Arkansas.

Afterword
Jubilee and Coronation

In 1952 Cam and Elaine Townsend celebrated an Easter sunrise service with the small group of SIL workers at the Yarinacocha base in Peru.[1] Later, Cam wrote:

> On Easter morning we gathered on the grounds between Haywood Hall and the lake to greet the sunrise with praise to God for the resurrection and all that it means. We faced toward the east, singing and watching for the sun to break through the bank of clouds along the horizon. Before us stretched the largest unevangelized area in the world [known at that time]. Three hundred tribes under nine different flags (including the three Guyanas) were waiting for the "Sun of righteousness to rise with healing in His wings" for them (Malachi 4:2). In a sense, this is dependent on the wings of JAARS airplanes, because they have already been carrying Christ's message far to the north and south and west. Someday they will fly to the east to reach all the 300 tribes.
>
> In the brightness of the tropical sunrise we claimed again the mandate of the gospel. Again came the assurance that the power that had brought Christ Jesus from the dead would carry us

through to victory not only to the 300 tribes of Amazonia's immensity, but to every tribe everywhere.

A few weeks later on June 12, Cam's brother Paul wrote Cam a lengthy letter outlining his latest theological thinking about the kingdom of God and how, "When people believe the good news of the Gospel they are translated out of Satan's tyrannical kingdom of darkness and oppression into the freedom and light of the kingdom of His dear Son." Paul wrote:

> I got to thinking about your Easter morning comments, as you looked eastward from Haywood Hall across that vast dark forest of the largest unevangelized area in the world, 300 tribes in nine countries. I thought, you are sending out little couplets of young people into that vast expanse with nothing more than a handful of seeds, but what potentialities are in those seeds! My prayer is that the precious seed will fall into prepared hearts and bring forth fruit for eternity, some 30 fold, some 60, and some 100.

Even in those early days in Peru Cam intuitively acted out what J.B. Phillips said of the early church, "The handful of men and women who constituted the early Church had explicit orders to expand. They had a command without limits to it, "Go into all the world and preach the gospel to every creature" (Mark 16:15).

One night camped out on a cold mountain ridge in Guatemala a young twenty-two-year-old Cameron Townsend, sensed a call by God that would change the entire direction of his life. With Cam on that ridge was his Cakchiquel colporteur companion and friend, Francisco Díaz. As the two men shared a simple meal of dried tortillas and a hard-boiled egg washed down with tepid water, Francisco shared (as he had done on several occasions before) his long-held dream for the Cakchiquels to have the Scriptures in the language of his birth. Francisco shared his puzzlement over why the Scriptures they were selling were only available in Spanish. Surely, he wondered, God could speak his Word to the Cakchiquels just as He had done to Spanish-speaking people.

Challenged to make Francisco's dream a reality Cam chose to respond in faith to whatever it was that God wanted of him. That choice often stretched Cam's faith to the limit. Yet while the essence of Cam's faith was a bold, active, assertive faith in the manner of Hebrews 11:33-34, his faith was sometimes subject to pain, discouragement, misunderstanding and ambiguity. Yet Cam's faith was never shattered. It remained intact through his long and productive life. This is not to say that Cam was never tempted to doubt or to wonder where God was. Early in his career in Guatemala, Cam contracted tuberculosis. He struggled with other health problems, he had sores that wouldn't heal and, like Job, he was afflicted with boils. His first wife Elvira was sickly and became at times an invalid, and always there was a financial struggle. Further, Cam knew if his vision of a viable linguistic school were to have credibility it would require men and women with Ph.Ds who could publish scholarly works for the scientific linguistic community, although he himself lacked a college degree. Yet without sufficient money for his personal needs, and in the midst of a worldwide economic depression, lacking the guaranteed support of a church or established organization, in 1934 Cam said, "With God's help this fledgling group of Bible translators will one day cause the scientific world to sit up and take notice!"

With this as his vision and what he believed was a mandate from God, Cam and L.L. Legters (co-founder of SIL) crossed the Mexico border (with great difficulty from the officials who did not want to let them into the country) on November 11, 1933. That evening in their motel room in Monterrey, Mexico, the two men read that day's reading from *Daily Light* and were renewed in spirit with the words from Exodus 23:20: "Behold, I send an angel before thee in the way, and to bring thee into the place which I have prepared."

Two years later, in 1935, with less than seventy dollars in his pocket Cam ventured again into Mexico. With him were seven new recruits and his young niece Evelyn Griset (later to become Evelyn Pike) to help care for Elvira, Cam's invalid wife. Their mode of transportation was an old Buick that "drank oil like gasoline" and struggled hard at every hill to pull their albatross of a house trailer. Both car and trailer fell victim to repeated breakdowns on their long journey to Mexico City.

This first part of their adventure to establish an SIL presence in Mexico took them to the impoverished Náhuatl Aztec village of Tetelcingo two hours south of Mexico City where Cam would begin his language study in preparation for the translation of the New Testament. Remem-

bering that event, long-time friend
and colleague Dr. Ken Pike said:
"Not since the third century has
there been a man like Cameron
Townsend who attempted so much
and saw so many dreams realized in
his own lifetime."

In the beginning days of Wycliffe,
some of Cam's colleagues and
friends often accused him of being
visionary to the point of impractical-
ity. When they questioned him about
his actions and asked him to explain
the rationale for his step or leap of
faith, Cam was often unable to respond with a logical explanation of
where he got his ideas. He simply
felt a deeper conviction than did
most of his colleagues, namely that
he sensed God was leading him and
that God is always above one's limitations. At times Cam refused to give

Cam and Elaine visited
many schools of the for-
mer USSR in an effort to
evaluate the effective-
ness of the extensive bilingual education program
being carried out in the
Soviet Union. Their
findings were consis-
tently positive.

in to realism. The word "impossibility" was not in his vocabulary and
he believed the word "no" was not necessarily a negative. He truly believed Wycliffe's early theme song:

> Faith, mighty faith the promise sees and looks to God alone,
> laughs at impossibilities, and shouts, "It shall be done!"

At the end of his tenure as general director in May 1971, when a few in
the Wycliffe leadership challenged some of the early Wycliffe policies,
Cam chose to trust God, and moved into a new area of ministry. Dr. Jim
Dean, former director for SIL in Papua New Guinea, board member in
1971 and director of Wycliffe Canada said of that moment:

> When our board felt it was time for Uncle Cam to lay down his title
> as general director and become simply our founder, I was im-

pressed with his willingness and humility to accept this directive and move vigorously ahead with a new outreach to the USSR.

In 1968, at age seventy-two Cam was still pioneering. He and Elaine began the first of eleven trips to the Soviet Union with the purpose of finding creative ways for SIL to work in the Caucasus. For five-and-a-half months Cam and Elaine traveled to five republics of the Caucasus without escort, visiting and interviewing educators, linguists, social workers, anthropologists and ordinary citizens as well as members of the Academy of Science of the Union of Soviet Socialist Republics. Cam wanted to write a book that would show the world the success of the USSR's bilingual education program and how literacy could build community and nationhood. Cam firmly believed the simple act of a person learning to read and write was the first step in personal spiritual renewal. Not only would literacy change that person's self-image, it could be the first step in allowing that person access to the Scriptures, and ultimately into a personal relationship with God.

The book that came out of that extensive research and travel was *They Found a Common Language,* published in 1972 by Harper & Row. The book received critical praise for Cam's insight and passion for universal literacy and bilingual education.

After Cameron Townsend died in Waxhaw on April 23, 1982, Wycliffe published a special edition of its bimonthly publication, *In Other Words,* in which a number of people remembered Cam's achievements as a Bible translator, linguist, servant/statesman, pioneer, man of faith, friend to all, including knowing and being a personal friend, and in some cases a confidant to thirty-eight presidents of eleven countries in Latin America. In addition to all of this he was a devoted husband, loving father and grandfather. Jim Dean was among those who remembered:

At first I wondered why Uncle Cam was making so many trips to the USSR. Then I discovered that he had personally financed and arranged for the translation and publication of the First Epistle of John into five USSR languages. Here was a man in his early seventies looking for new ways to accomplish the task God had given him so many years before.

Jim shared another memory that most profoundly illustrates one of the reasons Cam was so beloved by people who knew him. Said Jim:

> Whenever I was in his presence I was impressed with the way he gave his full attention to [another person]. On one occasion after his retirement he invited me to Waxhaw to a special celebration in honor of Dick Pittman. Cam not only entertained me in his home, he found time (amidst the many other people he was interacting with) to discuss Wycliffe affairs with me. When it came time for me to leave, he jumped in his car and drove me to my next appointment. This simple action demonstrated clearly that Uncle Cam was never too busy to serve people.

On a balmy Southern California evening in May 1981, with Billy Graham the principal speaker, with thousands of friends and supporters gathered at the Anaheim Convention Center, Wycliffe U.S. celebrated a Golden Jubilee for Bible translation. At the center of this celebration was Uncle Cam Townsend, who fifty years before had completed the New Testament translation for the Cakchiquel people. While Francisco Díaz, Cam's early friend and mentor, died before his dream of having the Scriptures in his own language became reality, Townsend's translation, and the work of colleagues who later built on his work became the foundation of the Cakchiquel church and scores of congregations that continue to this day.

In reviewing Uncle Cam's life that night of the Jubilee celebration Billy Graham paid him the ultimate compliment when he said, "Uncle Cam has touched the world in a way I never could."

Later, Dr. Ralph Winter of the U.S. Center for World Mission in Pasadena, California, said that he placed Townsend among the great missionary pioneers of history:

> If in our lifetime, there is anyone comparable to William Carey [believed to be the founder of modern missions] and Hudson Taylor [founder of the China Inland Mission, a man Cam had long admired] I believe it is William Cameron Townsend. He saw that there were still unreached frontiers and for more than half a century he waved the flag for overlooked tribal peoples of the world.

Dick Pittman [left] was the founding director of many SIL branches in southeast Asia and the South Pacific, in the Philippines, India, Nepal, Papua New Guinea and Indonesia. He worked closely with associate Jim Dean (right).

Note

1   On April 20, 2004, at 11:a.m.EST the Yarinacocha jungle center of the Peru Branch of SIL was donated in a public ceremony to the Ministry of Education for use as the new National Intercultural University of the Amazon (Universidad Nacional de la Amazonia.)

It was a long-standing vision of Uncle Cam Townsend to see the center used as an institute for higher education. The date of April 20 was chosen to remember the date in 1946 when Uncle Cam and his new wife Elaine arrived in Peru with the first group of linguist and support workers. The Peru Branch is grateful to God for 56 years of ministry among Peru's ethnic peoples.

Kenneth Pike [right] and Cameron Townsend often entered into lively discussions regarding the effectiveness of SIL work and workers.

Appendix A

Time Line

A WCT/SIL/WBT TIME LINE OF SIGNIFICANT EVENTS.

July 9, 1896 William Cameron Townsend (WCT) is born at home in Riverside County, near Corona, California. Dr. Huff of Corona attends his mother, Molly Cormack Townsend. WCT is named after his father, William Hammond Townsend, and Cameron after an uncle, Richard Cameron.

1900 The Will Townsend family of eight moves to Downey, California. Will was a farmer. He was stone deaf, the result of an accident.

September 1, 1907 WCT joins the Cumberland Presbyterian Church of Downey, California by profession of faith at age eleven.

June 1908 WCT is first academically in his sixth grade class at Downey Public School, WCT had perfect attendance the entire school year.

June 17, 1910 WCT is graduated from Downey Grammar School, valedictorian of his class of twenty-two.

October 6, 1912 WCT, along with his parents and brother Paul, joins the Clearwater Presbyterian Church of Clearwater, California.

1914 WCT graduates from Compton, California high school with highest average in the class. He enrolls in Occidental College.

1915 WCT joins the Student Volunteer Missions organization in his sophomore year. He is challenged to consider missions by John R. Mott and by reading the biography of Hudson Taylor, missionary to China.

October 7, 1916 WCT enlists in the California National Guard at Los Angeles, California during his junior year at Occidental College. He meets Elbert (Robby) Robinson at college.

January 1917 WCT contacts the Bible House of Los Angeles in response to their call for Bible salesmen in Central America. WCT and Robby Robinson meet Stella Zimmerman, missionary to Guatemala, who challenges them to go to Central America rather than going off to war.

March 1917 WCT and Robby, at their request, are honorably discharged from the California National Guard.

April 1917 After finishing their school year, WCT and Robby start working on a California ranch to earn their passage to Guatemala.

April 6, 1917 U.S. declares war on Germany.

July 1917 Elvira Malmstrom, future wife of WCT, arrives in Guatemala, serving as secretary with a Presbyterian mission.

September 15, 1917 Twenty-one-year-old WCT and Robby leave San Francisco aboard the *S.S. Pacific Mail* for Guatemala.

October 3, 1917 Cameron Townsend and his friend Robbie Robinson arrive in Guatemala.

October 1917 WCT contacts Cakchiquel Indians for the first time. He begins traveling with Francisco Díaz, faithful colleague and Cakchiquel believer.

August 1919 after marrying Elvira Malmstrom in July 1919, WCT and Elvira begin learning the Cakchiquel language of Guatemala in the town of Patzún.

1920 Leonard Livingston (L.L.) Legters was the guest speaker at the Cakchiquel Bible Conference. Returning to the U.S. Legters champions the work of WCT and becomes an enthusiastic recruiter and fundraiser.

August 1923 Townsend publishes trial copies of the Gospel of John in Cakchiquel.

February 1926 Townsend sends his analysis of the Cakchiquel grammar to Dr. Edward Sapir of the University of Chicago and receives a favorable evaluation from Sapir, renowned in the field of linguistics.

October 10, 1929 WCT and co-translators Trinidad Bac and Joe Chicol finish the New Testament in Cakchiquel and prepare it for printing.

May 31, 1931 The first copy of the Cakchiquel New Testament is presented to the President of Guatemala.

1933 In Keswick, New Jersey, and Keswick, England, the Lord gives a special burden for prayer for the unreached peoples of Mexico and the world.

November 11, 1933 Cam Townsend and Mr. and Mrs. L.L. Legters enter Mexico. November 11 becomes Wycliffe's annual day of prayer.

December 31, 1933 Townsend sets out on a six-week survey trip of Mexico's rural education, and at the same time prepares word lists and notes regarding the many minority language groups.

June 1934 The first session of Camp Wycliffe is held in an abandoned farmhouse near Sulphur Springs, Arkansas. Three students attend.[1]

June 8, 1935 The second session of Camp Wycliffe opens with five students, including Ken Pike.

September 1935 Townsend and Elvira with a party of ten young people, including Evelyn Griset (Cam's niece later to be married to Ken Pike) arrive in Mexico City just in time to attend the Seventh American Scientific Congress. They are accepted as official members of the congress.

October 15, 1935 Cam and Elvira set up their two-ton house trailer in the central square of the tiny, impoverished Aztec village of Tetelcingo, Mexico.

January 25, 1936 President Lázaro Cárdenas pays a surprise visit to the Townsends in Tetelcingo. Thus begins a lifelong friendship between WCT and Cárdenas. The president encourages Cam to bring more workers to Mexico.

June 30, 1937 Ken Pike enters the University of Michigan at WCT's urging to study linguistics under eminent linguists, Dr. Edward Sapir and Dr. Charles C. Fries.

October 1939 Uncle Cam begins writing a biography of President Lázaro Cárdenas, which is eventually published in 1952.

1940 There are thirty-seven SIL translators working in Mexico with eighteen language groups. L.L. Legters dies.

February 1942 Ken Pike receives his Ph.D. in linguistics from the University of Michigan.

June 10, 1942 The ninth session of Camp Wycliffe, renamed the Summer Institute of Linguistics (SIL), opens at the University of Oklahoma (at Norman), enrollment, 122 students. SIL accredited courses are held here each summer until the late 1970s.

June 1942 At a motel in Norman, Oklahoma WBT and SIL are formally organized and incorporated, by W.C. Townsend, Wm. G. Nyman, Kenneth Pike and Eugene Nida.

July 12, 1944 Uncle Cam flies to Mexico in search of a site for a training camp for new workers. A site in Tzeltal country of Southern Mexico is chosen. He directs the first Jungle Camp course in Nov-Dec 1945.

Summer 1944 SIL courses begin at Briercrest, Saskatchewan, Canada.

December 24, 1944 Elvira Townsend dies in Southern California.

May 15 - June 28, 1945 WCT flies to Peru at the invitation of the Peruvian Minister of Education, to carry out a six-week language and logistical survey by plane and riverboat of the vast Peruvian Amazonia.

June 28, 1945 Cam signs a contract with the Peruvian government.

April 4, 1946 WCT is married to Elaine Mielke. Former president Cárdenas is the best man.

April 1946 WCT, Elaine and 19 translators and support workers arrive in Lima, Peru.

July 12, 1946 Uncle Cam purchases SIL's first aircraft, a Canadian Grumman Duck. It is operated in Peru jointly under contract with various ministries of government. MAF lends pilot Betty Greene to SIL for one year to fly the Duck until pilot Larry Montgomery arrives in Peru.

February 25, 1947 Cam and Elaine are in a plane crash of a small commercial aircraft at Jungle Camp, Chiapas, Mexico. Both the Townsends and the pilot suffer injuries. Baby Grace is unharmed.

1948 Jungle Aviation and Radio Service (JAARS) is established to give aviation and radio support to translators living in remote areas.

June 1, 1951 The first complete SIL New Testament is published in the Mixtec dialect of San Miguel el Grande, Oaxaca, Mexico. Ken Pike, Don Stark, and Angel Merecias Sánchez are the translators.

Spring 1952 The first SIL team arrives in Guatemala under the leadership of Earl Adams. A contract with the government of Guatemala is signed by Don Burns Sept. 25, 1952.

June 23, 1952 SIL courses open at the University of North Dakota under the direction of Dr. Richard S. Pittman. He holds that post for 25 years.

Feb 28, 1953 Pittman signs a cooperative agreement between SIL and the Philippine government.

April 18, 1953 SIL's members first arrive in Manila.

May 1953 First contingent of six SIL members arrives in Ecuador under the direction of Bob Schneider.

July 6, 1953 SIL courses begin in Great Britain directed by Ken and Evelyn Pike.

March 9, 1954 Australian Council of WBT is established.

August 12, 1954 WCT signs a cooperative contract between SIL and the Bolivian government.

June 7, 1955 SIL's first members arrive in Riberalta, Bolivia, in SIL's Catalina aircraft under the direction of Harold Key with his wife Mary.

September 1955 Dr. Robert J. Story of Australia challenges SIL International Conference delegates regarding the previously "unknown" 1,000 Bibleless languages of the Pacific area. Conference authorizes SIL to seek an agreement with the government of Papua New Guinea to begin work among its estimated 600 language groups. The first SIL members arrive in October of 1956.

January 8, 1956 Five young pioneer missionaries, Jim Elliot, Nate Saint, Roger Youderian, Ed McCully and Pete Fleming are speared to death by Aucas (later named Waorani) in remote Ecuadorian jungle.

January 1956 The first of six editions of the Navajo NT is printed and distributed; WBT's second New Testament.

August 1, 1956 Dale Kietzman signs an Agreement of Cooperation between the National Museum of Brazil and SIL for fieldwork in that country.

September 1957 Ken Pike reports to the SIL Conference that 500 students attended the five SIL schools the previous summer.

December 1957 Dick Pittman and Dave Thomas arrive in Saigon, Vietnam seeking permission to begin SIL work in that country.

Fall 1958 John Beekman conducts the first SIL translation workshop in Mitla, Oaxaca, Mexico, a significant step forward in the translation program.

September 1959 SIL and WBT membership reaches 1,000 including first second-generation member, Marilou Pittman Weaver.

February 13, 1961 Ecuador's President José Velasco Ibarra meets Kimo, converted Auca assassin, and is deeply impressed by Kimo's character and understanding of spiritual matters.

November 1961 Businessman Henderson Belk and wife Anne deed 256 acres of farmland at Waxhaw, N.C. near Charlotte for construction of the JAARS technical services center.

December 1, 1961 Dr. John Bendor-Samuel, director of the first Africa branch of SIL, signs an agreement between the government of Ghana and SIL.

February 19, 1962 WCT signs a contract with the Government of Colombia, which is published officially on June 18, 1962.

October 31, 1962 A cooperative agreement between the University of Nigeria and SIL by Africa area director John Bendor-Samuel.

March 4, 1963 SIL translators in Viet Nam, Elwood and Vurnell Jacobsen with their baby daughter Kari and Gaspar and Josephine Makil with their twin baby children Janie and Jessie and three-year-old son Thomas, are ambushed on the road sixty-five miles north of Saigon. Elwood, Gaspar and his baby child Janie are shot and killed by Viet Cong. Thomas is shot in the thigh and recovers.

December 10, 1964 Dick Pittman signs an agreement between SIL and Deccan College of West India, facilitated by a visit to the college the previous year by Ken Pike and Colin Day.

May 1966 SIL now beginning a new language project every 14 days, working in 400 languages in 18 countries.

December. 20, 1966 Dick Pittman signs an agreement between SIL and Tribhuvan University, Nepal.

October 20, 1968 WCT and Elaine fly to Moscow 1968. This is the first of eleven trips undertaken by the Townsends between 1968 and 1979 to the USSR.

May 5, 1969 Wycliffe Associates is incorporated in California.

February 3, 1971 After nine visits over a period of 15 years by Dick Pittman and others, Dr. Jim Dean signs a contract with the University of Indonesia. SIL members soon arrive in Jakarta.

February 5, 1973 WCT and Elaine visit Zulfikar Ali Bhutto, President of Pakistan in Islamabad, to discuss implementation of bilingual education in that multilingual country. WCT sends President Bhutto a plan for promoting linguistic unification in Pakistan around Urdu, the majority language.

March 24, 1975 Ken Pike signs an Agreement of Cooperation between Cenderawasih University of Indonesia and SIL for a cooperative program in the province of Irian Jaya.

March 27, 1972 Dr. Frank Robbins signs a Memorandum of Agreement between SIL International Linguistic Center and the University of Texas at Arlington, Dallas, Texas.

March 19, 1975 John and Carolyn Miller and daughter LuAnn are captured by North Vietnamese forces at Banmethout and held captive for ten months.

April 16, 1975 All SIL staff leaves Vietnam because of heavy fighting and the imminent fall of Saigon.

July 21, 1975 First SIL linguistic courses are held in Japan.

June 3, 1976 SIL Contract with Tribhuvan University of Nepal is not renewed and SIL members leave the country.

October 31, 1977 Dr. Ken Smith signs a Memorandum of Understanding between the government of Sabah, Malaysia, and SIL.

February 9, 1979 Dr. Ken Pike signs a Memorandum of Understanding between Mahidol University of Thailand and SIL.

July 14, 1979 The New Testament in the Amuesha language of Peru is designated the one-hundredth New Testament translated under SIL auspices.

March 7, 1981 Terrorists in Bogotá assassinate Chet Bitterman, SIL member in Colombia.

January 1982 Dr. Ken Pike is nominated for the Nobel Peace Prize by the Executive Director of the Linguistics Association of Canada and the U.S.

April 1982 Bolivia branch of SIL is closed down, having finished the linguistic and translation work in the jungle area.

April 23, 1982 After nine days in hospital, William Cameron Townsend quietly slips out of his weary body and into the presence of Jesus Christ whom he loved and served.

Notes

1   There has been some confusion over the actual number of students who attended that first linguistic course in 1934. The texts say there were just two students in 1934. The course actually began with three students, Richmond McKinney, Edward Sywulka and Oral Van Horn. Several weeks into the course, Oral Van Horn dropped out. Teachers for that first course included L.L. Legters, Joe Chicol from Guatemala and Cameron Townsend. There were other guest lecturers as well.

Appendix B

Uncle Cam's Leadership Style
by George Cowan

He led from the front, not the rear, always out ahead of us, giving entrepreneurial direction and making decisions on the field, not from the home headquarters.

He led by faith, not by sight. He trusted God, and he trusted God to guide. Individuals, groups and governments also guided him. He delegated authority, but reserved the right to veto.

He led by example, not by argument or reasoning. In fact, he often found it difficult to answer the question "Why?" He would often answer with a story.

He led by suggestion, not by command, but expected suggestions to be taken seriously.

He led openly, without secrets, resisting things that had to be kept in confidence. But he recognized true confidentiality and kept that. He wanted meetings to be open to anyone—family, town-hall meeting atmosphere.

He led positively, not negatively. If he couldn't say something good, he would say nothing. He almost never "chewed us out" (Dick Pittman).

He led by providential guidance. He walked close to God, his Word, and, having committed his day to God, he interpreted unexpected circumstances, interruptions, and meetings with people as divinely ordered. Opportunities, not agendas ruled.

He led courageously, fearlessly, calmly, and doggedly. He had a fertile mind and was innovative but single-minded in goal and direction.

He led by warm personal friendships rather than by rule or contract.

He believed everyone could do something to help; never turned down an offer to help. He drew people to be involved. He latched on to specialists and harnessed their skills.

He led in prayer, in turning to Scripture, in obeying Scripture (e.g. loving enemies) and in faithful witnessing under all circumstances to all levels of people.

He excelled in giving God the glory and giving others thanks.

He led by consistently emphasizing the basics and demonstrating them. He never lost sight of the Lord or of the goal of translating the Bible.

Cameron Townsend was not perfect. He was aware of his own limitations, a "vessel of clay, that the excellency of the glory might be of God and not of man." He left an indelible imprint on many of us (outsiders comment on how much some of us act like Uncle Cam). He left a lasting imprint on the organizations he founded.

From a paper by Ben Elson, published in 1995, on the history of the development of Wycliffe and SIL:

> When the Mexico Branch [the first SIL branch to organize] decided to organize in a formal way and to work on a constitution for the branch, two important principles emerged. One was that the Director, Mr. Townsend, would be elected by the membership. He could have been director for life, but rather, chose to subject himself to the will of the membership, believing that God would lead them. The second was that there would be an executive committee of the branch that would have power to overrule the director in cases of disagreement. In looking at these two principles, it should be pointed out that Mr. Townsend was an experienced missionary and Bible translator with a vision for reaching Bibleless groups to translate the Bible for them, while those working with him were inexperienced novices, but he was to put himself under their ultimate authority. This was a truly historic decision! I am not sure later generations of Wycliffe members fully appreciated its significance.

A light-hearted moment at a board meeting of the Summer Institute of Linguistics held in Mexico City the fall of 1961 at the SIL headquarters. Left to right facing the camera: Phil Grossman, Dick Pittman, Cameron Townsend, Turner Blount, George Cowan, Ken Watters, Eugene Loos, Don Johnson. Facing the table: Earl Miller, Otis Leal, Ben Elson, Lorin Griset.

Appendix C

SIL International
Goodwill Airplanes

Donor	Recipient	Ceremony	Plane Name	Plane Type
Mexico	Peru	April 5, 1951	*Amauta Moisés Sáenz*	Catalina PBY
Chicago	Ecuador	December 17, 1955	*City of Chicago*	Helio Courier
Idaho	Brazil	November 1956	*Spirit of Idaho*	Helio Courier
Oklahoma	Bolivia	June 28, 1956	*Friendship of Oklahoma*	Helio Courier
Orange County, CA	Peru	September 6, 1956	*Friendship of Orange County*	Helio Courier
Kansas City, MO	Ecuador	January 19, 1958	*Spirit of Kansas City*	Helio Courier
Seattle	Philippines	June 20, 1958	*The Spirit of Seattle*	Helio Courier
Miami/Orlando	Brazil	June 22, 1959	*Mariscal Rondón*	Catalina PBY
Minnesota	Philippines	October 26, 1959	*Friendship of Minnesota*	Aero-Commander
Riverside, CA	Philippines	April 27, 1960	*Friendship of Riverside*	Hiller Helicopter
Pontiac, MI	Philippines	July 20, 1960	*Spirit of Pontiac*	Helio Courier
Philadelphia, PA	Brazil	November 28, 1961	*Spirit of Philadelphia*	Helio Courier
Greensboro, NC	Peru	May 12, 1962	*Spirit of Greensboro*	

continued

Donor	Recipient	Ceremony	Plane Name	Plane Type
San Diego, CA	Philippines	May 11, 1964	*The Spirit of San Diego*	Helio Courier
Indiana	Colombia	June 16, 1964	*Friendship of Indiana*	Helio Courier
Miami, FL	Colombia	December 12, 1965	*Friendship of Miami*	Helio Courier
Oregon	Brazil	January 27, 1970	*Spirit of Oregon*	Cessna 206
Georgia	Brazil	April 21, 1974	*Friendship of Georgia*	Cessna 206
Maine	Brazil	May 19, 1974	*Friendship of Maine*	Lake Amphibian
Denver, CO	Brazil	June 1974	*Denver Abrahamson*	Cessna 206
Oregon	Papua New Guinea	March 31, 1976	*Spirit of Linn*	Cessna 206
Tulsa, OK	Indonesia	April 23, 1977	*Friendship of Tulsa*	Helio Courier
Valparaiso, IN	Papua New Guinea	July 22, 1979	*Friendship of Valparaiso*	Cessna 206
N/S Carolina	Brazil	October 1981	*Spirit of the Carolinas*	Cessna 206

Appendix D

Bible Translators of History

O n September 30, 420 A.D., the great Eastern European biblical scholar **JEROME** died. The legacy of his life was the translation of the Old and New Testaments into the common Latin of his day (known as the *Vulgate*). Jerome's concern for ordinary people to have the Bible in their everyday language gave the Western church its principal vehicle of faith for the next thousand years.

JOHN WYCLIFFE (c.1319-1384) called the "morning star of the Reformation" and his colleagues translated the Scriptures into English for the first time. Before this, only Latin Bibles existed for English speakers. His simple explanation for translation was: "Now dear friends have I showed you that it is lawful for the people to know God's law and the faith of the holy church in their language. And that it is lawful and needful to him who can read to have God's law written in books, so they can read it and better understand."

MARTIN LUTHER (1483-1546) heard the truths of the Reformation crying out for release into the language of the people. He wanted to see Bibles in German and declared: "Would that this one book were in every language, in every land, before the eyes and in the ears and hearts of all men!"

WILLIAM TYNDALE (c. 1490-1536) translated the New Testament from Greek into English amid such opposition that he had to flee to Germany where the translation was printed in 1525. Eleven years later, Tyndale was burned at the stake. With words that would echo down through the centuries he wrote: "I perceive by experience how that it was impossible to establish the lay people in any truth except the scripture plainly laid before their eyes in their mother tongue."

JOHN ELIOT (1604-1690) left Britain for colonial New England where he translated the New Testament into the language of the Massachusetts Indians, a first for North America.

WILLIAM CAREY (1761-1834), "The Father of Modern Missions," paved the way for the noble line of modern missionary translators. Assisted by others, Carey's pioneer Bible translation work left the Word of God in thirty-five languages and dialects in India.

ROBERT MORRISON (1782-1834), despite great opposition and hardship, completed the translation of the Wenli Bible in China when he was just thirty-six.

WILLIAM CAMERON TOWNSEND (1896-1982), as a young twenty-one-year-old, sold scripture portions throughout Guatemala and Central America. He became aware that a great majority of Guatemala's people spoke languages other than Spanish. Townsend's friend and traveling companion, Francisco Díaz, a Cakchiquel Indian, challenged him to provide the scriptures in Cakchiquel. Townsend accepted the challenge, settled into a Cakchiquel community and learned the complex unwritten language. Ten years later, Townsend and his co-translators completed the Cakchiquel New Testament translation.

Townsend realized that he alone could not translate the Bible for all the language groups in Guatemala, much less the world, and set out to recruit a corps of linguists. Thus were born the Summer Institute of Linguistics (SIL) and Wycliffe Bible Translators(WBT).

Since the first Wycliffe translators were trained in 1934, the ever growing team has begun work in more than sixty countries.

Wycliffe and its partners have an enormous task ahead of them. At least 6,800 languages are spoken throughout the earth, and only 2,300 of these have even a portion of God's Word.

In 1967, the significance of the worldwide Bible translation task prompted the U.S. Senate and House of Representatives to declare September 30 "Bible Translation Day," inviting communities in the U.S. to observe the day with appropriate ceremonies.

Over 300,000,000 people still wait for the first verse of Scripture in their own language. What John Wycliffe said six hundred years ago still applies: "Christ and His apostles taught the people in the tongue that was most known to the people. Why shouldn't men [and women] do so now?"

William Cameron Townsend with Mexican diplomats April 19, 1964. Mexico City dedication of the Moisés Sáenz Publication Building. Left to right: WCT, Dr. Ramón Beteta (Secretary of Finance), President Adolfo López Mateos, Dr. Jaime Torres Bodet (Secretary of Education), Dr. Alfonso Caso (Director of the Mexican Indian Institute), and Dr. Ben Elson (Director of SIL in Mexico), inspecting the building.

Appendix E

Townsend's Reply to the Roman Catholic Archbishop, Peru, 1953

This is a portion of Cameron Townsend's reply to the August 8, 1953 attack from the Roman Catholic hierarchy. The article is translated from Spanish. It was printed in Peru's leading newspaper *El Comercio*, the same newspaper that ran articles attacking SIL. After it was published, Elaine Townsend wrote her parents the following:

> The leading newspaper kindly published Cameron's long letter that explained who we were and what our mission was about. God enabled Cam to write this letter in love, avoiding any contentious argument. The letter has met with enthusiastic approval from government officials, university professors and our Peruvian friends. Someone said "this was the most open and far-reaching gospel witness that the evangelicals had ever secured in a Peruvian newspaper (and for free). The newspapers have steadfastly refused to

accept paid advertisement from any evangelical source." Whether that is true or not, the evangelical cause and the whole cause for religious liberty has benefited from the Government's courageous stand in our defense. We thank you for your prayers for us and for the officials.

Cameron Townsend's Letter

Director of *El Comercio*, Lima. August 18, 1953.

An article has been published in your esteemed newspaper in which the Summer Institute of Linguistics is attacked on the supposition that it is sectarian and proselytizing in nature, as well as not very scientific and very dangerous for the sovereignty of the nation. In the face of a series of such attacks from the same source I have maintained silence because I was endeavoring to follow the example of Him who is the Example for every Christian, "*Who, when He was reviled, reviled not again: when He suffered, He threatened not, but committed himself to Him that judges righteously,*" (I Peter 2:23). The great respect in which I hold the high office of the author of these attacks has also restrained me. But now that he [the author] is persisting in his mistaken opinion and also trying to persuade all of our gracious friends to have nothing to do with us, I have decided to publish this one reply.

I have a letter from a noble Franciscan missionary with whom I have been acquainted for more than six years that eloquently expresses the spirit that ought to prevail in every discussion among Christians. This letter was sent, January 12, 1953. Among other things he says:

[See Padre Alegre's letter in chapter eleven.]

In this spirit, so clearly and sincerely expressed by my friend, a priest in the jungle of Peru, I shall attempt to clarify those points about which doubts have been raised.

I wish to emphasize that all the members of the Summer Institute of Linguistics are true believers in our Lord Jesus Christ. They have offered their lives so that they might dedicate their training and earnest effort to the service of the indigenous peoples of the jungle which to this day have retained their interesting aboriginal languages. Each of our members believes in the Apostles' Creed and with gratitude humbly embraces the truth which by divine inspiration, is set forth in the Gospel of John, chapter three, verse sixteen: "For God so loved the world that He gave His only begotten son, that whosoever believeth in him, should not perish but have everlasting life."

Thus it is not a question of "wolves," but of believers in the only Savior of the world. Nor is it a question of a sectarian organization, since all our members must promise that their service will be multilateral, without distinction as to race, or creed and be completely free from ecclesiasticism. Because of this, no ordained minister, whether Catholic or Protestant, may become a member of the Summer Institute of Linguistics unless he is willing to leave his [ecclesiastical duties] to follow ours.

This non-sectarian attitude of the Summer Institute of Linguistics is in my opinion so essential to the nature of our organization that when, on one occasion some of our members wanted to alter it slightly, I proffered my resignation as General Director. A large majority defeated the proposal and we continue to be non-sectarian. Because of this fact no religious denomination contributes funds toward our work. Our support comes from individuals and independent groups. This is why we can be both friends to all and servants to all. Why should it be considered strange that a member of one religion can be a friend of someone who holds some other belief? If it were impossible for a sincere Christian to befriend a Jew, a Muslim or an atheist, then the United Nations would be unable to function. Benito Juárez, that great Mexican statesman, said, "Peace is respect for the rights of others." If each believer holds in respect the opinions of other believers, then peace and friendly relations can reign between them.

It was not incongruous that a great Catholic statesman (I suppose Bolívar was a Catholic) should have labored so energetically hard for the union of all America, including the Protestant elements. Think also of Franklin Roosevelt, himself a Protestant, who labored hard to strengthen the bonds of union of all nations of the Americas, calling his policy that of the "Good Neighbor." Likening it to the attitude of the man whom our Lord spoke about in His parable of the Samaritan who, although a member of a religion that was antagonistic to the Jews, gave help and comfort to a Jew.

I, your servant, do not belong to any denomination. However, I respect them all and try to be a good neighbor to all. The Summer Institute of Linguistics, founded by me and directed by me, does not protest against anything and does not attack anyone. On the contrary, endeavoring to promote a spirit of love and brotherhood, we try to serve all. We don't call ourselves Protestants, but simply believers in Christ. The success which we have attained in the matter of neighborly harmony is evidenced by the fact that, while the majority of the nations of the world were preparing for war, and while the roar of artillery in Korea spread fear and hate on all sides, the government and people of Mexico, in a fraternal gesture, donated a large Catalina airplane to Peru for the work of the Summer Institute of Linguistics, to use among the tribes of Amazonia. This was done in recognition of the many years of service the Summer Institute of Linguistics has rendered the Mexican government among its ethnic minorities.

Our firm adherence to this non-sectarian principle upon which I founded the Institute in 1934, has triumphed to such a degree that five Republics in various parts of the world have signed agreements with us, and we are affiliated with two large State Universities in the United States. However, while we hold to a non-sectarian attitude it does not preclude our recognizing and accepting the Christian's duty of making Christianity known to the peoples whose languages and customs we study.

Index

C

Llushin River in Ecuador 156-157
London Bible College 110

M
___

Machiguenga Indians, Peru 9-10
MAF xii, 6, 9, 17, 21-23, 28-32, 37, 39, 41, 46, 48-52, 55, 60, 67, 120,
        137, 147, 149, 152, 156-157, 263 See also Missionary Aviation
        Fellowship
Magsaysay, Ramón 109, 116, 184, 208
Makil, Gaspar 265
Malmstrom, Adele Cecilia, Elvira Townsend's nice 68-69, 75, 84, 260
Marañón River, Peru
Matteson, Esther xxii, 11, 48, 76, 82, 140, 246
May, Bernie 26, 177
Mayoruna 11
Mazatec Tribe of Mexico 89
McAlister, Jack 97-98
McCarter, Dr. Pete Kyle 191
McCully, Ed 149, 193, 264
McGinness, Irene 11
McKinney, Richmond 212, 220, 267
McNickel, Darcy 125
Mears, Henrietta 54, 60
Melbourne, Australia 78
Mellis, Charlie 21-23, 51
Merecias, Angel 263
Michigan, University of 126, 135, 262
Michoacán 42 See also Pátzcuaro
Mickelson, E.H. 34
Micronesia 78
Mielke, Elaine (maiden name of Elaine Townsend) 1, 263
Miller, Carolyn and John 129, 266
Miller, Earl 245
Missionary Aviation Fellowship 6, 28, 137 See also MAF
Mitla 114, 265 See also Oaxaca
Mixtec Tribe of Mexico 89-90, 96-98, 115, 132, 263
Mixtec New Testament 89-90, 96-98, 115, 132

Q

R

S

Truxton, Jim 6, 9, 39, 67
Tulsa, Oklahoma 65, 170, 172-173, 175, 272
Turner, Glen 156, 270
Twentyman, John and Isabel 86-87
Tzeltal tribe in Mexico 13, 82, 93, 97-100, 145, 194-196, 199, 240, 244, 262

U

Ucayali river 36, 64-65, 91
UCLA 132
Urquidi, Joe 13
Urubamba river Peru 6, 9, 76, 117

V

Valcárcel, Dr. Luis 4
Vanuatu 78
Venezuela 23, 30-31, 39, 77, 101-104, 165, 189
Vietnam 161, 223, 225-226, 249, 265-266

W

Wallis, Ethel 140, 153, 193, 199
Waorani 153-154, 264 See also Auca(s)
WASP (Women's Air Force Service Pilots) 9
Watkins, Grace 153
Watters, Ken and Vivian 11, 44, 165, 204, 229, 270
Witt, Eleanor (daughter of William G. Nyman) 230
Wycliffe Chronicle 64
Wycliffe, John 219, 275
Wyzenbeck, Andrew 83

X-Y-Z

Yarinacocha, Peru 4, 38, 62, 64, 67-69, 72, 75, 78, 81, 90-91, 93, 118, 130, 138, 186, 235, 251
Yaxoquintelá, Jungle Camp Location Mexico 13
Yine 82, 93 See also Piro
Youderian, Roger 149, 264

Index addendum *Yours to Finish the Task*

References to prayer, praying, praise